THE PARADISE LOST OF MILTON

THE PARADISE LOST OF MILTON

BY

John Milton

GenNext Publication

Published by

GenNext Publication
5, Ansari Road
New Delhi-110002

Distribution Network
gyanbooks.com
India, USA, Canada, UK, Australia, France

ISBN: 978-93-9386-325-6 (HB)

15 impression 2023

Printed at: Goyal Offset Printers, Delhi.

CONTENTS

BOOK - I

The First Book proposes, first in brief, the whole subject, man's disobedience, and the loss thereupon of Paradise, wherein he was placed; then touches the prime cause of his fall, the Serpent, or rather Satan in the Serpent; who, revolting from God, and drawing to his side many legions of angels, was, by the command of God, driven out of Heaven, with all his crew, into the great deep. Which action passed over, the Poem hastens into the midst of things, presenting Satan with his angels now falling into Hell, described here, not in the centre, for Heaven and Earth may be supposed as yet not made, certainly not yet accursed, but in a place of utter darkness, fitliest called Chaos. Here Satan, with his angels, lying on the burning lake, thunderstruck and astonished, after a certain space recovers, as from confusion, calls up to him who next in order and dignity lay by him; they confer of their miserable fall; Satan awakens all his legions, who lay till then in the same manner confounded. They rise; their numbers; array of battle; their chief leaders named, according to the idols known afterward in Canaan and the countries adjoining. To these Satan directs his speech, comforts them with hope yet of regaining Heaven, but tells them lastly of a new world, and a new kind of creature to be created, according to an ancient prophecy, or report in Heaven; for, that angels were long before this visible creation, was the opinion of many ancient fathers. To find out the truth of this prophecy, and what to determine thereon, he refers to a full council. What his associates thence attempt. Pandemonium, the palace of Satan, rises, suddenly built out of the deep : the infernal peers there sit in council.

OF man's first disobedience, and the fruit[1]
Of that forbidden tree, whose mortal taste
Brought death into the world, and all our woe.
With loss of Eden, till one greater Man
Restore us, and regain the blissful seat.
Sing, heavenly Muse,[2] that on the secret top
Of Oreb, or of Sinai, didst inspire
That shepherd, who first taught the chosen seed
In the beginning how the heavens and earth

1. Few things are so fatal to the pleasant and profitable reading of an author, as the distraction occasioned by profuse, and often trivial, notes upon his text. Commentators on Milton have assigned a large space to coincidences between him and preceding writers–a wonderfully larger space than we should have thought it worth while so to occupy. We doubt not that much the greater part of those coincidences are coincidences of which the author was wholly unconscious; and where it was otherwise, the matter is either so trivial as not to deserve to be mentioned, or the metal borrowed is borrowed almost invariably that it might receive an impress which the genius of Milton only could have given to it. In the annotation we submit to the reader, we hope to distinguish between what may be really useful, and what would be felt as only so much incumbrance and impediment.

2. *Sing, heavenly Muse.*–Prayer for the inspiration breathed into the old Hebrew prophets. Milton's third wife, who survived him many years, related of him that he used to compose his poetry chiefly in winter; and on his waking in a morning would make her write down sometimes twenty or thirty verses. Being asked whether he did not often read Homer and Virgil, she understood the question as indicating a suspicion that he may have made an undue use in some instances of those authors, and answered with eagerness–"He stole from nobody but the Muse who inspired him;" and being asked by a lady present who the Muse was, she replied–"It was God's grace, and the Holy Spirit that visited him nightly."– *Newton's Life of Milton.* Richardson also says–"Milton would sometimes lie awake whole nights, but not a verse could he make; and on a sudden his poetic fancy would rush upon him with an impetus or *cpstrum.*"

Rose out of Chaos : or, if Sion hill
Delight thee more, and Siloa's brook that flowed
Fast by the oracle of God, I thence
Invoke thy aid to my adventurous song,
That, with no middle flight, intends to soar
Above the Aonian mount,[1] while it pursues
Things unattempted yet in prose or rhyme.
And chiefly Thou, O Spirit,[2] that dost prefer
Before all temples the upright heart and pure,
Instruct me, for Thou know'st : Thou from the first
Wast present, and with mighty wings outspread.
Dove-like, sat'st brooding on the vast abyss,
And madest it pregnant. What in me is dark,
Illumine; what is low, raise and support;
That to the height of this great argument
I may assert Eternal Providence,
And justify the ways of God to men.
Say first – for Heaven hides nothing from thy view,
Nor the deep tract of Hell – say first, what cause
Moved our grand parents,[3] in that happy state.
Favoured of Heaven so highly, to fall off
From their Creator, and transgress His will
For one restraint, lords of the world besides ?
Who first seduced them to that foul revolt ?
The infernal Serpent; he it was, whose guile,
Stirred up with envy and revenge, deceived
The mother of mankind; what time his pride
Had cast him out from Heaven, with all his host

---

1. *Above the Aonian mount.*–Mount Helicon, the seat of the Greek Muses. The poet aims at higher things than could have come from their inspiration.
2. *And chiefly Thou, O Spirit.*–It is thus that Milton seeks, not only the inspiration which has given us Hebrew poetry, but that which has given us Hebrew sanctity.
3. *Grand parents.*–First, or great parents.

Of rebel Angels; by whose aid, aspiring
To set himself in glory above his peers.
He trusted to have equalled the Most High,
As far removed from God and light of heaven,
As from the centre thrice to the utmost pole.
Oh, how unlike the place from whence they fell !
There the companions of his fall, o'erwhelmed
With floods and whirlwinds of tempestuous fire,
He soon discerns; and weltering by his side
One next himself in power, and next in crime,
Long after known in Palestine,[1] and named
Beelzebub : to whom the arch-enemy.
And thence in Heaven called Satan,[2] with bold words
Breaking the horrid silence, thus began :
 If thou beest he; but oh, how fallen ! how changed
From him, who, in the happy realms of light,
Clothed with transcendent brightness, didst outshine
Myriads, though bright ! If he, whom mutual league,
United thoughts and counsels, equal hope
And hazard in the glorious enterprise.
Joined with me once, now misery hath joined
In equal ruin; into what pit thou seest
From what height fallen, so much the stronger proved
He with his thunder. And till then who knew
The force of those dire arms ? Yet not for those,
Nor what the potent Victor in his rage
Can else inflict, do I repent or change,
Though changed in outward lustre, that fixed mind,
And high disdain from sense of injured merit.
That with the Mightiest raised me to contend,
And to the fierce contention brought along

1. *Long after known in Palestine.*–Milton often speaks of the heathen gods as being .the fallen angels, practising their frauds in that form upon their victims.

2. *Satan.*–Enemy, in Hebrew.

Innumerable force of Spirits armed.
That durst dislike his reign, and, me preferring,
His utmost power with adverse power opposed
In dubious battle on the plains of Heaven,
And shook his throne. What though the field be lost
All is not lost; the unconquerable will,
And study of revenge, immortal hate,
And courage never to submit or yield,
And what is else not to be overcome;
That glory never shall his wrath or might
Extort from me. To bow and sue for grace
With suppliant knee, and deify His power
Who from the terror of this arm so late
Doubted his empire – that were low indeed.
That were an ignominy, and shame beneath
This downfall. Since, by fate, the strength of gods,
And this empyreal substance, cannot fail;
Since, through experience of this great event.
In arms not worse, in foresight much advanced,
We may with more successful hope resolve
To wage, by force or guile, eternal war,
Irreconcilable to our grand Foe,
Who now triumphs, and, in the excess of joy
Sole reigning, holds the tyranny of Heaven.
    So spake the apostate angel, though in pain,
Vaunting aloud, but racked with deep despair;
And him thus answered soon his bold compeer :
    O prince, O chief of many-throned powers,
That led the embattled seraphim to war
Under thy conduct, and, in dreadful deeds
Fearless, endanger'd heaven's perpetual King,
And put to proof His high supremacy,
Whether upheld by strength, or chance, or fate;
Too well I see and rue the dire event,
That with sad overthrow and foul defeat,
Hath lost us Heaven, and all this mighty host
In horrible destruction laid thus low,

As far as gods and heavenly essences
Can perish : for the mind and spirit remain
Invincible, and vigour soon returns,
Though all our glory extinct, and happy state
Here swallowed up in endless misery.
But what if He our Conqueror – whom I now
Of force believe Almighty – since no less
Than such could have o'erpowered such force as ours –
Have left us this our spirit and strength entire,
Strongly to suffer and support our pains.
That we may so suffice[1] His vengeful ire.
Or do Him mightier service as His thralls[2]
By right of war, whate'er His business be,
Here in the heart of hell to work in fire,
Or to His errands in the gloomy Deep ?
What can it then avail, though yet we feel
Strength undiminished, or eternal being.
To undergo eternal punishment ?
Whereto with speedy words the arch-fiend replied :
 Fallen cherub ! to be weak is miserable,
Doing or suffering : but of this be sure,
To do aught good never will be our task,
But ever to do ill our sole delight.
As being the contrary to His high will
Whom we resist. If then His providence
Out of our evil seek to bring forth good,
Our labour must be to pervert that end.
And out of good still to find means of evil;
Which oft-times may succeed, so as perhaps
Shall grieve Him, if I fail not, and disturb
His inmost counsels from their destined aim.
But see ! the angry Victor hath recalled
His ministers of vengeance and pursuit
Back to the gates of Heaven. The sulphurous hail.

1. *Sufice.*–Satisfy.

2. *Thralls.*–Anglo-Saxon for slaves. Hence our word thraldom.

Shot after us in storm, o'erblown, hath laid
The fiery surge, that from the precipice
Of Heaven received us falling, and the thunder,
Winged with red lightning and impetuous rage,
Perhaps hath spent his shafts, and ceases now
To bellow through the vast and boundless Deep.
Let us not slip the occasion, whether scorn,
Or satiate furry yield it from our Foe.
Seest thou the dreary plain, forlorn and wild,
The seat of desolation, void of light.
Save what the ghmmering of these livid flames
Cast pale and dreadful ? Thither let us tend
From off the tossing of these fiery waves,
There rest – if any rest can harbour there –
And, re-assembling our afflicted powers,
Consult how we may henceforth most offend
Our Enemy, our own loss how repair,
How overcome this dire calamity.
What reinforcement we may gain from hope.
If not, what resolution from despair.
Thus Satan, talking to his nearest mate,
With head uplift above the wave, and eyes
That sparkling blazed, his other parts besides
Prone on the flood, extended long and large.
Lay floating many a rood, in bulk as huge
As whom[1] the fables name of monstrous size,
Titanian,[2] or Earth-born, that warred on Jove;
Briareus,[3] or Typhon,[4] whom the den

1. *As whom.*–As his whom.
2. *Titanian.*–The Titans, or giants, who according to the Greek mythology, made war upon the god".
3. *Briareus.*–One of three monster brothers, described as possessing a hundred arms and fifty heads. They are said to have given victory to the gods over the Titans.
4. *Typhon.*–A tempest-producing, and sometimes a fire-breathing giant. Hesiod makes Typhaon and Typhceus two distinct monster powers of the primitive world.

By ancient Tarsus held; or that sea-beast
Leviathan, which God of all His works
Created hugest that swim the ocean stream :
Him, haply, slumbering on the Norway foam,
The pilot of some small night-foundered skiff,
Deeming some island, oft, as seamen tell,
With fixed anchor in his scaly rind.
Moors by his side under the lea, while night
Invests the sea, and wished morn delays : –
So stretched out huge in length the Arch-fiend lay
Chained on the burning lake, nor ever thence
Had risen, or heaved his head, but that the will
And high permission of all-ruling Heaven
Left him at large to his own dark designs.
That with reiterated crimes he might
Heap on himself damnation, while he sought
Evil to others; and, enraged, might see
How all his malice served but to brinor forth
Infinite goodness, grace, and mercy, shown
On man by him seduced; but on himself
Treble confusion, wrath, and vengeance, poured.
    Forthwith upright he rears from off the pool
His mighty stature. On each hand the flames.
Driven backward, slope their pointing spires, and, rolled
In billows, leave in the midst a horrid vale.
Then with expanded wings he steers his flight
Aloft, incumbent on the dusky air,
That felt unusual weight, till on dry land
He lights – if it were land that ever burned
With solid, as the lake with liquid, fire :
And such appeared in hue as when the force
Of subterranean wind transports a hill
Torn from Pelorus,[1] or the shattered side
Of thundering Ætna, whose combustible

1. *Pelorus*.–The northern cape of Sicilv.

And fuelled entrails thence conceiving fire,
Sublimed with mineral fury, aid the winds
And leave a singed bottom, all involved[1]
With stench and smoke. Such resting found the sole
Of unblessed feet. Him followed his next mate:
Both glorying to have 'scaped the Stygian[2] flood
As gods, and by their own recovered strength,
Not by the sufferance of supernal Power.
Is this the region, this the soil, the clime,
Said then the lost archangel, this the seat
That we must change for Heaven; this mournful gloom
For that celestial light ? Be it so ! Since He,
Who now is Sovran, can dispose and bid
What shall be right : furthest from Him is best,
Whom reason hath equalled, force hath made supreme
Above His equals. Farewell, happy fields,
Where joy for ever dwells ! Hail, horrors ! hail.
Infernal world ! And thou, profoundest Hell,
Receive thy new possessor ! One who brings
A mind not to be changed by place -or time.
The mind is its own place, and in itself
Can make a Heaven of Hell, a Hell of Heaven.
What matter where, if I be still the same.
And what I should be, all but less than He
Whom thunder hath made greater ? Here at least
We shall be free; the Almighty hath not built
Here for His envy; will not drive us hence.
Here we may reign secure, and, in my choice,[3]
To reign is worth ambition, though in Hell.
Better to reign in Hell than serve in Heaven.
But wherefore let we then our faithful friends,
The associates and copartners of our loss,

1. *All involved.*–Involved in, or along with.

2. *Stygian.*–From Styx–the name of the great river which is said to flow round the nether world seven times.

3. *In my choice.*–In my judgment–to me.

Lie thus astonished on the oblivious pool,
And call them not to share with us their part
In this unhappy mansion; or once more
With rallied arms to try what may be yet
Regained in Heaven, or what more lost in Hell ?
So Satan spake; and him Beelzebub
Thus answered : Leader of those armies bright,
Which but the Omnipotent none could have foiled !
If once they hear that voice, their liveliest pledge
Of hope in fears and dangers, heard so oft
In worse extremes, and on the perilous edge
Of battle, when it raged, m all assaults
Their surest signals, they will soon resume
New courage and revive, though now they lie
Grovelling and prostrate on yon lake of fire.
As we erewhile, astounded and amazed.
No wonder, fallen such a pernicious height.
He scarce had ceased, when the superior fiend
Was moving towards the shore, his ponderous shield,
Ethereal temper, massy, large, and round,
Behind him cast. The broad circumference
Hung on his shoulders like the moon, whose orb
Through optic glass the Tuscan artist[1] views
At evening from the top of Fesole[2]
Or in Valdarno,[3] to descry new lands.
Rivers, or mountains, in her spotty globe.
His spear, to equal which the tallest pine,
Hewn on Norwegian hills, to be the mast
On some great ammiral,[4] were but a wand

1. *The Tuscan artist.*–Galileo, the inventor of the telescope.
2. *Fesole.*–A hill overlooking Florence and the surrounding country.
3. *Valdarno.*–The seat of Florence.
4. *Ammiral.*–An Italian form of expression for admiral. The admiral's ship was often called the admiral.

He walked with to support uneasy steps
Over the burning marl, not like those steps
On Heaven's azure, and the torrid clime
Smote on him sore besides, vaulted with fire.
Nathless he so endured, till on the beach
Of that inflamed sea he stood, and called
His legions, angel forms, who lay entranced[1]
Thick as autumnal leaves that strew the brooks
In Vallambrosa,[2] where the Etrurian shades
High overarched embower, or scattered sedge
Afloat, when with fierce winds Orion armed
Hath vexed the Red Sea coast, whose waves overthrew
Busiris[3] and his Memphian chivalry,[4]
While with perfidious hatred they pursued
The sojourners of Goshen, who beheld
From the safe shore their floating carcases
And broken chariot-wheels : so thick bestrewn,
Abject and lost lay these, covering the flood,
Under amazement of their hideous change.
He called so loud, that all the hollow deep
Of Hell resounded : Princes, potentates,
Warriors, the flower of Heaven, once yours, now lost,
If such astonishment as this can seize
Eternal spirits. Or have ye chosen this place
After the toil of battle to repose
Your wearied virtue, for the ease you find
To slumber here, as in the vales of Heaven ?
Or in this abject posture have ye sworn
To adore the Conqueror ? – who now beholds
Cherub and seraph rolling in the flood.
With scattered arms and ensigns; till anon

1. *Entranced.*–Bereft of mental power–incapable of action.
2. *Vallambrosa.*–A wooded district about eighteen miles from Florence.
3. *Busiris.*–Name given to the Pharaohs of the Red Sea.
4. *Memphian chivalry.*–The horsemen and charioteers who followed the Israelites.

His swift pursuers from Heaven-gates discern
The advantage, and descending, tread us down
Thus drooping, or with linked thunderbolts
Transfix us to the bottom of this gulf?
Awake, arise, or be for ever fallen !
They heard, and were abashed, and up they sprung
Upon the wing – as when men, wont to watch
On duty, sleeping found by whom they dread,
Rouse and bestir themselves ere well awake.
Nor did they not perceive the evil plight
In which they were, or the fierce pains not feel.
Yet to their general's voice they soon obeyed
Innumerable. As when the potent rod
Of Amram's son,[1] in Egypt's evil day,
Waved round the coast, up called a pitchy cloud
Of locusts, warping on the eastern wind
That o'er the realm of impious Pharaoh hung
Like night, and darkened all the land of Nile :
So numberless were those bad Angels seen,
Hovering on wing, under the cope of Hell,
'Twixt upper, nether, and surrounding fires,–
Till, at a signal given, the uplifted spear
Of their great sultan waving to direct
Their course, in even balance down they light
On the firm brimstone, and fill all the plain,
A multitude, like which the populous North
Poured never from her frozen loins, to pass
Rhene or the Danaw,[2] when her barbarous sons
Came like a deluge on the south, and spread
Beneath Gibraltar to the Libyan sands.
Forthwith from every squadron and each band,
The heads and leaders thither haste where stood

1. *Amram's son.*–Moses.

2. *Rhene or the Danaw.*– The Rhine or Danube.

Their great commander. Godlike shapes, and forms
Excelling human; princely dignities;
And powers that erst in Heaven sat on thrones,
Though of their names in heavenly records now
Be no memorial, blotted out and rased
By their rebellion from the Book of Life.
Nor had they yet among the sons of Eve
Got them new names; till, wandering o'er the earth,
Through God's high sufferance, for the trial of man,
By falsities and lies the greatest part
Of mankind they corrupted to forsake
God their Creator, and the invisible
Glory of Him that made them to transform
Oft to the image of a brute, adorned
With gay religions, full of pomp and gold,
And devils to adore for deities:
Then were they known to men by various names.
And various idols through the heathen world.
 Say, Muse, their names then known. Who first, who
Roused from the slumber, on that fiery couch.
At their great emperor's call, as next in worth
Came singly where he stood on the bare strand.
While the promiscuous crowd stood yet aloof
The chief were those, who, from the pit of Hell,
Roaming to seek their prey on earth, durst fix
Their seats long after next the seat of God,
Their altars by His altar; gods adored
Among the nations round; and durst abide
Jehovah thundering out of Sion, throned
Between the cherubim; yea, often placed
Within His sanctuary itself their shrines,
Abominations, and with cursed things
His holy rites and solemn feasts profaned,
And with their darkness durst affront His light.
First, Moloch, horrid king, besmeared with blood
Of human sacrifice, and parents' tears;

Though, for the noise of drums and timbrels loud,
Their children's cries unheard, that passed through fire
To his grim idol. Him the Ammonite
Worshipped in Rabba[1] and her watery plain,
In Argob and in Basan, to the stream
Of utmost Arnon. Nor content with such
Audacious neighbourhood, the wisest heart
Of Solomon he led by fraud to build
His temple right against the temple of God,
On that opprobrious hill,[2] and made his grove
The pleasant valley of Hinnom, Tophet thence
And black Gehenna called, the type of Hell.[3]
Next, Chemos, the obscene dread of Moab's sons,
From Aroer to Nebo, and the wild
Of southmost Abarim; in Hesebon,
And Horonaim, Seon's realm, beyond
The flowery dale of Sibma, clad with vines,
And Elealé to the asphaltic pool.[4]
Peor his other name, when he enticed
Israel in Sittim, on their march from Nile,
To do him wanton rites, which cost them woe.
Yet thence his lustful orgies he enlarged
Even to that hill of scandal, by the grove
Of Moloch homicide; lust hard by hate;
Till good Josiah drove them hence to Hell.
With these came they, who, from the bordering flood
Of old Euphrates to the brook that parts
Egypt from Syrian ground, had general names

1. *In Rabba.*–Capital of the Ammonites.
2. *That opprobrious hill.*–Made opprobrious by the uses to which it was thus applied.
3. *Type of Hell.*–Tophet was originally a beautiful royal residence in the Valley of Hinnom; but from the abominations which came to be practised there, the later Jews were wont to burn the bodies of malefactors in that quarter, and took from it their "type of hell."
4. *Asphaltic pool.*–The Dead Sea.

Of Baalim and Ashtaroth; those male,
These feminine; for spirits, when they please,
Can either sex assume, or both, – so soft
And uncompounded is their essence pure,
Not tied or manacled with joint or limb,
Nor founded on the brittle strength of bones.
Like cumbrous flesh, but, in what shape they choose.
Dilated or condensed, bright or obscure,
Can execute their aery purposes.
And works of love or enmity fulfil.
For those the race of Israel oft forsook
Their Living Strength, and unfrequented left
His righteous altar, bowing lowly down
To bestial gods; for which their heads as low
Bowed down in battle, sunk before the spear
Of despicable foes. With these in troop
Came Astoreth, whom the Phoenicians called
Astarte, queen of heaven, with crescent horns,
To whose bright image nightly by the moon
Sidonian virgins paid their vows and songs;
In Sion also not unsung, where stood
Her temple on the offensive mountain, built
By that uxorious king, whose heart, though large,
Beguiled by fair idolatresses, fell
To idols foul. Thammuz came next behind,
Whose annual wound, to Lebanon allured
The Syrian damsels to lament his fate
In amorous ditties all a summer's day,
While smooth Adonis from his native rock
Ran purple to the sea, supposed with blood
Of Thammuz[1] yearly wounded : the love-tale

1. *Thammuz.*–A god of the Syrians–the Adonis of that people–said to die every year and to live again. Women professed yearly to lament his fate, and great sensual vice, as the mode of doing him homage, was the result. (See Ezek. viii. 13, 14.)

Infected Sion's daughters with like heat,
Whose wanton passions in the sacred porch
Ezekiel saw, when, by the vision led,
His eye surveyed the dark idolatries
Of alienated Judah.[1] Next came one
Who mourned in earnest, when the captive ark
Maimed his brute image, heads and hands lopped off
In his own temple, on the grunsel edge,[2]
Where he fell flat, and shamed his worshippers.
Dagon his name, sea-monster, upward man
And downward fish : yet had his temple high
Reared in Azotus, dreaded through the coast
Of Palestine, in Gath and Ascalon,
And Accaron and Gaza's frontier bounds.
Him followed Rimmon, whose delightful seat
Was fair Damascus, on the fertile banks
Of Abbana and Pharphar, lucid streams.
He also 'gainst the house of God was bold :
A leper once he lost, and gained a king;
Ahaz, his sottish conqueror, whom he drew
God's altar to disparage and displace.
For one of Syrian mode, whereon to burn
His odious offerings, and adore the gods
Whom he had vanquished. After these appeared
A crew, who, under names of old renown,
Osiris, I sis, Orus, and their train,
With monstrous shapes and sorceries abused
Fanatic Egypt, and her priests, to seek
Their wandering aods disguised in brutish forms
Rather than human. Nor did Israel 'scape
The infection, when their borrowed gold composed
The calf in Oreb; and the rebel king
Doubled that sin in Bethel and in Dan,

1. Ezek. viii. 12.

2. *Grunsel edge.*–Threshold.

Likening his Maker to the grazed ox,
Jehovah, who, in one night, when He passed
From Egypt marching, equalled with one stroke
Both her first-born and all her bleating gods.
Belial came last, than whom a spirit more lewd
Fell not from heaven, or more gross to love
Vice for itself : to him no temple stood.
Or altar smoked : yet who more oft than he
In temples and at altars, when the priest
Turns atheist, as did Eli's sons, who filled
With lust and violence the house of God ?
In courts and palaces he also reigns,
And in luxurious cities, where the noise
Of riot ascends above their loftiest towers,
And injury, and outrage : and when night
Darkens the streets, then wander forth the sons
Of Belial, flown with insolence and wine.
Witness the streets of Sodom, and that night
In Gibeah, when the hospitable door
Exposed a matron, to avoid worse rape.
These were the prime in order and in might;
The rest were long to tell, though far renowned,
The Ionian gods, of Javan's issue held
Gods, yet confessed later than heaven and earth.
Their boasted parents : Titan, heaven's first-born,
With his enormous brood, and birthright seized
By younger Saturn; he from mightier Jove,
His own and Rhea's son, like measure found.
So Jove usurping reigned. These first in Crete
And Ida known, thence on the snowy top
Of cold Olympus ruled the middle air.
Their highest heaven; or on the Delphian cliff.
Or in Dodona,[1] and through all the bounds

---

1. *The Delphian cliff, or in Dodona.*–There was an oracle to Apollo at Delphi, and one to Jupiter at Dodona.

Of Doric land; or who with Saturn old
Fled over Adria to the Hesperian fields,
And o'er the Celtic roamed the utmost isles.
All these and more came flocking; but with looks
Downcast and damp; yet such wherein appeared
Obscure some glimpse of joy, to have found their chief
Not in despair, to have found themselves not lost
In loss itself, – which on his countenance cast
Like doubtful hue. But he, his wonted pride
Soon recollecting, with high words, that bore
Semblance of worth, not substance, gently raised
Their fainting courage, and dispelled their fears.
Then straight commands, that at the warlike sound
Of trumpets loud and clarions, be upreared
His mighty standard. That proud honour claim'd
Azazel as his right; a cherub tall,
Who forthwith from the glittering staff unfurled
The imperial ensign, which, full high advanced,
Shone like a meteor streaming to the wind,
With gems and golden lustre rich emblazed,
Seraphic arms and trophies; all the while
Sonorous metal blowing martial sounds,
At which the universal host up sent
A shout, that tore Hell's concave, and beyond
Frighted the reign of Chaos and old Night.
All in a moment, through the gloom were seen
Ten thousand banners rise into the air,
With orient colours waving. With them rose
A forest huge of spears; and thronging helms
Appeared, and serried shields in thick array,
Of death immeasurable : anon they move
In perfect phalanx to the Dorian mood[1]
Of flutes and soft recorders, – such as raised
To height of noblest temper heroes old

1. *The Dorian mood.*–In the Greek or Spartan manner.

Arming to battle; and instead of rage
Deliberate valour breathed, firm and unmoved
With dread of death to flight or foul retreat :
Nor wanting power to mitigate and 'suage
With solemn touches troubled thoughts, and chase
Anguish, and doubt, and fear, and sorrow, and pain,
From mortal or immortal minds. Thus they,
Breathmg united force, with fixed thought.
Moved on in silence to soft pipes, that charmed
Their painful steps o'er the burnt soil. And now
Advanced in view they stand, a horrid front
Of dreadful length and dazzling arms, in guise
Of warriors old with ordered spear and shield,
Awaiting what command their mighty chief
Had to impose. He through the armed files
Darts his experienced eye, and soon traverse[1]
The whole battalion views, their order due,
Their visages and stature as of gods,
Their number last he sums. And now his heart
Distends with pride, and hardening in his strength
Glories. For never, since created man,
Met such embodied force, as named with these
Could merit more than that small infantry
Warred on by cranes, though all the giant brood
Of Phlegra[2] with the heroic race were joined
That fought at Thebes and Ilium,[3] on each side
Mixed with auxiliar gods; and what resounds
In fable or romance of Uther's son
Begirt with British and Armoric knights;
And all who since, baptized or infidel,
Jousted in Aspramont, or Montalban,

1. *Traverse.*–From end to end.
2. *Of Phlegra.*–Some make the giant war in which Hercules was engaged to have taken place in Phlegra.
3. *Thebes and Ilium.*– The Greek Thebes and Troy.

Damasco, or Morocco, or Trebisond,
Or whom Biserta sent from Afric shore.
When Charlemain with all his peerage fell
By Fontarabia. Thus far these beyond
Compare of mortal prowess, yet observed
Their dread commander. He, above the rest
In shape and gesture proudly eminent,
Stood like a tower. His form had yet not lost
All its original brightness; nor appeared
Less than Archangel ruined, and the excess
Of glory obscured, – as when the sun, new risen,
Looks through the horizontal misty air,
Shorn of his beams; or from behind the moon,
In dim eclipse, disastrous twilight sheds
On half the nations, and with fear of change
Perplexes monarchs. Darkened so, yet shone
Above them all the Archangel. But his face
Deep scars of thunder had intrenched, and care
Sat on his faded cheek, but under brows
Of dauntless courage, and considerate pride
Waiting revenge. Cruel his eye, but cast
Signs of remorse and passion, to behold
The fellows of his crime, the followers rather –
Far other once beheld in bliss – condemned
For ever now to have their lot in pain,
Millions of spirits for his fault amerced
Of Heaven, and from eternal splendours flung
For his revolt, yet faithful how they stood,
Their glory withered : as when heaven's fire
Hath scathed the forest oaks, or mountain pines,
With singed top, their stately growth, though bare,
Stands on the blasted heath. He now prepared
To speak; whereat their doubled ranks they bend
From wing to wing, and half enclose him round
With all his peers : attention held them mute.
Thrice he essayed, and thrice, in spite of scorn,

Tears, such as angels weep, burst forth : at last
Words, interwove with sighs, found out their way.
O myriads of immortal spirits ! O powers
Matchless, but with the Almighty ! and that strife
Was not inglorious, though the event was dire,
As this place testifies, and this dire change,
Hateful to utter ! But what power of mind,
Foreseeing or presaging, from the depth
Of knowledge past or present, could have feared,
How such united force of gods, how such
As stood like these, could ever know repulse ?
For who can yet believe, though after loss,
That all these puissant legions, whose exile
Hath emptied heaven, shall fail to re-ascend
Self-raised, and re-possess their native seat ?
For me, be witness all the host of heaven,
If counsels different, or dangers shunned
By me, have lost our hopes. But He who reigns
Monarch in heaven, till then as one secure
Sat on His throne, upheld by old repute.
Consent or custom, and His regal state
Put forth at full, but still His strength concealed.
Which tempted our attempt, and wrought our fall.
Henceforth His might we know, and know our own;
So as not either to provoke, or dread
New war provoked. Our better part remains
To work in close design, by fraud or guile,
What force effected not, that He no less
At length from us may find, who overcomes
By force, hath overcome but half his foe.
Space may produce new worlds; whereof so rife
There went a fame in heaven that he ere long
Intended to create, and therein plant
A generation whom his choice regard
Should favour equal to the sons of heaven.
Thither, if but to pry, should be perhaps

Our first eruption. Thither or elsewhere,
For this infernal pit shall never hold
Celestial spirits in bondage, nor the abyss
Long under darkness cover. But these thoughts
Full counsel must mature. Peace is despaired;
For who can think submission ? War then, war,
Open or understood, must be resolved.
He spake: and to confirm his words, out flew
Millions of flaming swords, drawn from the thighs
Of mighty cherubim; the sudden blaze
Far round illumined Hell. Highly they raged
Against the Highest, and fierce with grasped arms
Clashed on their sounding shields the din of war,
Hurling defiance toward the vault of Heaven.
There stood a hill not far, whose grisly top
Belched fire and rolling smoke; the rest entire
Shone with a glossy scurf; undoubted sign
That in his womb was hid metallic ore,
The work of sulphur. Thither, winged with speed,
A numerous brigade hastened : as when bands
Of pioneers, with spade and pickaxe arm'd,
Forerun the royal camp, to trench a field,
Or cast a rampart. Mammon led them on.
Mammon, the least erected spirit that fell
From heaven, – for e'en in heaven his looks and thoughts
Were always downward bent, admiring more
The riches of heaven's pavement, trodden gold,
Than aught divine or holy, else enjoyed
In vision beatific. By him first
Men also, and by his suggestion taught,
Ransacked the centre, and with impious hands
Rifled the bowels, of their mother earth
For treasures, better hid. Soon had his crew
Opened into the hill a spacious wound,
And digged out ribs of gold. Let none admire
That riches grow in Hell, – that soil may best

Deserve the precious bane. And here let those
Who boast in mortal things, and wondering tell
Of Babel, and the works of Memphian kings,
Learn how their greatest monuments of fame,
And strength, and art, are easily outdone
By spirits reprobate, and in an hour,
What in an age they, with incessant toil
And hands innumerable, scarce perform.
Nigh on the plain, in many cells prepared,
That underneath had veins of liquid fire
Sluiced from the lake, a second multitude,
With wondrous art, founded the massy ore,
Severing each kind, and scummed the bullion dross.
A third as soon had formed within the ground
A various mould, and from the boiling cells,
By strange conveyance, filled each hollow nook,
As in an organ, from one blast of wind,
To many a row of pipes the soundboard breathes.
Anon, out of the earth, a fabric huge
Rose like an exhalation, with the sound
Of dulcet symphonies and voices sweet,
Built like a temple, where pilasters round
Were set, and Doric pillars overlaid
With golden architrave. Nor did there want
Cornice or frieze, with bossy sculptures graven.
The roof was fretted gold. Not Babylon,
Nor great Alcairo,[1] such magnificence
Equalled in all their glories, to enshrine
Belus or Serapis, their gods, or seat
Their kings, when Egypt with Assyria strove
In wealth and luxury. The ascending pile
Soon fixed her stately height; and straight the doors,
Opening their brazen folds, discover, wide
Within, her ample spaces, o'er the smooth

1. *Alcairo*.–Memphis.

And level pavement. From the arched roof,
Pendent by subtle magic, many a row
Of starry lamps and blazing cressets, fed
With naphtha and asphaltus, yielded light
As from a sky. The hasty multitude
Admiring entered; and the work some praise,
And some the architect. His hand was known
In heaven by many a towered structure high,
Where sceptred angels held their residence,
And sat as princes, whom the supreme King
Exalted to such power, and gave to rule,
Each in his hierarchy, the orders bright.
Nor was his name unheard or unadored
In ancient Greece; and in the Ausonian land
Men called him Mulciber; and how he fell
From heaven, they fabled, thrown by angry Jove
Sheer o'er the crystal battlements : from morn
To noon he fell, from noon to dewy eve,
A summer's day; and with the setting sun
Dropped from the zenith, like a falling star,
On Lemnos, Ægean isle. Thus they relate,
Erring ;[1] for he with this rebellious rout
Fell long before; nor aught availed him now
To have built in heaven high towers, nor did he 'scape
By all his engines, but was headlong sent
With his industrious crew to build in Hell.
    Meanwhile the winged heralds, by command
Of sovereign power, with awful ceremony
And trumpet's sound, throughout the host proclaim
A solemn council, forthwith to be held
At Pandemonium, the high capital
Of Satan and his peers. Their summons called
From every band and squared regiment,
By place or choice the worthiest; they anon,

1. *Erring.*–Milton thus hnks the tradition concerning Vulcan in the Greek mythology with that of a workman of a higher order.

With hundreds and with thousands, trooping came,
Attended. All access was thronged; the gates
And porches wide, but chief the spacious hall –
Though like a covered field, where champions bold
Wont ride in armed, and at the Soldan's[1] chair
Defied the best of Panim[2] chivalry
To mortal combat, or career with lance –
Thick swarmed, both on the ground and in the air,
Brushed with the hiss of rustling wings. As bees
In spring-time, when the sun with Taurus rides,
Pour forth their populous youth about the hive
In clusters; they among fresh dews and flowers
Fly to and fro, or on the smoothed plank,
The suburb of their straw-built citadel.
New rubbed with balm, expatiate and confer
Their state affairs, – so thick the aery crowd
Swarmed and were straitened, till, the signal given,
Behold a wonder ! They but now who seemed
In bigness to surpass earth's giant sons,
Now less than smallest dwarfs, in narrow room
Throng numberless like that Pygmean race
Beyond the Indian mount; or fairy elves,
Whose midnight revels by a forest side
Or fountain, some belated peasant sees,
Or dreams he sees, while overhead the moon
Sits arbitress, and nearer to the earth
Wheels her pale course; they, on their mirth and dance
Intent, with jocund music charm his ear;
At once with joy and fear his heart rebounds.
Thus incorporeal spirits to smallest forms
Reduced their shapes immense, and were at large,
Though without number still, amidst the hall

1. *Soldan.*–Sultan.

2. *Panim.*–Pagan–not Christian.

Of that infernal court. But far within,
And in their own dimensions, like themselves,
The great seraphic lords and cherubim
In close recess and secret conclave sat;
A thousand demi-gods, on golden seats,
Frequent and full. After short silence then.
And summons read, the great consult began.

BOOK - II

The consultation begun, Satan debates whether another battle be to be hazarded for the recovery of heaven. Some advise it, others dissuade: a third proposal is preferred, mentioned before by Satan, to search the truth of that prophecy or tradition in heaven concerning another world, and another kind of creature, equal or not much inferior to themselves, about this time to be created. Their doubt, who shall be sent on this difficult search; Satan, their chief, undertakes alone the voyage, is honoured and applauded. The council thus ended, the rest betake them several ways, and to several employments, as their inclinations lead them, to entertain the time till Satan return. He passes on his journey to hell-gates; finds them shut, and who sat there to guard them; by whom at length they are opened, and discover to him the great gulf between hell and heaven; with what difficulty he passes through, directed by Chaos, the power of that place, to the sight of this new world which he sought.

HIGH on a throne of royal state, which far
Outshone the wealth of Ormus and of Ind,[1]
Or where the gorgeous East, with richest hand,
Showers on her kings barbaric pearl and gold,
Satan exalted sat, by merit raised
To that bad eminence; and, from despair
Thus high uplifted beyond hope, aspires
Beyond thus high; insatiate to pursue
Vain war with Heaven; and, by success untaught,[2]
His proud imaginations thus displayed :

---

1. *Wealth of Ormus and of Ind.*–Precious stones which came from India, and of which Ormus, an island in the Red Sea, was the great mart.
2. *By success untaught.*–A classical form of expression, meaning untaught by events–by experience.

Powers and Dominions, Deities of Heaven!
For since no deep within her gulf can hold
Immortal vigour, though oppressed and fallen,
I give not Heaven for lost. From this descent
Celestial virtues rising, will appear
More glorious and more dread than from no fall,
And trust themselves to fear no second fate.
Me though just right, and the fixed laws of Heaven.
Did first create your leader; next, free choice,
With what besides, in counsel or in fight,
Hath been achieved of merit; yet this loss,
Thus far at least recovered, hath much more
Established in a safe unenvied throne,
Yielded with full consent. The happier state
In Heaven, which follows dignity, might draw
Envy from each inferior; but who here
Will envy whom the highest place exposes
Foremost to stand against the Thunderer's aim,
Your bulwark, and condemns to greatest share
Of endless pain ? Where there is then no good
For which to strive, no strife can grow up there
From faction. For none sure will claim in Hell
Precedence, – none, whose portion is so small
Of present pain, that with ambitious mind
Will covet more. With this advantage then
To union, and firm faith, and firm accord,
More than can be in Heaven, we now return
To claim our just inheritance of old,
Surer to prosper than prosperity
Could have assured us; and, by what best way,
Whether of open war, or covert guile,
We now debate : who can advise, may speak.
He ceased; and next him Moloch, sceptred king,
Stood up, the strongest and the fiercest spirit
That fought in Heaven, now fiercer by despair.

His trust was with the Eternal to be deemed
Equal in strength, and rather than be less,
Cared not to be at all. With that care lost
Went all his fear; of God, or hell, or worse,
He recked not; and these words thereafter spake:
  My sentence is for open war. Of wiles,
More unexpert, I boast not; them let those
Contrive who need, or when they need, not now.
For, while they sit contriving, shall the rest,
Millions that stand in arms, and longing wait
The signal to ascend, sit lingering here,
Heaven's fugitives, and for their dwelling-place
Accept this dark opprobrious den of shame,
The prison of his tyranny who reigns
By our delay ? No ! let us rather choose,
Armed with hell flames and fury, all at once,
O'er Heaven's high towers to force resistless way,
Turning our tortures into horrid arms
Against the torturer; when, to meet the noise
Of his almighty engine, he shall hear
Infernal thunder, and, for lightning, see
Black fire and horror shot with equal rage
Among his Angels, and his throne itself
Mixed with Tartarean sulphur and strange fire,
His own invented torments. But perhaps
The way seems difficult and steep to scale
With upright wing against a higher foe.
Let such bethink them, if the sleepy drench
Of that forgetful lake benumb not still,
That in our proper motion we ascend
Up to our native seat : descent and fall
To us is adverse. Who but felt of late,
When the fierce foe hung on our broken rear
Insulting, and pursued us through the deep,
With what compulsion and laborious flight
We sunk thus low ? The ascent is easy then.

The event is feared; should we again provoke
Our stronger, some worse way his wrath may find
To our destruction, – if there be in hell
Fear to be worse destroyed. What can be worse
Than to dwell here, driven out from bliss, condemned
In this abhorred deep to utter woe,
Where pain of unextinguishable fire
Must exercise us[1] without hope of end,
The vassals of his anger, when the scourge
Inexorable, and the torturing hour,
Call us to penance ? More destroyed than thus
We should be quite abolished, and expire.
What fear we, then ? What doubt we to incense
His utmost ire, which, to the height enraged,
Will either quite consume us, and reduce
To nothing this essential – happier far
Than miserable to have eternal being –
Or, if our substance be indeed divine,
And cannot cease to be, we are at worst
On this side nothing; and by proof we feel
Our power sufficient to disturb his heaven,
And with perpetual inroads to alarm,
Though inaccessible, his fatal throne,
Which, if not victory, is yet revenge.
He ended, frowning, and his look denounced[2]
Desperate revenge, and battle dangerous
To less than gods. On the other side up rose
Belial, in act more graceful and humane;
A fairer person lost not heaven; he seemed
For dignity composed, and high exploit :
But all was false and hollow; though his tongue
Dropt manna, and could make the worse appear
The better reason, to perplex and dash

1. *Exercise us.*–Torment or try us–the Latin sense of the word.

2. *Denounced.*–Menaced, proclaimed

Maturest counsels : for his thoughts were low :
To vice industrious, but to nobler deeds
Timorous and slothful; yet he pleased the ear,
And with persuasive accent thus began :
    I should be much for open war, O peers,
As not behind in hate; if what was urged
Main reason to persuade immediate war,
Did not dissuade me most, and seem to cast
Ominous conjecture on the whole success;
When he, who most excels in fact of arms,
In what he counsels, and in what excels,
Mistrustful grounds his courage on despair
And utter dissolution, as the scope
Of all his aim, after some dire revenge.
First, what revenge ? The towers of heaven are filled
With armed watch, that render all access
Impregnable. Oft on the bordering deep
Encamp their legions; or, with obscure wing
Scout, far and wide into the realm of night.
Scorning surprise. Or could we break our way
By force, and at our heels all hell should rise
With blackest insurrection, to confound
Heaven's purest light; yet our great Enemy,
All incorruptible, would on his throne
Sit unpolluted, and the ethereal mould,
Incapable of stain, would soon expel
Her mischief, and purge off the baser fire.
Victorious. Thus repulsed, our final hope
Is flat despair: we must exasperate
The Almighty Victor to spend all His rage.
And that must end us; that must be our cure, –
To be no more. Sad cure ! for who would lose.
Though full of pain, this intellectual being,
Those thoughts that wander through eternity,
To perish rather, swallowed up and lost
In the wide womb of uncreated night,

Devoid of sense and motion ? And who knows,
Let this be good, whether our angry Foe
Can give it, or will ever? How he can,
Is doubtful : that he never will, is sure.
Will he, so wise, let loose at once his ire,
Belike through impotence, or unaware,
To give his enemies their wish, and end
Them in his anger, whom his anger saves
To punish endless ? Wherefore cease we then ?
Say they who counsel war – We are decreed,
Reserved, and destined to eternal woe :
Whatever doing, what can we suffer more,
What can we suffer worse ? Is this then worst,
Thus sitting, thus consulting, thus in arms ?
What ! when we fled amain, pursued, and struck
With heaven's afflicting thunder, and besought
The deep to shelter us ? This hell then seemed
A refuge from those wounds, or when we lay
Chained on the burning lake ? That sure was worse.
What if the breath that kindled those grim fires
Awaked, should blow them into sevenfold rage,
And plunge us in the flames ? Or, from above,
Should intermitted vengeance arm again
His red right hand to plague us ? What if all
Her stores were opened, and this firmament
Of Hell should spout her cataracts of fire,
Impendent horrors, threatening hideous fall
One day upon our heads, while we, perhaps,
Designing or exhorting glorious war,
Caught in a fiery tempest, shall be hurled
Each on his rock transfixed, the sport and prey
Of racking whirlwinds, or for ever sunk
Under yon boiling ocean, wrapped in chains,
There to converse with everlasting groans,
Unrespited, unpitied, unreprieved.
Ages of hopeless end ? This would be worse.

War, therefore, open or concealed, alike
My voice dissuades; for what can force or guile
With him, or who deceive his mind, whose eye
Views all things at one view ? He from heaven's height
All these our motions vain sees, and derides;
Not more almighty to resist our might,
Than wise to frustrate all our plots and wiles.
Shall we then live thus vile, the race of heaven
Thus trampled, thus expelled to suffer here
Chains and these torments ? Better these than worse,
By my advice; since fate inevitable
Subdues us, and omnipotent decree,
The Victor's will. To suffer, as to do,
Our strength is equal, nor the law unjust
That so ordains : this was at first resolved,
If we were wise, against so great a Foe
Contending, and so doubtful what might fall.
I laugh, when those who at the spear are bold
And venturous, if that fail them, shrink and fear
What yet they know must follow, to endure
Exile, or ignominy, or bonds, or pain.
The sentence of their Conqueror. This is now
Our doom; which if we can sustain and bear.
Our Supreme Foe in time may much remit
His anger, and perhaps, thus far removed,
Not mind us not offending, satisfied
With what is punished; whence these raging files
Will slacken, if His breath stir not their flames.
Our purer essence then will overcome
Their noxious vapour; or, inured, not feel;
Or, changed at length, and to the place conformed
In temper and in nature, will receive
Familiar the fierce heat, and void of pain.
This horror will grow mild, this darkness light :
Besides what hope the never-ending flight
Of future days may bring, what chance, what change

Worth waiting : since our present lot appears
For happy, though but ill; for ill, not worst;
If we procure not to ourselves more woe.
Thus Belial, with words clothed in reason's garb.
Counselled ignoble ease, and peaceful sloth,
Not peace : And after him thus Mammon spake :
Either to disenthrone the King of Heaven
We war, if war be best, or to regain
Our own right lost. Him to unthrone we then
May hope, when everlasting Fate shall yield
To fickle Chance, and Chaos judge the strife.
The former, vain to hope, argues as vain
The latter; for what place can be for us
Within heaven's bound, unless heaven's Lord supreme
We overpower ? Suppose he should relent.
And publish grace to all, on promise made
Of new subjection; with what eyes could we
Stand in his presence humble, and receive
Strict laws imposed, to celebrate his throne
With warbled hymns, and to his Godhead sing
Forced hallelujahs, while he lordly sits
Our envied Sovereign, and his altar breathes
Ambrosial odours and ambrosial flowers,
Our servile of lerings ? This must be our task
In heaven, this our delight. How wearisome
Eternity so spent, in worship paid
To whom we hate ! Let us not then pursue
By force impossible, by leave obtained
Unacceptable, though in heaven, our state
Of splendid vassalage; but rather seek
Our own good from ourselves, and from our own
Live to ourselves, though in this vast recess,
Free, and to none accountable, preferring
Hard liberty before the easy yoke
Of servile pomp. Our greatness will appear
Then most conspicuous, when great things of small,

Useful of hurtful, prosperous of adverse,
We can create; and in what place soe'er
Thrive under evil, and work ease out of pain,
Through labour and endurance. This deep world
Of darkness do we dread ? How oft amidst
Thick clouds and dark doth heaven's all-ruling Sire
Choose to reside, his glory unobscured,
And with the majesty of darkness round
Covers his throne; from whence deep thunders roar,
Mustering their rage, and heaven resembles hell ?
As he our darkness, cannot we his light
Imitate, when we please ? This desert soil
Wants not her hidden lustre, gems and gold;
Nor want we skill or art, from whence to raise
Magnificence; and what can heaven show more ?
Our torments also may in length of time
Become our elements; these piercing fires
As soft as now severe, our temper changed
Into their temper; which must needs remove
The sensible of pain. All things invite
To peaceful counsels, and the settled state
Of order, how in safety best we may
Compose our present evils, with regard
Of what we are, and where, dismissing quite
All thoughts of war. Ye have what I advise.
He scarce had finished, when such murmur filled
The assembly, as when hollow rocks retain
The sound of blustering winds, which all night long
Had roused the sea, now with hoarse cadence lull
Seafaring men o'erwatched, whose bark by chance
Or pinnace, anchors in a craggy bay
After the tempest, such applause was heard
As Mammon ended, and his sentence pleased,
Advising peace. For such another field
They dreaded worse than hell, so much the fear
Of thunder and the sword of Michael

Wrought still within them. And no less desire
To found this nether empire, which might rise
By policy, and long process of time,
In emulation opposite to heaven.
Which when Beelzebub perceived, than whom,
Satan except, none higher sat, with grave
Aspect he rose, and in his rising seemed
A pillar of state. Deep on his front engraven
Deliberation sat, and public care;
And princely counsel in his face yet shone,
Majestic, though in ruin. Sage he stood.
With Atlantean shoulders, fit to bear
The weight of mightiest monarchies. His look
Drew audience and attention still as night
Or summer's noontide air, while thus he spake :
    Thrones, and imperial powers, offspring of heaven,
Ethereal virtues ! or these titles now
Must we renounce, and, changing style, be called
Princes of hell ? For so the popular vote
Inclines, here to continue, and build up here
A growing empire. Doubtless, while we dream.
And know not that the Kine of Heaven hath doomed
This place our dungeon, not our safe retreat
Beyond his potent arm, to live exempt
From heaven's high jurisdiction, in new league
Banded against his throne, but to remain
In strictest bondage, though thus far removed.
Under the inevitable curb reserved.
His captive multitude : for he, be sure,
In height or depth, still first and last will reign
Sole king, and of His kingdom lose no part
By our revolt, but over hell extend
His empire, and with iron sceptre rule
Us here, as with his golden those in heaven.
What sit we then projecting peace and war ?
War hath determined us, and foiled with loss

Irreparable; terms of peace yet none
Vouchsafed or sought; for what peace will be given
To us enslaved, but custody severe,
And stripes, and arbitrary punishment,
Inflicted ? and what peace can we return,
But to our power hostility and hate,
Untamed reluctance, and revenge, though slow,
Yet ever plotting how the Conqueror least
May reap his conquest, and may least rejoice
In doing what we most in suffering feel?
Nor will occasion want, nor shall we need
With dangerous expedition to invade
Heaven, whose high walls fear no assault or siege,
Or ambush from the deep. What if we find
Some easier enterprise ? There is a place –
If ancient and prophetic fame in heaven
Err not, – another world, the happy seat
Of some new race, called Man, about this time
To be created like to us, though less
In power and excellence, but favoured more
Of him who rules above. So was his will
Pronounced among the gods, and by an oath.
That shook Heaven's whole circumference, confirmed.
Thither let us bend all our thoughts, to learn
What creatures there inhabit, of what mould
Or substance, how endued, and what their power,
And where their weakness, how attempted best,
By force or subtlety. Though heaven be shut,
And heaven's high Arbitrator sit secure
In his own strength, this place may He exposed,
The utmost border of his kingdom, left
To their defence who hold it. Here perhaps
Some advantageous act may be achieved
By sudden onset, either with hell-fire
To waste his whole creation, or possess
All as our own, and drive, as we were driven,

The puny habitants. Or, if not drive,
Seduce them to our party, that their God
May prove their foe, and with repenting hand
Abolish his own works. This would surpass
Common revenge, and interrupt his joy
In our confusion, and our joy upraise
In his disturbance; when his darling sons,
Hurled headlong to partake with us, shall curse
Their frail original, and faded bliss,
Faded so soon. Advise, if this be worth
Attempting, or to sit in darkness here
Hatching vain empires. – Thus Beelzebub
Pleaded his devilish counsel, first devised
By Satan, and in part proposed. For whence,
But from the author of all ill, could spring
So deep a malice, to confound the race
Of mankind in one root, and earth with hell
To mingle and involve, done all to spite
The great Creator ? But their spite still serves
His glory to augment. The bold design
Pleased highly those infernal states, and joy
Sparkled in all their eyes. With full assent
They vote. Whereat his speech he thus renews :
    Well have ye judged, well ended long debate,
Synod of gods ! and, like to what ye are, .
Great things resolved, which, from the lowest deep,
Will once more lift us up, in spite of fate,
Nearer our ancient seat. Perhaps in view
Of those bright confines, whence, with neighbouring arms,
And opportune excursion, we may chance
Re-enter heaven; or else in some mild zone
Dwell, not unvisited of heaven's fair light
Secure, and at the brightening orient beam
Purge off this gloom : the soft delicious air,
To heal the scar of these corrosive fires,
Shall breathe her balm. But first, whom shall we send

In search of this new world ? Whom shall we find
Sufficient ? Who shall tempt with wandering feet
The dark, unbottomed, infinite abyss,
And through the palpable obscure find out
His uncouth way, or spread his aery flight,
Upborne with indefatigable wings,
Over the vast abrupt, ere he arrive
The happy isle? What strength, what art, can then
Suffice, or what evasion bear him safe
Through the strict sentries and stations thick
Of Angels watching round ? Here he had need
All circumspection; and we now no less
Choice in our suffrage; for, on whom we send,
The weight of all, and our last hope, relies.
    This said, he sat; and expectation held
His look suspense, awaiting who appeared
To second, or oppose, or undertake,
The perilous attempt. But all sat mute,
Pondering the danger with deep thoughts; and each
In other's countenance read his own dismay.
Astonished. None among the choice and prime
Of those heaven-warring champions could be found
So hardy, as to proffer or accept
Alone the dreadful voyage; till at last
Satan, whom now transcendent glory raised
Above his fellows, with monarchal pride.
Conscious of highest worth, unmoved thus spake :
    O progeny of Heaven ! empyreal Thrones !
With reason hath deep silence and demur
Seized us, though undismayed. Long is the way
And hard, that out of hell leads up to light;
Our prison strong; this huge convex of fire,
Outrageous to devour, immures us round
Ninefold, and gates of burning adamant,
Barred over us, prohibit all egress.
These passed, if any pass, the void profound

Of unessential night receives him next
Wide gaping, and with utter loss of being
Threatens him, plunged in that abortive gulf.
If thence he 'scape into whatever world.
Or unknown region, what remains him less
Than unknown dangers, and as hard escape ?
But I should ill become this throne, O peers.
And this imperial sovereignty, adorned
With splendour, armed with power, if aught proposed
And judged of public moment, in the shape
Of difficulty or danger, could deter
Me from attempting. Wherefore do I assume
These royalties, and not refuse to reign,
Refusing to accept as great a share
Of hazard as of honour, due alike
To him who reigns, and so much to him due
Of hazard more, as he above the rest
High honoured sits ? Go, therefore, mighty powers,
Terror of heaven, though fallen ! intend at home –
While here shall be our home, – what best may ease
The present misery, and render Hell
More. tolerable; if there be cure or charm.
To respite, or deceive, or slack the pain
Of this ill mansion. Intermit no watch
Against a wakeful Foe, while I abroad.
Through all the coasts of dark destruction seek
Deliverance for us all. This enterprise
None shall partake with me. Thus saying, rose
The monarch, and prevented all reply;
Prudent, lest, from his resolution raised.
Others among the chief might offer now –
Certain to be refused – what erst they feared,
And, so refused, might in opinion stand
His rivals, winning cheap the high repute,
Which he through hazard huge must earn. But they
Dreaded not more the adventure, than his voice

Forbidding; and at once with him they rose.
Their rising all at once was as the sound
Of thunder heard remote. Toward him they bend
With awful reverence prone; and as a god
Extol him equal to the Highest in heaven.
Nor failed they to express how much they praised,
That for the general safety he despised
His own. For neither do the spirits damned
Lose all their virtue; lest bad men should boast
Their specious deeds on earth, which glory excites,
Or close ambition, varnished o'er with zeal.
Thus they their doubtful consultations dark
Ended, rejoicing in their matchless chief
As when from mountain-tops the dusky clouds
Ascending, while the north wind sleeps, o'erspread
Heaven's cheerful face, the louring element[1]
Scowls o'er the darkened landskip snow, or shower,
If chance the radiant sun, with farewell sweet.
Extend his evening beam, the fields revive,
The birds their notes renew, and bleating herds
Attest their joy, that hill and valley rings.
O shame to men ! Devil with devil damned
Firm concord holds, men only disagree
Of creatures rational, though under hope
Of heavenly grace; and, God proclaiming peace,
Yet live in hatred, enmity, and strife.
Among themselves, and levy cruel wars.
Wasting the earth, each other to destroy :
As if – which might induce us to accord –
Man had not hellish foes enow besides,
That day and night for his destruction wait.
The Stygian council thus dissolved, and forth
In order came the grand infernal peers.

1. *Element.* – The higher atmosphere, the elements filling it.

Midst came their mighty paramount,[1] and seemed
Alone the antagonist of Heaven, nor less
Than Hell's dread emperor, with pomp supreme,
And god-like imitated state. Him round
A globe of fiery seraphim enclosed
With bright emblazonry, and horrent arms.
Then, of their session ended, they bid cry
With trumpets' regal sound the great result.
Toward the four winds four speedy cherubim
Put to their mouths the sounding alchemy,[2]
By herald's voice explained; the hollow abyss
Heard far and wide, and all the host of Hell
With deafening shout returned them loud acclaim.
Thence more at ease their minds, and somewhat raised
By false presumptuous hope, the ranged powers
Disband, and, wandering, each his several way
Pursues, as inclination or sad choice
Leads him, perplexed where he may likeliest find
Truce to his restless thoughts, and entertain
The irksome hours, till his great chief return.
Part on the plain, or in the air sublime
Upon the wing, or in swift race contend.
As at the Olympian games or Pythian fields;[3]
Part curb their fiery steeds, or shun the goal
With rapid wheels, or fronted brigads form.
As when, to warn proud cities, war appears
Waged in the troubled sky, and armies rush
To battle in the clouds, before each van
Prick forth the aery knights, and couch their spears
Till thickest legions close; with feats of arms

1. *Paramount.*– Chief – lord paramount.

2. *Sounding alchemy.*–The metal of which trumpets are made.

3. *As at the Olympian games or Pythian fields.*–The Olympic games, in part described in the text, had descended as a custom from early times in Greek history, and were celebrated every four years. An Olympiad in Greek chronology consisted of these four years.

From either end of heaven the welkin burns.
Others, with vast Typhoean rage, more fell,
Rend up both rocks and hills, and ride the air
In whirlwind. Hell scarce holds the wild uproar.
As when Alcides,[1] from Œchalia crowned
With conquest, felt the envenomed robe, and tore
Through pain up by the roots Thessalian pines,
And Lichas from the top of Œta threw
Into the Euboic sea. Others, more mild,
Retreated in a silent valley, sing
With notes angelical to many a harp
Their own heroic deeds, and hapless fall
By doom of battle; and complain that fate
Free virtue should enthral to force or chance.
Their song was partial; but the harmony –
What could it less when spirits immortal sing ? –
Suspended Hell,[2] and took with ravishment
The thronging audience. In discourse more sweet –
For eloquence the soul, song charms the sense –
Others apart sat on a hill retired,
In thoughts more elevate, and reasoned high
Of providence, foreknowledge, will, and fate;
Fixed fate, free will, foreknowledge absolute,
And found no end, in wandering mazes lost.
Of good and evil much they argued then,
Of happiness and final misery
Passion and apathy, and glory and shame,
Vain wisdom all, and false philosophy.
Yet, with a pleasing sorcery, could charm
Pain for a while, or anguish, and excite
Fallacious hope, or arm the obdured breast
With stubborn patience, as with triple steel.
Another part, in squadrons and gross bands,
On bold adventure to discover wide

1. *As when Alcides.*–A name given to Hercules.

2. *Suspended Hell.*–Helped them to forget it.

That dismal world, if any clime perhaps
Might yield them easier habitation, bend
Four ways their flying march, along the banks
Of four infernal rivers, that disgorge
Into the burning lake their baleful streams :
Abhorred Styx, the flood of deadly hate;
Sad Acheron,[1] of sorrow, black and deep;
Cocytus, named of lamentation loud
Heard on the rueful stream; fierce Phlegethon,[2]
Whose waves of torrent fire inflame with rage.
Far off from these, a slow and silent stream,
Lethe, the river of oblivion, rolls
Her watery labyrinth, whereof who drinks.
Forthwith his former state and being forgets.
Forgets both joy and grief, pleasure and pain.
Beyond this flood a frozen continent
Lies dark and wild, beat with perpetual storms
Of whirlwind and dire hail, which on firm land
Thaws not, but gathers heap, and ruin seems
Of ancient pile; or else deep snow and ice,
A gulf profound as that Serbonian bog[3]
Betwixt Damiata and mount Casius old.
Where armies whole have sunk. The parching air
Burns frore,[4] and cold performs the effect of fire.
Thither, by harpy-footed furies haled.
At certain revolutions, all the damned
Are brought; and feel by turns the bitter change

---

1. *Sad Acheron.*–A river in the region of the lost, also called Cocytus, and said to utter a wail of sorrow as it flows.
2. *Fierce Phlegethon.*–Another of the infernal rivers, sometimes described as the fierce and bloody.
3. *Serbonian bog.*–A lake, with its adjacent marsh, near one of the mouths of the Nile.
4. *Burns frore.*–Burns *frosty.* Intense cold becomes heat. "When the cold north wind bloweth, it devoureth the mountains, and *burneth* the wilderness, and consumeth the grass *as fire.*" (Ecclus. xlii. 20, 21.)

Of fierce extremes, extremes by change more fierce;
From beds of raging fire, to starve in ice
Their soft ethereal warmth, and there to pine
Immovable, infixed, and frozen round,
Periods of time; thence hurried back to fire.
They ferry over this Lethean sound
Both to and fro, their sorrow to augment,
And wish and struggle, as they pass, to reach
The tempting stream, with one small drop to lose
In sweet forgetfulness all pain and woe,
All in one moment, and so near the brink;
But fate withstands, and to oppose the attempt
Medusa[1] with Gorgonian terror guards
The ford, and of itself the water flies
All taste of living wight, as once it fled
The lip of Tantalus. Thus roving on
In confused march forlorn, the adventurous bands,
With shuddering horror pale, and eyes aghast,
Viewed first their lamentable lot, and found
No rest. Through many a dark and dreary vale
They passed, and many a region dolorous,
O'er many a frozen, many a fiery Alp,
Rocks, caves, lakes, fens, bogs, dens, and shades of death,
A universe of death, which God by curse
Created evil, for evil only good;
Where all life dies, death lives, and Nature breeds
Perverse, all monstrous, all prodigious things.
Abominable, unutterable, and worse
Than fables yet have feigned, or fear conceived,
Gorgons, and Hydras, and Chimeras dire.[2]

1. *Medusa.*– One of the three fearful sisters known by the name of Gorgons. Their heads are said to have been covered with hissing serpents in place of hair, and they had brazen claws, enormous teeth, and wings.

2. *Gorgons and Hydras, and Chimeras dire.*–Virgil and Tasso had fixed all these monstrous existences in their hell long since.

Meanwhile, the adversary of God and man,
Satan, with thoughts inflamed of highest design.
Puts on swift wings, and towards the gates of hell
Explores his solitary flight. Sometimes
He scours the right-hand coast, sometimes the left;
Now shaves with level wing the deep, then soars
Up to the fiery concave towering high.
As when far off at sea a fleet descried
Hangs in the clouds, by equmoxial winds
Close sailing from Bengala, or the isles
Of Ternate and Tidore, whence merchants bring
Their spicy drugs; they on the trading flood,
Through the wide Ethiopian to the Cape,
Ply stemming nightly toward the pole : so seemed
Far off the flying fiend. At last appear
Hell-bounds, high reaching to the horrid roof,
And thrice threefold the gates. Threefolds were brass,
Three iron, three of adamantine rock
Impenetrable, impaled with circling fire,
Yet unconsumed. Before the gates there sat
On either side a formidable shape;
The one seemed woman to the waist, and fair;
But ended foul in many a scaly fold
Voluminous and vast, a serpent armed
With mortal sting. About her middle round
A cry of hell-hounds never-ceasing barked.
With wide Cerberian mouths,[1] full loud, and rung
A hideous peal. Yet when they list, would creep,
If aught disturbed their noise, into her womb,
And kennel there; yet there still barked and howled
Within, unseen. Far less abhorred than these
Vexed Scylla, bathing in the sea that parts

1. *Cerberian mouths.*–Cerberus, the name given to the dog said to guard the entrance to the infernal regions. Commonly described as having three heads, but by some poets as having many more.

Calabria from the hoarse Trinacrian[1] shore.
Nor uglier follow the night-hag, when, called
In secret, riding through the air she comes.
Lured with the smell of infant blood, to dance
With Lapland witches, while the labouring moon
Eclipses at their charms. The other shape.
If shape it might be called that shape had none
Distinguishable in member, joint, or limb.
Or substance might be called that shadow seemed,
For each seemed either – black it stood as Night,
Fierce as ten Furies, terrible as Hell,
And shook a dreadful dart; what seemed his head
The likeness of a kingly crown had on.
Satan was now at hand, and from his seat
The monster moving onward, came as fast
With horrid strides; Hell trembled as he strode.
The undaunted fiend what this might be admired,[2]
Admired, not feared. God and His Son except,
Created thing nought valued he, nor shunned;
And with disdainful look thus first began :
Whence, and what art thou, execrable shape !
That darest, though grim and terrible, advance
Thy miscreated front athwart my way
To yonder gates ? Through them I mean to pass,
That be assured, without leave asked of thee.
Retire, or taste thy folly, and learn by proof,
Hell-born, not to contend with spirits of heaven!
To whom the goblin, full of wrath, replied :
Art thou that traitor-angel, art thou he.
Who first broke peace in Heaven, and faith, till then
Unbroken; and in proud rebellious arms,
Drew after him the third part of heaven's sons
Conjured against the Highest; for which both thou

1. *Trinacrian.*–Sicilian.

2. *Admired.*–Wondered.

And they, outcast from God, are here condemned
To waste eternal days in woe and pain ?
And reckonest thou thyself with Spirits of Heaven,
Hell-doomed, and breathest defiance here and scorn.
Where I reign king, and, to enrage thee more,
Thy king and lord? Back to thy punishment,
False fugitive, and to thy speed add wings,
Lest with a whip of scorpions I pursue
Thy lingering, or with one stroke of this dart
Strange horror seize thee, and pangs unfelt before.
So spake the grizzly Terror, and in shape.
So speaking and so threatening, grew tenfold
More dreadful and deform. On the other side,
Incensed with indignation, Satan stood
Unterrified, and like a comet burned,
That fires the length of Ophiuchus huge[1]
In the arctic sky, and from his horrid hair
Shakes pestilence and war. Each at the head
Levelled his deadly aim; their fatal hands
No second stroke intend; and such a frown
Each cast at the other, as when two black clouds,
With heaven's artillery fraught, come rattling on
Over the Caspian, then stand front to front,
Hovering a space, till winds the signal blow
To join their dark encounter in mid-air :
So frowned the mighty combatants, that Hell
Grew darker at their frown; so matched they stood,
For never but once more was either like
To meet so great a Foe : And now great deeds
Had been achieved, whereof all Hell had rung,
Had not the snaky sorceress that sat
Fast by hell-gate, and kept the fatal key.
Risen, and with hideous outcry rushed between.
O father ! what intends thy hands, she cried.

1. *Ophiuchus huge.* – i.e., serpent- holder; one of the northern constellations.

Against thy only son ? What fury, O son !
Possesses thee to bend that mortal dart
Against thy father's head ? and know'st for whom;
For Him who sits above, and laughs the while
At thee ordained his drudge, to execute
Whate'er His wrath, which He calls justice, bids;
His wrath, which one day will destroy ye both!
 She spake, and at her words the hellish pest
Forbore; then these to her Satan returned :
 So strange thy outcry, and thy words so strange
Thou interposest, that my sudden hand.
Prevented, spares to tell thee yet by deeds
What it intends, till first I know of thee,
What thing thou art, thus double-formed, and why,
In this infernal vale first met, thou call'st
Me father, and that phantasm call'st my son :
I know thee not, nor ever saw till now
Sight more detestable than him and thee.
 To whom thus the portress of hell-gate replied :
Hast thou forgot me then, and do I seem
Now In thine eye so foul, once deemed so fair
In Heaven ? when at the assembly, and in sight
Of all the seraphim with thee combined
In bold conspiracy against Heaven's King,
All on a sudden miserable pain
Surprised thee; dim thine eyes, and dizzy swum
In darkness, while thy head flames thick and fast
Threw forth; till, on the left side opening wide,
Likest to thee in shape and countenance bright,
Then shining heavenly fair, a goddess armed,
Out of thy head I sprung. Amazement seized
All the host of heaven; back they recoiled afraid
At first, and called me Sin, and for a sign
Portentous held me; but, familiar grown,
I pleased, and with attractive graces won
The most averse, thee chiefly, who full oft

Thyself in me thy perfect image viewing,
Became enamoured, and such joy thou took'st
With me in secret, that my womb conceived
A growing burden. Meanwhile war arose,
And fields were fought in heaven; wherein remained –
For what could else ? – to our Almighty Foe
Clear victory; to our part loss and rout.
Through all the Empyrean. Down they fell,
Driven headlong from the pitch of heaven, down
Into this deep; and in the general fall,
I also; at which time, this powerful key
Into my hand was given, with charge to keep
These gates for ever shut, which none can pass
Without my opening. Pensive here I sat
Alone; but long I sat not, till my womb.
Pregnant by thee, and now excessive grown,
Prodigious motion felt, and rueful throes.
At last this odious offspring whom thou seest,
Thine own begotten, breaking violent way,
Tore through my entrails, that, with fear and pain
Distorted, all my nether shape thus grew
Transformed. But he my inbred enemy
Forth issued, brandishing his fatal dart.
Made to destroy. I fled, and cried out Death !
Hell trembled at the hideous name, and sighed
Far from her caves, and back resounded. Death !
I fled; but he pursued – though more, it seems.
Inflamed with lust than rage – and, swifter far.
Me overtook, his mother, all dismayed,
And in embraces forcible and foul
Ingendering with me, of that rape begot
These yelling monsters, that with ceaseless cry
Surround me, as thou sawest; hourly conceived
And hourly born, with sorrow infinite
To me; for, when they list, into the womb

That bred them they return, and howl, and gnaw
My bowels, their repast; then bursting forth
Afresh, with conscious terrors vex me round,
That rest or intermission none I find.
Before mine eyes in opposition sits
Grim Death, my son and foe, who sets them on,
And me his parent would full soon devour
For want of other prey, but that he knows
His end with mine involved;[1] and knows that
Should prove a bitter morsel, and his bane,
Whenever that shall be; so fate pronounced.
But thou, O father, I forewarn thee, shun
His deadly arrow; neither vainly hope
To be invulnerable in those bright arms,
Though tempered heavenly; for that mortal dint,
Save He who reigns above, none can resist.
She finished; and the subtle fiend his lore
Soon learned, now milder, and thus answered smooth :
Dear daughter, since thou claim'st me for thy sire,
And my fair son here show'st me, the dear pledge
Of dalliance had with thee in heaven, and joys
Then sweet, now sad to mention, through dire change
Befallen us, unforeseen, unthought of; know,
I come no enemy, but to set free
From out this dark and dismal house of pain
Both him and thee, and all the heavenly host
Of spirits, that, in our just pretences armed,
Fell with us from on high. From them I go
This uncouth errand sole; and, one for all.
Myself expose, with lonely steps to tread
The unfounded deep, and through the void immense
To search with wandering quest a place foretold
Should be, and, by concurring signs, ere now
Created, vast and round, a place of bliss

1. *His end with mine involved.*–As death came by sin, the destruction of sin would bring an end to death.

In the purlieus[1] of heaven, and therein placed
A race of upstart creatures, to supply
Perhaps our vacant room; though more removed,
Lest heaven, surcharged with potent multitude.
Might hap to move new broils. Be this or aught
Than this more secret now designed, I haste
To know; and, this once known, shall soon return.
And bring ye to the place where thou and Death
Shall dwell at ease, and up and down unseen
Wing silently the buxom air,[2] embalmed
With odours; there ye shall be fed and filled
Immeasurably, all things shall be your prey.
He ceased, for both seemed highly pleased; and Deadi
Grinned horrible a ghasdy smile, to hear
His famine should be filled; and blessed his maw
Destined to that good hour. No less rejoiced
His mother bad, and thus bespake her sire :
The key of this infernal pit by due.
And by command of heaven's all-powerful King,
I keep, by him forbidden to unlock
These adamantine gates; against all force
Death ready stands to interpose his dart,
Fearless to be o'ermatched by living might.
But what owe I to His commands above
Who hates me, and hath hither thrust me down
Into this gloom of Tartarus profound.
To sit in hateful office here confined,
Inhabitant of heaven, and heavenly born,
Here, in perpetual agony and pain.
With terrors and with clamours compassed round
Of mine own brood, that on my bowels feed ?
Thou art my lather, thou my author, thou
My being gavest me; whom should I obey

1. *Purlieus.*–Adjacent and open parts.

2. *The buxom air.*–Light, yielding.

But thee ? whom follow ? Thou wilt bring me soon
To that new world of light and bliss, among
The gods who live at ease, where I shall reign
At thy right hand voluptuous, as beseems
Thy daughter and thy darling, without end.
Thus saying, from her side the fatal key,
Sad instrument of all our woe, she took;
And towards the gate rolling her bestial train,
Forthwith the huge portcullis high updrew.
Which but herself, not all the Stygian powers
Could once have moved; then in the key-hole turns
The intricate wards, and every bolt and bar
Of massy iron or solid rock with ease
Unfastens. On a sudden open fly,
With impetuous recoil and jarring sound,
The infernal doors, and on their hinges grate
Harsh thunder, that the lowest bottom shook
Of Erebus.[1] She opened, but to shut
Excelled her power : the gates wide open stood,
That with extended wings a bannered host.
Under spread ensigns marching, might pass through,
With horse and chariots ranked in loose array;
So wide they stood, and like a furnace-mouth
Cast forth redounding smoke and ruddy flame.
Before their eyes in sudden view appear
The secrets of the hoary deep; a dark
Illimitable ocean, without bound,
Without dimension, where length, breadth, and height,
And time, and place, are lost; where eldest Night
And Chaos, ancestors of Nature, hold
Eternal anarchy, amidst the noise
Of endless wars, and by confusion stand.
For Hot, Cold, Moist, and Dry, four champions fierce.
Strive here for mastery, and to battle bring

1. *Erebus.*–Dark shades below, through which spirits were supposed to pass into Hades.

Their embryon atoms; they around the flag
Of each his faction, in their several clans,
Light-armed or heavy, sharp, smooth, swift, or slow,
Swarm populous, unnumbered as the sands
Of Barca or Cyrene's torrid soil.
Levied to side with warring winds, and poise
Their lighter wings. To whom these most adhere
He rules a moment. Chaos umpire sits,
And by decision more embroils the fray
By which he reigns. Next him, high arbiter
Chance governs all. Into this wild abyss,
The womb of Nature, and perhaps her grave,
Of neither sea, nor shore, nor air, nor fire,
But all these in their pregnant causes mixed
Confusedly, and which thus must ever fight,
Unless the Almighty Maker them ordain
His dark materials to create more worlds;
Into this wild abyss, the wary fiend
Stood on the brink of hell, and looked awhile,
Pondering his voyage; for no narrow frith
He had to cross. Nor was his ear less pealed
With noises loud and ruinous – to compare
Great things with small – than when Bellona storms
With all her battering engines bent to raze
Some capital city; or less than if this frame
Of heaven were falling, and these elements
In mutiny had from her axle torn
The steadfast earth. At last his sail-broad vans
He spreads for flight, and in the surging smoke
Uplifted spurns the ground; thence many a league.
As in a cloudy chair, ascending, rides
Audacious; but, that seat soon failing, meets
A vast vacuity. All unawares.
Fluttering his pennons vain, plumb down he drops
Ten thousand fathom deep; and to this hour
Down had been falling, had not, by ill chance,

The strong rebuff of some tumultuous cloud,
Instinct with fire and nitre, hurried him
As many miles aloft. That fury stayed,
Quenched in a boggy syrtis, neither sea.
Nor good dry land; nigh foundered, on he fares,
Treading the crude consistence, half on foot,
Half flying. Behoves him now both oar and sail.
As when a gryphon, through the wilderness
With winged course, o'er hill or moory dale,
Pursues the Arimaspian,[1] who by stealth
Had from his wakeful custody purloined
The guarded gold : so eagerly the fiend
O'er bog, or steep, through strait, rough, dense, or rare.
With head, hands, wings, or feet, pursues his way.
And swims, or sinks, or wades, or creeps, or flies.
At length a universal hubbub wild.
Of stunning sounds, and voices all confused,
Borne through the hollow dark, assaults his ear
With loudest vehemence. Thither he plies,
Undaunted, to meet there whatever power
Or spirit of the nethermost abyss
Might in that noise reside, of whom to ask
Which way the nearest coast of darkness lies
Bordering on light; when straight behold the throne
Of Chaos,[2] and his dark pavilion spread
Wide on the wasteful deep; with him enthroned
Sat sable-vested Night, eldest of things,[3]
The consort of his reign; and by them stood

1. *A gryphon...pursues the Arimaspian.*–Gryphons were fabulous animals, half eagle, half lion, and supposed to be the special guardians of gold mines; while the Arimaspians were a people skilled and brave in possessing themselves of that sort of treasure.

2. *Chaos.*–The spirit supposed to have its home amidst the "unformed and void."

3. *Night, eldest of things.*–The command, "Let there be light," supposes darkness–night to be older than day, than creation.

Orcus and Hades,[1] and the dreaded name
Of Demogorgon ;[2] Rumour next, and Chance,
And Tumult, and Confusion, all embroiled.
And Discord, with a thousand various mouths.
To whom Satan turning boldly, thus : Ye powers
And spirits of this nethermost abyss.
Chaos and ancient Night, I come no spy,
With purpose to explore or to disturb
The secrets of your realm; but, by constraint
Wandering this darksome desert, as my way
Lies through your spacious empire up to light,
Alone, and without guide, half lost, I seek
What readiest path leads where your gloomy bounds
Confine with heaven; or, if some other place.
From your dominion won, the ethereal King
Possesses lately, thither to arrive
I travel this profound; direct my course;
Directed, no mean recompense it brings
To your behoof, if I that region lost.
All usurpation thence expelled, reduce
To her original darkness, and your sway –
Which is my present journey – and once more
Erect the standard there of ancient Night.
Yours be the advantage all, mine the revenge.
Thus Satan : and him thus the Anarch old,
With faltering speech and visage incomposed.
Answered : I know thee, stranger, who thou art;
That mighty leading Angel, who of late
Made head 'gainst heaven's King, though overthrown.
I saw and heard; for such a numerous host
Fled not in silence through the frighted deep.

1. *Orcus and Hades.*–Orcus is supposed to mean Pluto–Hades his dark home.

2. *Demogorgon.*–An infernal deity, believed to be of great power; the most frightful effects were supposed to follow from the skilled use of his name.

With ruin upon ruin, rout on rout,
Confusion worse confounded; and heaven-gates
Poured out by millions her victorious bands.
Pursuing. I upon my frontiers here
Keep residence; if all I can will serve
That little which is left so to defend.
Encroached on still through your intestine broils
Weakening the sceptre of old Night. First Hell,
Your dungeon, stretching far and wide beneath;
Now lately heaven and earth another world.
Hung o'er my realm, linked in a golden chain,
To that side heaven, from whence your legions fell.
If that way be your walk, you have not far;
So much the nearer danger; go, and speed;
Havoc, and spoil, and ruin, are my gain.
    He ceased; and Satan stayed not to reply,
But, glad that now his sea should find a shore,
With fresh alacrity and force renewed.
Springs upward, like a pyramid of fire,
Into the wild expanse, and, through the shock
Of fighting elements, on all sides round
Environed, wins his way; harder beset
And more endangered, than when Argo passed
Through Bosphorus, betwixt the justling rocks;
Or when Ulysses on the larboard shunned
Charybdis, and by the other whirlpool steered.
So he with difficulty and labour hard
Moved on, with difficulty and labour he;
But he once passed, soon after, when man fell –
Strange alteration ! – Sin and Death amain
Following his track, such was the will of Heaven
Paved after him a broad and beaten way
Over the dark abyss, whose boiling gulf
Tamely endured a bridge of wondrous length.
From hell continued, reaching the utmost orb
Of this frail world : by which the spirits perverse

With easy intercourse pass to and fro
To tempt or punish mortals, except whom
God and good Angels guard by special grace.
But now at last the sacred influence
Of light appears, and from the walls of heaven
Shoots far into the bosom of dim Night
A glimmering dawn. Here Nature first begins
Her farthest verge, and Chaos to retire,
As from her outmost works, a broken foe,
With tumult less, and with less hostile din.
That Satan with less toil, and now with ease
Wafts on the calmer wave by dubious light,
And, like a weather-beaten vessel, holds
Gladly the port, though shrouds and tackle torn;
Or in the emptier waste, resembling air,
Weighs his spread wings, at leisure to behold
Far off the empyreal heaven, extended wide
In circuit, undetermined square or round.
With opal towers and battlements adorned
Of living sapphire, once his native seat;
And fast by, hanging in a golden chain.
This pendent world, in bigness as a star
Of smallest magnitude, close by the moon.
Thither, full fraught with mischievous revenge,
Accursed, and in a cursed hour, he hies.

BOOK - III

GOD, sitting on His throne, sees Satan flying towards this world, then newly created: shows him to the Son, who sat at His right hand; foretells the success of Satan in perverting mankind; clears His own justice and wisdom from all imputation, having created man free, and able enough to have withstood his tempter; yet declares His purpose of grace towards him, in regard he fell not of his own malice, as did Satan, but by him seduced. The Son of God renders praise to His Father for the manifestation of His gracious purpose towards man; but God again declares that grace cannot be extended towards man without the satisfaction of Divine justice. Man hath offended the majesty of God by aspiring to Godhead, and, therefore, with all his progeny, devoted to death, must die, unless some one can be found sufficient to answer for his offence, and undergo his punishment. The Son of God freely offers Himself a ransom for man: The Father accepts Him, ordains His incarnation, pronounces His exaltation above all names in heaven and earth; commands all the angels to adore Him. They obey, and by hymning to their harps in full quire, celebrate the Father and the Son. Meanwhile, Satan alights upon the bare convex of this world's outermost orb; where wandering, he first finds a place, since called the Limbo of Vanity: what persons and things fly up thither: thence comes to the gate of heaven, described ascending by stairs, and the waters above the firmament that few about it: his passage thence to the orb of the sun; he finds there Uriel, the regent of that orb, but first changes himself into the shape of a meaner angel; and, pretending a zealous desire to behold the new creation, and man, whom God had placed there, inquires of him the place of his habitation, and is directed: alights first on Mount Niphates.

HAIL, holy Light! offspring of Heaven first-born![1]
Or of the Eternal co-eternal beam,
May I express thee unblamed ? since God is light,
And never but in unapproached light
Dwelt from eternity, dwelt then in thee,
Bright effluence of bright essence increate !
Or hear'st thou rather, pure ethereal stream,
Whose fountain who shall tell ? Before the sun,
Before the heavens thou wert, and at the voice
Of God, as with a mantle, didst invest
The rising world of waters dark and deep,.
Won from the void and formless infinite.
Thee I revisit now with bolder wing,
Escaped the Stygian pool, though long detained
In that obscure sojourn, while in my flight
Through utter and through middle darkness borne,
With other notes than to the Orphean lyre,
I sung of Chaos and eternal Night;
Taught by the heavenly muse to venture down
The dark descent, and up to reascend,
Though hard and rare; – thee I revisit safe.
And feel thy sovereign vital lamp; but thou
Revisit'st not these eyes, that roll in vain
To find thy piercing ray, and find no dawn;
So thick a drop serene hath quenched their orbs,
Or dim suffusion veiled. Yet not the more
Cease I to wander where the Muses haunt.
Clear spring, or shady grove, or sunny hill,
Smit with the love of sacred song; but chief
Thee, Sion, and the flowery brooks beneath.
That wash thy hallowed feet, and warbling flow,
Nightly I visit: nor sometimes forget

1. *Offspring of Heaven first-born.*–The reader will remember that Milton was a blind bard while giving us the inspirations of "Paradise Lost." Literature has nothing more beautiful or affecting than the touching lament which here comes from the heart of the poet.

Those other two equalled with me in fate,
So were I equalled with them in renown.
Blind Thamyris, and blind Mæonides,[1]
And Tiresias, and Phineus,[2] prophets old :
Then feed on thoughts, that voluntary move
Harmonious numbers; as the wakeful bird
Sings darkling, and in shadiest covert hid,
Tunes her nocturnal note.[3] Thus with the year
Seasons return; but not to me returns
Day, or the sweet approach of even or morn,
Or sight of vernal bloom, or summer's rose.
Or flocks, or herds, or human face divine;
But cloud instead, and ever-during dark
Surrounds me, from the cheerful ways of men
Cut off, and for the book of knowledge fair
Presented with a universal blank
Of Nature's works, to me expunged and rased,
And wisdom at one entrance quite shut out.
So much the rather thou, celestial light,
Shine inward, and the mind through all her powers
Irradiate; there plant eyes, all mist from thence
Purge and disperse, that I may see and tell
Of things invisible to mortal sight.
    Now had the Almighty Father from above,
From the pure Empyrean where he sits
High throned above all height, bent down his eye,
His own works, and their works at once to view:
About him all the sanctities of heaven
Stood thick as stars, and from his sight received

1. *Thamyris and blind Mæonides.*–Thamyris was a Thracian poet, mentioned by Homer. Mæonides was a name given to Homer himself, from his father, Meon.

2. *Tiresias and Phineus.*–The first a Theban, the second a King of Arcadia, both celebrated in antiquity as men who gave prophecies in verse when blind.

3. *Nocturnal note.*–The nightingale.

Beatitude past utterance; on his right
The radiant image of his glory sat,
His only Son. On earth he first beheld
Our two first parents, yet the only two
Of mankind, in the happy garden placed.
Reaping immortal fruits of joy and love.
Uninterrupted joy, unrivalled love,
In blissful solitude. He then surveyed
Hell and the gulf between, and Satan there
Coasting the wall of heaven on this side Night
In the dun air sublime, and ready now
To stoop with wearied wings, and willing feet,
On the bare outside of this world, that seemed
Firm land imbosomed, without firmament,
Uncertain which, in ocean or in air.
Him God beholding from his prospect high,
Wherein past, present, future, he beholds.
Thus to his only Son foreseeing spake :
Only-begotten Son, seest thou what rage
Transports our adversary whom no bounds
Prescribed, no bars of Hell, nor all the chains
Heaped on him there, nor yet the main abyss
Wide interrupt, can hold; so bent he seems
On desperate revenge, that shall redound
Upon his own rebellious head. And now,
Through all restraint broke loose, he wings his way
Not far off heaven, in the precincts of light,
Directly towards the new-created world.
And man there placed, with purpose to essay
If him by force he can destroy, or, worse.
By some false guile pervert; and shall pervert;
For man will hearken to his glozing lies.
And easily transgress the sole command.
Sole pledge of his obedience. So will fall
He and his faithless progeny. Whose fault ?
Whose but his own? Ingrate, he had of me

All he could have. I made him just and right,
Sufficient to have stood, though free to fall.
Such I created all the ethereal powers
And spirits, both them who stood, and them who failed;
Freely they stood who stood, and fell who fell.
Not free, what proof could they have given sincere
Of true allegiance, constant faith, or love.
Where only what they needs must do appeared.
Not what they would ? What praise could they receive
What pleasure I from such obedience paid ?
When will and reason – reason also is choice –
Useless and vain, of freedom both despoiled,
Made passive both, had served necessity.
Not me ? They therefore, as to right belonged,
So were created, nor can justly accuse
Their maker, or their making, or their fate,
As if predestination overruled
Their will, disposed by absolute decree
Or high foreknowledge. They themselves decreed
Their own revolt, not I. If I foreknew,
Foreknowledge had no Influence on their fault,
Which had no less proved certain unforeknown.
So without least impulse or shadow of fate,
Or aught by me immutably foreseen,
They trespass, authors to themselves in all
Both what they judge, and what they choose; for so
I formed them free : and free they must remain.
Till they enthrall themselves; I else must change
Their nature, and revoke the high decree
Unchangeable, eternal, which ordained
Their freedom; they themselves ordained their fall.
The first sort by their own suggestion fell,
Self-tempted, self-depraved : Man falls, deceived
By the other first : Man therefore shall find grace,
The other none. In mercy and justice both,
Through heaven and earth, so shall my glory excel;

But mercy first and last shall brightest shine.
Thus while God spake, ambrosial fragrance filled
All heaven, and in the blessed spirits elect
Sense of new joy ineffable diffused.
Beyond compare the Son of God was seen
Most glorious : in him all his Father shone
Substantially expressed; and in his face
Divine compassion visibly appeared.
Love without end, and without measure grace,
Which uttering, thus he to his Father spake :
O Father, gracious was that word which closed
Thy sovereign sentence, that man should find grace;
For which both heaven and earth shall high extol
Thy praises, with the innumerable sound
Of hymns and sacred songs, wherewith thy throne
Encompassed shall resound thee ever blessed.
For should Man finally be lost, should Man,
Thy creature late so loved, thy youngest son,
Fall circumvented thus by fraud, though joined
With his own folly ? That be from thee far,
That far be from thee. Father, who art judge
Of all things made, and judgest only right.
Or shall the Adversary thus obtain
His end, and frustrate thine? Shall he fulfil
His malice, and thy goodness bring to nought;
Or proud return, though to his heavier doom.
Yet with revenge accomplished, and to Hell
Draw after him the whole race of mankind,
By him corrupted ? Or wilt thou thyself
Abolish thy creation, and unmake,
For him, what for thy glory thou hast made ?
So should thy goodness and thy greatness both
Be questioned and blasphemed without defence.
To whom the great Creator thus replied:
O Son, in whom my soul hath chief delight,
Son of my bosom. Son who art alone

My word, my wisdom, and effectual might,
All hast thou spoken as my thoughts are, all
As my eternal purpose hath decreed.
Man shall not quite be lost, but saved who will;
Yet not of will in him, but grace in me
Freely vouchsafed. Once more I will renew
His lapsed powers, though forfeit, and enthralled
By sin to foul exorbitant desires;
Upheld by me, yet once more he shall stand
On even ground against his mortal foe;
By me upheld, that he may know how frail
His fallen condition is, and to me owe
All his deliverance, and to none but me.
Some I have chosen of peculiar grace,
Elect above the rest; so is my will :
The rest shall hear me call, and oft be warned
Their sinful state, and to appease betimes
The incensed Deity, while offered grace
Invites; for I will clear their senses dark,
What may suffice, and soften stony hearts
To pray, repent, and bring obedience due.
To prayer, repentance, and obedience due,
Though but endeavoured with sincere intent,
Mine ear shall not be slow, mine eye not shut.
And I will place within them as a guide
My umpire. Conscience; whom if they will hear.
Light after light, well used, they shall attain,
And to the end persisting, safe arrive.
This my long sufferance, and my day of grace,
They who neglect and scorn, shall never taste;
But hard be hardened, blind be blinded more.
That they may stumble on, and deeper fall;
And none but such from mercy I exclude.
But yet all is not done; man disobeying,
Disloyal, breaks his fealty, and sins
Against the high supremacy of Heaven,

Affecting Godhead, and, so losing all,
To expiate his treason hath nought left.
But to destruction sacred and devote,[1]
He, with his whole posterity, must die.
Die he or Justice must; unless for him
Some other able, and as willing, pay
The rigid satisfaction, death for death.
Say, heavenly Powers, where shall we find such love ?
Which of ye will be mortal, to redeem
Man's mortal crime, and just the unjust to save
Dwells in all Heaven charity so dear?
He asked, but all the heavenly quire stood mute,
And silence was in Heaven. On man's behalf
Patron or intercessor none appeared,
Much less than durst upon his own head draw
The deadly forfeiture, and ransom set.
And now without redemption all mankind
Must have been lost,[2] adjudged to Death and Hell
By doom severe, had not the Son of God,
In whom the fulness dwells of love divine,
His dearest mediation thus renewed:
Father, thy word is passed, man shall find grace;
And shall grace not find means, that finds her way,
The speediest of thy winged messengers,
To visit all thy creatures, and to all
Comes unprevented, unimplored, unsought ?
Happy for Man, so coming; he her aid
Can never seek, once dead in sins, and lost;
Atonement for himself, or offering meet.
Indebted and undone, hath none to bring.
Behold me, then; me for him, life for life

1. *Sacred and devote*–A phrase from the Roman law, denoting one justly exposed to death.

2. *All mankind must have been lost.*–This assumes that the human race *must* have been perpetuated notwithstanding the entrance of sin. But was that necessary? Was it probable ?

I offer; on me let thine anger fall;
Account me Man : I for his sake will leave
Thy bosom, and this glory next to Thee
Freely put off, and for him lastly die
Well pleased; on me let Death wreak all his rage;
Under his gloomy power I shall not long
Lie vanquished. Thou hast given me to possess
Life in myself for ever; by thee I live,
Though now to Death I yield, and am his due,
All that of me can die. Yet, that debt paid.
Thou wilt not leave me in the loathsome grave.
His prey, nor suffer my unspotted soul
For ever with corruption there to dwell :
But I shall rise victorious, and subdue
My vanquisher, spoiled of his vaunted spoil;
Death his death's wound shall then receive, and stoop
Inglorious, of his mortal sting disarmed.
I, through the ample air, in triumph high
Shall lead Hell captive, maugre Hell, and show
The powers of darkness bound. Thou, at the sight
Pleased, out of Heaven shalt look down, and smile,
While, by thee raised, I ruin all my foes,
Death last, and with his carcass glut the grave;
Then, with the multitude of my redeemed,
Shall enter heaven, long absent, and return,
Father, to see thy face, wherein no cloud
Of anger shall remain, but peace assured
And reconcilement; wrath shall be no more
Thenceforth, but in thy presence joy entire.
    His words here ended, but His meek aspect
Silent, yet spake, and breathed immortal love
To mortal men, above which only shone
Filial obedience; as a sacrifice
Glad to be offered. He attends the will
Of his great Father. Admiration seized
All heaven, what this might mean, and whither tend

Wondering; but soon the Almighty thus replied :
O Thou in heaven and earth the only peace
Found out for mankind under wrath ! O Thou,
My soul complacence ! – well thou knowest how dear
To me are all my works, nor man the least.
Though last created; that for him I spare
Thee from my bosom and right hand, to save,
By losing thee awhile, the whole race lost.
Thou, therefore, whom thou only canst redeem,
Their nature also to thy nature join;
And be thyself Man among men on earth.
Made flesh, when time shall be, of virgin seed,
By wondrous birth; be thou in Adam's room
The head of all mankind, though Adam's son.
As in him perish all men, so in thee,
As from a second root, shall be restored
As many as are restored, without thee none.
His crime makes guilty all his sons. Thy merit,
Imputed, shall absolve them who renounce
Their own both righteous and unrighteous deeds,
And live in thee transplanted, and from thee
Receive new life. So Man, as is most just,
Shall satisfy for man, be judged, and die,
And dying rise, and rising with him, raise
His brethren, ransomed with his own dear life.
So heavenly love shall outdo hellish hate,
Giving to death, and dying to redeem,
So dearly to redeem, what hellish hate
So easily destroyed, and still destroys
In those who, when they may, accept not grace.
Nor shalt thou, by descending to assume
Man's nature, lessen or degrade thine own.
Because thou hast, though throned in highest bliss
Equal to God, and equally enjoying
Godlike fruition, quitted all, to save
A world from utter loss, and hast been found

By merit more than birthright. Son of God,
Found worthiest to be so, by being good,
Far more than great or high; because in thee
Love hath abounded more than glory abounds,
Therefore thy humiliation shall exalt
With thee thy manhood also to this throne;
Here shalt thou sit incarnate, here shalt reign
Both God and man. Son both of God and man.
Anointed universal king; all power
I give thee; reign for ever, and assume
Thy merits; under thee, as head supreme.
Thrones, Princedoms, Powers, Dominions, I reduce :
All knees to thee shall bow, of them that bide
In heaven, or earth, or under earth in hell.
When thou, attended gloriously from heaven,
Shalt in the sky appear, and from thee send
The summoning Archangels to proclaim
Thy dread tribunal; forthwith from all winds
The living, and forthwith the cited dead
Of all past ages, to the general doom
Shall hasten; such a peal shall rouse their sleep.
Then, all thy saints assembled, thou shalt judge
Bad men and Angels. They arraigned, shall sink
Beneath thy sentence. Hell, her numbers full,
Thenceforth shall be for ever shut. Meanwhile
The world shall burn, and from her ashes spring
New heaven and earth, wherein the just shall dwell,
And, after all their tribulations long,
See golden days, fruitful of golden deeds,
With joy and love triumphing, and fair truth.
Then thou thy regal sceptre shalt lay by.
For regal sceptre then no more shall need;
God shall be all in all. But, all ye gods,
Adore Him, who to compass all this, dies;
Adore the Son, and honour Him as Me.
　　No sooner had the Almighty ceased, but all

The multitude of angels, with a shout,
Loud as from numbers without number, sweet
As from blessed voices, uttering joy, heaven rung
With jubilee, and loud hosannas filled
The eternal regions. Lowly reverent
Towards either throne they bow, and to the ground,
With solemn adoration, down they cast
Their crowns, inwove with amarant and gold; –
Immortal amarant, a flower which once
In Paradise, fast by the tree of life.
Began to bloom; but soon for man's offence
To heaven removed, where first it grew, there grows,
And flowers aloft, shading the fount of life.
But where the River of Bliss through midst of Heaven
Rolls o'er Elysian flowers her amber stream;
With these, that never fade, the spirits elect
Bind their resplendent locks, inwreathed with beams.
Now in loose garlands thick thrown off, the bright
Pavement, that like a sea of jasper shone,
Impurpled with celestial roses, smiled.
Then, crowned again, their golden harps they took,
Harps ever tuned, that glittering by their side
Like quivers hung, and with preamble sweet
Of charming symphony they introduce
Their sacred song, and waken raptures high :
No voice exempt, no voice but well could join
Melodious part, such concord is in heaven.
    Thee, Father, first they sung, Omnipotent,
Immutable, Immortal, Infinite,
Eternal King; thee. Author of all being,
Fountain of light, thyself invisible
Amidst the glorious brightness, where thou sittest
Throned inaccessible, but when thou shadest
The full blaze of thy beams, and, through a cloud
Drawn round about thee, like a radiant shrine,
Dark with excessive bright thy skirts appear,

Yet dazzle heaven, that brightest seraphim
Approach not, but with both wings veil their eyes.
Thee, next they sang, of all creation first.
Begotten Son, Divine Similitude,
In whose conspicuous countenance, without cloud
Made visible, the Almighty Father shines,
Whom else no creature can behold : on thee
Impressed the effulgence of his glory abides,
Transfused on thee his ample Spirit rests.
He heaven of heavens, and all the powers therein
By thee created; and by thee threw down
The aspiring dominations : thou that day
Thy Father's dreadful thunder didst not spare,
Nor stop thy flaming chariot-wheels, that shook
Heaven's everlasting frame, while o'er the necks
Thou drovest of warring angels disarrayed.
Back from pursuit thy powers with loud acclaim
Thee only extolled. Son of thy Father's might,
To execute fierce venjreance on his foes.
Not so on Man : him, through their malice fallen
Father of mercy and grace, thou didst not doom
So strictly, but much more to pity incline,
No sooner did thy dear and only Son
Perceive thee purposed not to doom frail man
So strictly, but much more to pity inclined.
He, to appease thy wrath, and end the strife
Of mercy and justice in thy face discerned.
Regardless of the bliss wherein he sat
Second to thee, offered Himself to die
For man's offence. Oh, unexampled love !
Love nowhere to be found less than Divine !
Hail, Son of God, Saviour of men ! Thy name
Shall be the copious matter of my song
Henceforth, and never shall my heart thy praise
Forget, nor from thy Father's praise disjoin.
    Thus they in heaven, above the starry sphere

Their happy hours in joy and hymning spent.
Meanwhile upon the firm opacous globe
Of this round World, whose first convex divides
The luminous inferior orbs, enclosed
From Chaos, and the inroad of Darkness old,
Satan alighted walks. A globe far off
It seemed, now seems a boundless continent,
Dark, waste, and wild, under the frown of Night
Starless, exposed, and ever-threatening storms
Of Chaos blustering round, inclement sky;
Save on that side which, from the wall of heaven,
Though distant far, some small reflection gains
Of glimmering air less vexed with tempest loud.
Here walked the Fiend at large in spacious field.
As when a vulture, on Imaüs[1] bred,
Whose snowy ridge the roving Tartar bounds,
Dislodging Irom a region scarce of prey,
To gorge the flesh of lambs or yearling kids,
On hills where flocks are fed, flies toward the springs
Of Ganges or Hydaspes, Indian streams;
But in his way lights on the barren plains
Of Sericana, where Chineses drive
With sails and wind their cany wagons[2] light :
So, on this windy sea of land, the Fiend
Walked up and down alone, bent on his prey;
Alone, for other creature in this place.
Living or lifeless, to be found was none;
None yet, but store hereafter from the earth
Up hither, like aerial vapours, flew
Of all things transitory and vain, when sin
With vanity had filled the works of men;
Both all things vain, and all who in vain things
Built their fond hopes of glory or lasting fame,
Or happiness in this or the other life.

1. *Imaüs*– The snow-crowned Himalaya mountains.
2. *Cany wagons.*–Light vehicles, constructed of *bamboo*.

All who have their reward on earth, the fruits
Of painful superstition and blind zeal,
Nought seeking but the praise of men, here find
Fit retribution, empty as their deeds;
All the unaccomplished works of Nature's hand,
Abortive, monstrous, or unkindly mixed.
Dissolved on earth, flee thither, and in vain,
Till final dissolution, wander here;
Not in the neighbouring moon, as some have dreamed;
Those argent fields more likely habitants.
Translated saints, or middle spirits, hold,
Betwixt the angelical and human-kind.[1]
Hither of ill-joined sons and daughters born
First from the ancient world those giants came,
With many a vain exploit, though then renowned;
The builders next of Babel on the plain
Of Sennaar,[2] and still with vain design
New Babels, had they wherewithal, would build :
Others came single; he, who to be deemed
A god, leaped fondly into Ætna flames,
Empedocles ;[3] and he who, to enjoy
Plato's Elysium, leaped into the sea,
Cleombrotus;[4] and many more too long,[5]
Embryos, and idiots, eremites, and friars
White, black, and gray, with all their trumpery.
Here pilgrims roam, that strayed so far to seek

1. *Betwixt the angelical and human-kind.*–See Gen. vi. 4.

2. *Sennaar.*–Shinar, in Babylonia.

3. *Empedocles.*–A scholar of Pythagoras, who cast himself into Etna, in hope that his mysterious disappearance would lead to his being worshipped as a god. But Etna threw back the iron pattens he wore, and the end was ridicule, not worship. (Horace, *De Art. Poet.,* v. 464.)

4. *Cleombrotus.*–A Greek youth, so enamoured with Plato's doctrine of immortality, that he drowned himself in hope of realising it.

5. *Many more too long:*–Too long to tell. Some suppose a line to be wanting here.

In Golgotha Him dead who lives in Heaven;
And they, who, to be sure of Paradise,
Dying put on the weeds of Dominic,
Or in Franciscan think to pass disguised;
They pass the planets seven, and pass the fixed,
And that crystalline sphere whose balance weighs
The trepidation talked, and that first moved;
And now Saint Peter at Heaven's wicket seems
To wait them with his keys, and now at foot
Of Heaven's ascent they lift their feet, when, lo !
A violent cross-wind from either coast
Blows them transverse, ten thousand leagues awry
Into the devious air; then might ye see
Cowls, hoods, and habits, with their wearers, tossed
And fluttered into rags; then relics, beads,
Indulgences, dispenses, pardons, bulls.
The sport of winds : all these, upwhirled aloft,
Fly o'er the backside of the world far off.
Into a Limbo large and broad, since called
The Paradise of Fools, to few unknown
Long after, now unpeopled, and untrod.
    All this dark globe the Fiend found as he pass
And long he wandered, till at last a gleam
Of dawning light turned thitherward in haste
His travelled steps. Far distant he descries,
Ascending by degrees magnificent
Up to the wall of heaven, a structure high;
At top whereof, but far more rich, appeared
The work as of a kingly palace-gate,
With frontispiece of diamond and gold
Embellished; thick with sparkling orient gems
The portal shone, inimitable on earth
By model, or by shading pencil drawn.
The stairs were such as whereon Jacob saw
Angels ascending and descending, bands
Of guardians bright, when he from Esau fled

To Padan-Aram, in the field of Luz,
Dreaming by night under the open sky,
And waking cried, "This is the gate of Heaven."
Each stair mysteriously was meant, nor stood
There always, but drawn up to Heaven sometimes
Viewless; and underneath a bright sea flowed
Of jasper, or of liquid pearl, whereon
Who after came from earth, sailing arrived,
Wafted by Angels, or flew o'er the lake
Wrapped in a chariot drawn by fiery steeds.
The stairs were then let down, whether to dare
The Fiend by easy ascent, or aggravate
His sad exclusion from the doors of bliss:
Direct against which opened from beneath.
Just o'er the blissful seat of Paradise,
A passage down to the earth, a passage wide,
Wider by far than that of after-times
Over Mount Sion, and, though that were large,
Over the Promised Land, to God so dear;
By which, to visit oft those happy tribes,
On high behests his angels to and fro
Pass frequent, and his eye with choice regard
From Paneas, the fount of Jordan's flood,
To Beersaba, where the Holy Land
Borders on Egypt and the Arabian shore;
So wide the opening seemed, where bounds were set
To darkness, such as bound the ocean wave.
 Satan from hence, now on the lower stair,
That scaled by steps of gold to Heaven-gate,
Looks down with wonder at the sudden view
Of all this world at once. As when a scout.
Through dark and desert ways with peril gone
All night, at last by break of cheerful dawn
Obtains the brow of some high-climbing hill,
Which to his eye discovers unaware
The goodly prospect of some foreign land

First seen, or some renowned metropolis,
With glistering spires and pinnacles adorned,
Which now the rising sun gilds with his beams;
Such wonder seized, though after heaven seen,
The spirit malign, but much more envy seized,
At sight of all this world beheld so fair.
Round he surveys – and well might, where he stood
So high above the circling canopy
Of night's extended shade – from eastern point
Of Libra to the fleecy star that bears
Andromeda[1] far off Atlantic seas,
Beyond the horizon; then from pole to pole
He views in breadth, and without longer pause
Down right into the world's first remon throws
His flight precipitant, and winds with ease
Through the pure marble air[2] his oblique way
Amongst innumerable stars, that shone
Stars distant, but nigh hand seemed other worlds;
Or other worlds they seemed, or happy isles,
Like those Hesperian gardens famed of old.
Fortunate fields, and groves, and flowery vales.
Thrice-happy isles; but who dwelt happy there
He stayed not to inquire. Above them all
The golden sun, in splendour likest heaven.
Allured his eye; thither his course he bends
Through the calm firmament, – but up or down.
By centre or eccentric, hard to tell.
Or longitude, – where the great luminary
Aloof the vulgar constellations thick.
That from his lordly eye keep distance due.

1. *Andromeda.*–One of the six signs of the zodiac, which are supposed for the first time to hold out their lamps celestial to the gaze of the fiend.

2. *The pure marble air.*–Marble is a word from the Greek and signifies to shine or glisten. The word is used by Milton, not as denoting hardness, but brightness and clearness.

Dispenses light from far : they, as they move
Their starry dance in numbers that compute
Days, months, and years, towards his all-cheering lamp
Turn swift their various motions, or are turned
By his magnetic beam, that gently warms
The universe, and to each inward part
With gentle penetration, though unseen.
Shoots invisible virtue even to the deep;
So wondrously was set his station bright.
There lands the Fiend, a spot like which perhaps
Astronomer in the sun's lucent orb
Through his glazed optic tube yet never saw.
The place he found beyond expression bright.
Compared with aught on earth, metal or stone;
Not all parts like, but all alike informed
With radiant light, as glowing iron with fire;
If metal, part seemed gold, part silver clear:
If stone, carbuncle most or chrysolite.
Ruby or topaz, or the twelve that shone
In Aaron's breastplate, and a stone besides
Imagined rather oft than elsewhere seen.
That stone, or like to that, which here below
Philosophers in vain so long have sought.
In vain, though by their powerful art they bind
Volatile Hermes,[1] and call up unbound
In various shapes old Proteus[2] from the sea,
Drained through a limbec to his native form.
What wonder then if fields and regions here
Breathe forth elixir pure, and rivers run
Potable gold, when with one virtuous touch
The arch-chymic sun, so far from us remote,

1. *Volatile Hermes.–i.e.,* can make mercury or quicksilver do their will.

2. *Old Proteus.*–A person who baffles his pursuers by assuming all shapes, but who is said to have been fixed in his true shape at last. So chemistry passes through changing phenomena to fixedness and certainty.

Produces, with terrestrial humour mixed,
Here in the dark so many precious things
Of colour glorious, and effect so rare ?
Here matter new to o-aze the Devil met
Undazzled. Far and wide his eye commands;
For sight no obstacle found here, nor shade,
But all sunshine, as when his beams at noon
Culminate from the equator, as they now
Shot upward still direct, whence no way round
Shadow from body opaque can fall and the air,
Nowhere so clear, sharpened his visual ray
To objects distant far, whereby he soon
Saw within ken a glorious angel stand,
The same whom John saw also in the sun.
His back was turned, but not his brightness hid;
Of beaming sunny rays a golden tiar
Circled his head, nor less his locks behind
Illustrious on his shoulders, fledge with wings,
Lay waving round. On some great charge employed
He seemed, or fixed in cogitation deep.
    Glad was the spirit impure, as now in hope
To find who might direct his wandering flight
To Paradise, the happy seat of Man,
His journey's end, and our beginning woe.
But first he casts[1] to change his proper shape,
Which else might work him danger or delay.
And now a stripling cherub he appears.
Not of the prime, yet such as in his face
Youth smiled celestial, and to every limb
Suitable grace diffused, so well he feigned.
Under a coronet his flowing hair
In curls on either cheek played; wings he wore.
Of many a coloured plume, sprinkled with gold;
His habit fit for speed succinct, and held

1. *He casts.*– Considers–forecasts

Before his decent steps a silver wand.
He drew not nigh unheard; the angel bright,
Ere he drew nigh, his radiant visage turned,
Admonished by his ear, and straight was known
The Archangel Uriel, one of the seven
Who in God's presence, nearest to his throne,
Stand ready at command, and are his eyes
That run through all the Heavens, or down to the Earth
Bear his swift errands over moist and dry.
O'er sea and land : him Satan thus accosts :
Uriel, for thou of those seven spirits that stand
In sight of God's high throne, gloriously bright,
The first art wont his great authentic will
Interpreter through highest heaven to bring.
Where all his sons thy embassy attend;
And here art likeliest by supreme decree
Like honour to obtain, and as his eye[1]
To visit oft this new creation round;
Unspeakable desire to see, and know
All these his wondrous works, but chiefly Man,
His chief delight and favour, him for whom
All these his works so wondrous he ordained.
Hath brought me from the quires of cherubim
Alone thus wandering. Brightest seraph, tell
In which of all these shininor orbs hath Man
His fixed seat, or fixed seat hath none.
But all these shining orbs his choice to dwell;
That I may find him, and with secret gaze,
Or open admiration, him behold.
On whom the great Creator hath bestowed
Worlds, and on whom hath all these graces poured;
That both in him and all things, as is meet.
The universal Maker we may praise.
Who justly hath driven out his rebel foes

1. *As his eye.*–As being his eye.

To deepest Hell, and, to repair that loss,
Created this new happy race of men
To serve him better : wise are all his ways.
So spake the false dissembler unperceived;
For neither man nor angel can discern
Hypocrisy, the only evil that walks
Invisible, except to God alone,
By his permissive will, through heaven and earth.
And oft, though wisdom wake, suspicion sleeps
At wisdom's gate, and to simplicity
Resigns her charge, while goodness thinks no ill
Where no ill seems : which now for once beguiled
Uriel, though regent of the sun, and held
The sharpest-sighted spirit of all in Heaven;
Who to the fraudulent impostor foul,
In his uprightness, answer thus returned:
Fair angel, thy desire, which tends to know
The works of God, thereby to glorify
The great Work-Master, leads to no excess
That reaches blame, but rather merits praise
The more it seems excess, that led thee hither
From thy empyreal mansion thus alone,
To witness with thine eyes what some perhaps,
Contented with report, hear only in heaven :
For wonderful indeed are all His works,
Pleasant to know, and worthiest to be all
Had in remembrance always with delight:
But what created mind can comprehend
Their number, or the wisdom infinite
That brought them forth, but hid their causes deep.
I saw, when at His word the formless mass.
This world's material mould, came to a heap :
Contusion heard His voice and wild uproar
Stood ruled, stood vast infinitude confined;
Till at his second bidding darkness fled,
Light shone, and order from disorder sprung.

Swift to their several quarters hasted then
The cumbrous elements, earth, flood, air, fire;
And this ethereal quintessence of heaven
Flew upward, spirited with various forms,
That rolled orbicular, and turned to stars
Numberless, as thou seest, and how they move.
Each had his place appointed, each his course;
The rest in circuit walls this universe.
Look downward on that globe, whose hither side
With light from hence, though but reflected, shines;
That place is Earth, the seat of Man; that light
His day, which else, as the other hemisphere.
Night would invade; but there the neighbouring moon-
So call that opposite fair star – her aid
Timely interposes, and her monthly round
Still ending, still renewing, through mid heaven,
With borrowed light her countenance triform
Hence fills and empties to enlighten the earth,
And in her pale dominion checks the night.
That spot to which I point is Paradise,
Adam's abode; those lofty shades, his bower.
Thy way thou canst not miss, me mine requires.
Thus said, he turned; and Satan, bowing low,
As to superior spirits is wont in heaven,
Where honour due and reverence none neglects,
Took leave, and towards the coast of Earth beneath,
Down from the ecliptic, sped with hoped success,
Throws his steep flight in many an aery wheel.
Nor stayed, till on Niphates' top he lights.[1]

1. *On Niphates' he lights.*–A mountain in Armenia, near which Milton places Paradise.

BOOK - IV

SATAN, now in prospect of Eden, and nigh the place where he must now attempt the bold enterprise which he undertook alone against God and man, falls into many doubts with himself, and many passions, fear, envy, and despair; but at length confirms himself in evil, journeys on to Paradise, whose outward prospect and situation is described; over-leaps the bounds; sits in the shape of a cormorant on the tree of life, as the highest in the garden, to look about him. The garden described; Satan's first sight of Adam and Eve; his wonder at their excellent form and happy state, but with resolution to work their fall; overhears their discourse, thence gathers that the tree of knowledge was forbidden them to eat of, under penalty of death; and thereon intends to found his temptation, by seducing them to ransgress; then leaves them awhile to know farther of their state by some other means. Meanwhile, Uriel, descending on a sunbeam, warns Gabriel, who had in charge the gate of Paradise, that some evil spirit had escaped the deep, and passed at noon by his sphere, in the shape of a good angel, down to Paradise, discovered after by his furious gestures in the mount. Gabriel promises to find him ere morning. Night coming on, Adam and Eve discourse of going to their rest: their bower described; their evening worship. Gabriel, drawing forth his bands of night-watch to walk the rounds of Paradise, appoints two strong angels to Adam's bower, lest the evil spirit should be there doing some harm to Adam or Eve sleeping; there they find him at the ear of Eve, tempting her in a dream, and bring him, though unwilling, to Gabriel; by whom questioned, he scornfully answers; prepares resistance; but, hindered by a sign from heaven, flies out of Paradise.

Oh, for that warning voice, which he, who saw
The Apocalypse, heard cry in heaven aloud,
Then when the Dragon, put to second rout.
Came furious down to be revenged on men,

"Woe to the inhabitants on earth !" that now.
While time was, our first parents had been warned
The coming of their secret foe, and 'scaped.
Haply so 'scaped his mortal snare. For now
Satan, now first inflamed with rage, came down,
The tempter ere the accuser of mankind,
To wreak on innocent frail man his loss
Of that first battle, and his flight to Hell.
Yet not rejoicing in his speed, though bold
Far off and fearless, nor with cause to boast.
Begins his dire attempt; which, nigh the birth
Now rolling, boils in his tumultuous breast,
And like a devilish engine back recoils
Upon himself Horror and doubt distract
His troubled thoughts, and from the bottom stir
The hell within him; for within him hell
He brings, and round about him, nor from hell
One step, no more than from himself, can fly
By change of place. Now conscience wakes despair
That slumbered; wakes the bitter memory
Of what he was, what is, and what must be –
Worse; of worse deeds worse sufferings must ensue.
Sometimes towards Eden, which now in his view
Lay pleasant, his grieved look he fixes sad;
Sometimes towards heaven and the full-blazing sun,
Which now sat high in his meridian tower;
Then, much revolving, thus in sighs began :
O thou, that, with surpassing glory crowned,
Look'st from thy sole dominion, like the God
Of this new world; at whose sight all the stars
Hide their diminished heads; to thee I call,
But with no friendly voice, and add thy name,
O sun ! to tell thee how I hate thy beams.
That bring to my remembrance from what state
I fell, how glorious once above thy sphere;

Till pride and worse ambition threw me down,
Warring in heaven against heaven's matchless King:
Ah, wherefore? He deserved no such return
From me, whom he created what I was
In that bright eminence, and with his good
Upbraided none; nor was his service hard.
What could be less than to afford Him praise,
The easiest recompense, and pay Him thanks ?
How due ! Yet all his good proved ill in me.
And wrought but malice. Lifted up so high
I 'sdained subjection, and thought one step higher
Would set me highest, and in a moment quit .
The debt immense of endless gratitude,
So burdensome; still paying, still to owe;
Forgetful what from Him I still received,
And understood not that a grateful mind
By owing owes not, but still pays, at once
Indebted and discharged; what burden then?
Oh, had his powerful destiny ordained
Me some inferior Angel, I had stood
Then happy; no unbounded hope had raised
Ambition. Yet why not ? some other Power
As great might have aspired, and me, though mean,
Drawn to his part. But other powers as great
Fell not, but stand unshaken, from within
Or from without, to all temptations armed.
Hadst thou the same free will and power to stand ?
Thou hadst : whom hast thou then or what to accuse.
But Heaven's free love dealt equally to all ?
Be then his love accursed, since love or hate
To me alike it deals eternal woe.
Nay, cursed be thou; since against His thy will
Chose freely what it now so justly rues.
Me miserable ! which way shall I fly
Infinite wrath, and infinite despair?

Which way I fly is Hell; myself am Hell;
And, in the lowest deep, a lower deep
Still threatening to devour me opens wide.
To which the hell I suffer seems a heaven.
Oh, then, at last relent. Is there no place
Left for repentance, none for pardon left ?
None left but by submission; and that word
Disdain forbids me, and my dread of shame
Among the spirits beneath, whom I seduced
With other promises and other vaunts
Than to submit, boasting I could subdue
The Omnipotent. Ah me ! they little know
How dearly I abide that boast so vain,
Under what torments inwardly I groan.
While they adore me on the throne of hell,
With diadem and sceptre high advanced,
The lower still I fall, only supreme
In misery : such joy ambition finds.
But say I could repent, and could obtain,
By act of grace, my former state; how soon
Would height recall high thoughts, how soon unsay
What feigned submission swore ! Ease would recant
Vows made in pain, as violent and void :
For never can true reconcilement grow
Where wounds of deadly hate have pierced so deep :
Which would but lead me to a worse relapse,
And heavier fall : so should I purchase dear
Short intermission, bought with double smart.
This knows my Punisher; therefore as far
From granting He, as I from begging, peace :
All hope excluded thus, behold, instead
Of us, outcast, exiled, his new delight,
Mankind, created, and for him this world.
So farewell hope; and with hope farewell fear;
Farewell remorse: all good to me is lost.

Evil, be thou my good : by thee at least
Divided empire with heaven's king I hold,
By thee, and more than half perhaps will reign.
As man ere long, and this new world shall know.
Thus while he spake, each passion dimmed his face.
Thrice changed with pale, ire, envy, and despair;
Which marred his borrowed visage, and betrayed
Him counterfeit, if any eye beheld :
For heavenly minds from such distempers foul
Are ever clear. Whereof he soon aware.
Each perturbation smoothed with outward calm.
Artificer of fraud; and was the first
That practised falsehood under saintly show,
Deep malice to conceal, couched with revenge.
Yet not enough had practised to deceive
Uriel, once warned; whose eye pursued him down
The way he went, and on the Assyrian mount
Saw him disfigured, more than could befall
Spirit of happy sort : his gestures fierce
He marked, and mad demeanour, then alone
As he supposed, all unobserved, unseen.
So on he fares, and to the border comes
Of Eden, where delicious Paradise,
Now nearer, crowns with her enclosure green,
As with a rural mound, the champaign head
Of a steep wilderness, whose hairy sides
With thicket overgrown, grotesque and wild,
Access denied; and overhead up grew
Insuperable height of loftiest shade.
Cedar, and pme, and fir, and branching palm,
A sylvan scene; and, as the ranks ascend
Shade above shade, a woody theatre
Of stateliest view. Yet higher than their tops
The verdurous wall of Paradise up-sprung;
Which to our general sire gave prospect large
Into his nether empire neighbouring round.

And higher than that wall a circling row
Of goodliest trees, loaden with fairest fruit,
Blossoms and fruits at once, of golden hue.
Appeared, with gay enamelled colours mixed;
On which the sun more glad impressed his beams.
Than in fair evening cloud, or humid bow,
When God hath showered the earth : so lovely seem
That landscape; and of pure now purer air
Meets his approach, and to the heart inspires
Vernal delight and joy, able to drive
All sadness but despair. Now gentle gales,
Fanning their odoriferous wings, dispense
Native perfumes, and whisper whence they stole
Those balmy spoils. As when to them who sail
Beyond the Cape of Hope, and now are past
Mozambic, off at sea north-east winds blow
Sabean odours from the spicy shore
Of Araby the Blest; with such delay
Well pleased they slack their course, and many a league
Cheered with the grateful smell, old Ocean smiles.
So entertained those odorous sweets the Fiend,
Who came their bane[1] though with them better pleased
Than Asmodeus with the fishy fume
That drove him, though enamoured, from the spouse
Of Tobit's son,[2] and with a vengeance sent
From Media post to Egypt, there fast bound.
    Now to the ascent of that steep savage hill
Satan hath journeyed on, pensive and slow;
But further way found none, so thick entwined,
As one continued brake, the undergrowth

1. *Who came their bane.*–These odours floating from the spice islands, far upon the evening or morning breeze, were known to the ancients, and are better known to the moderns.

2. *Of Tobit's son.*–Objection is justly taken to this use of the Apocrypha.legend. It degrades, in place of adorning the subject.

Of shrubs and tangling bushes had perplexed
All path of man or beast that passed that way.
One gate there only was, and that looked east
On the other side, which when the arch-felon saw,
Due entrance he disdained, and, in contempt,
At one slight bound high overleaped all bound
Of hill or highest wall, and sheer within
Lights on his feet. As when a prowling wolf,
Whom hunger drives to seek new haunt for prey,
Watching where shepherds pen their flocks at eve
In hurdled cotes amid the field secure,
Leaps o'er the fence with ease into the fold :
Or as a thief bent to unhoard the cash
Of some rich burgher, whose substantial doors.
Cross-barred and bolted fast, fear no assault,
In at the window climbs, or o'er the tiles :
So clomb this first grand thief into God's fold;
So since into his church lewd hirelings climb.
Thence up he flew, and on the tree of life,
The middle tree and highest there that grew,
Sat like a cormorant; yet not true life
Thereby regained, but sat devising death
To them who lived; nor on the virtue thought
Of that life-giving plant, but only used
For prospect, what, well used, had been the pledge
Of immortality. So little knows
Any, but God alone, to value right
The good before him, but perverts best things
To worst abuse, or to their meanest use.
 Beneath him with new wonder now he views,
To all delight of human sense exposed.
In narrow room, nature's whole wealth, yea more,
A heaven on earth : for blissful Paradise
Of God the garden was, by him in the east
Of Eden planted. Eden stretched her line
From Auran eastward to the royal towers

Of great Seleucia, built by Grecian kings;
Or where the sons of Eden long before
Dwelt in Telassar. In this pleasant soil
His far more pleasant garden God ordained.
Out of the fertile ground he caused to grow
All trees of noblest kind for sight, smell, taste;
And all amid them stood the tree of life,
High eminent, bloomiing ambrosial fruit
Of vegetable gold; and next to life,
Our death, the Tree of Knowledge, grew fast by,
Knowledge of good, bought dear by knowing ill.
Southward through Eden went a river large,
Nor changed his course, but through the shaggy hill
Passed underneath ingulfed; for God had thrown
That mountain as his garden mould, high raised
Upon the rapid current, which through veins
Of porous earth with kindly thirst up-drawn.
Rose a fresh fountain, and with many a rill
Watered the garden; thence united fell
Down the steep glade, and met the nether flood,
Which from his darksome passage now appears;
And now, divided into four main streams,
Runs diverse, wandering many a famous realm
And country, whereof here needs no account;
But rather to tell how, if art could tell,
How from that sapphire fount the crisped brooks,
Rolling on orient pearl and sands of gold,
With mazy error under pendent shades
Ran nectar, visiting each plant, and fed
Flowers worthy of Paradise, which not nice art
In beds and curious knots, but nature boon
Poured forth profuse on hill, and dale, and plain.
Both where the morning sun first warmly smote
The open field, and where the unpierced shade
Imbrowned the noontide bowers. Thus was this place
A happy rural seat of various view;

Groves whose rich trees wept odorous gums and balm;
Others whose fruit, burnished with golden rind,
Hung amiable,[1] Hesperian fables true.
If true, here only, and of delicious taste.
Betwixt them lawns, or level downs, and flocks
Grazing the tender herb, were interposed;
Or palmy hillock, or the flowery lap
Of some irriguous valley spread her store,
Flowers of all hue, and without thorn the rose.
Another side, umbrageous grots and caves
Of cool recess, o'er which the mantling vine
Lays forth her purple grape, and gently creeps
Luxuriant. Meanwhile murmuring waters fall
Down the slope hills, dispersed, or in a lake.
That to the fringed bank with myrtle crowned
Her crystal mirror holds, unite their streams.
The birds their quire apply; airs, vernal airs.
Breathing the smell of field and grove, attune
The trembling leaves, while universal Pan,[2]
Knit with the Graces and the Hours[3] in dance.
Led on the Eternal Spring. Not that fair field
Of Enna, where Prosorpine[4] gathering flowers,
Herself a fairer flower, by gloomy Dis[5]
Was gathered, which cost Ceres all that pain
To seek her through the world; nor that sweet grove
Of Daphne by Orontes, and the inspired
Castilian spring, might with this Paradise

1. *Amiable.*–Lovely, so as to call forth affection, desire.
2. *Universal Pan.–Hav,* all. The symbol with the ancients of all nature–the universe.
3. *The Graces and the Hours.*–Female divinities, accepted as emblems of the beauty, joy, and harmony of the seasons, especially of the spring.
4. *Prosorpine* has the accent here on the second syllable, as in the Latin.
5. *Gloomy Dis.*–Pluto.

Of Eden strive; nor that Nyseian isle[6]
Girt with the river Triton, where old Cham,
Whom Gentiles Ammon call and Lybian Jove,
Hid Amalthea, and her florid son.
Young Bacchus from his stepdame Rhea's eye :
Nor where Abassin kings[2] their issue guard,
Mount Amara,[3] though this by some supposed
True Paradise, under the Ethiop line
By Nilus's head, enclosed with shining rock,
A whole day's journey high, but wide remote
From this Assyrian garden, where the Fiend
Saw, undelighted, all delight, all kind
Of living creatures, new to sight and strange. .
Two of far nobler shape, erect and tall,
Godlike erect, with native honour clad,
In naked majesty seemed lords of all,
And worthy seemed : for in their looks divine
The image of their glorious Maker shone,
Truth, wisdom, sanctitude severe and pure.
Severe, but in true filial freedom placed.
Whence true authority in men; though both
Not equal, as their sex not equal seemed;
For contemplation he, and valour formed;
For softness she, and sweet attractive grace;
He for God only, she for God in him.
His fair large front and eye sublime declared
Absolute rule; and hyacinthine locks
Round from his parted forelock manly hung
Clustering, but not beneath his shoulders broad.
She, as a veil, down to the slender waist

1. *Nyseian isle.*–Enna, the grave of Daphne, and the Nyseian isle, were all places celebrated for their beauty by the Greek and Roman poets.

2. *Abassin kings.*–Abyssinian.

3. *Mount Amara.*–A mountain seclusion, to which some of the later emperors sent their younger sons for education.

Her unadorned golden tresses wore
Dishevelled, but in wanton ringlets waved.
As the vine curls her tendrils, which implied
Subjection, but required with gentle sway.
And by her yielded, by him best received.
Yielded with coy submission, modest pride.
And sweet, reluctant, amorous delay.
Nor those mysterious parts were then concealed,
Then was not guilty shame. Dishonest shame
Of nature's works, honour dishonourable,
Sin-bred, how have ye troubled all mankind
With shows instead, mere shows of seeming pure,
And banished from man's life his happiest life,
Simplicity and spotless innocence !
So passed they naked on, nor shunned the sight
Of God or angel; for they thought no ill :
So hand in hand they passed, the loveliest pair
That ever since in love's embraces met;
Adam the goodliest Man of Men since born
His sons, the fairest of her daughters Eve.
    Under a tuft of shade that on a green
Stood whispering soft, by a fresh fountain side
They sat them down; and, after no more toil
Of their sweet gardening labour than sufficed
To recommend cool zephyr, and made ease
More easy, wholesome thirst and appetite
More grateful, to their supper-fruits they fell,
Nectarine fruits, which the compliant boughs
Yielded them, sidelong as they sat reclined
On the soft downy bank damasked with flowers :
The savoury pulp they chew, and in the rind.
Still as they thirsted, scoop the brimming stream;
Nor gentle purpose, nor endearing smiles.
Wanted, nor youthful dalliance, as beseems
Fair couple, linked in happy nuptial league.
Alone as they. About them frisking played

All beasts of the earth, since wild, and of all chase
In wood or wilderness, forest or den;
Sporting the lion ramped, and in his paw
Dandled the kid; bears, tigers, ounces, pards.
Gambolled before them; the unwieldly elephant,
To make them mirth, used all his might, and wreathed
His lithe proboscis; close the serpent sly,
Insinuating, wove with Gordian twine
His braided train, and of his fatal guile
Gave proof unheeded; others on the grass
Couched, and, now filled with pasture, gazing sat,
Or bedward ruminating; for the sun.
Declined, was hasting now with prone career
To the ocean isles, and in the ascending scale
Of heaven the stars that usher evening rose;
When Satan, still in gaze, as first he stood.
Scarce thus at length failed speech recovered sad : –
O Hell ! what do mine eyes with grief behold ?
Into our room of bliss thus high advanced
Creatures of other mould, earth-born perhaps,
Not spirits, yet to heavenly spirits bright
Little inferior; whom my thoughts pursue
With wonder, and could love, so lively shines
In them Divine resemblance, and such grace
The hand that formed them on their shape hath poured.
Ah ! gentle pair, ye little think how nigh
Your change approaches, when all these delights
Will vanish, and deliver ye to woe;
More woe, the more your taste is now of joy;
Happy, but for so happy ill secured
Long to continue, and this high seat, your heaven
Ill fenced for heaven to keep out such a foe
As now is entered; yet no purposed foe
To you, whom I could pity thus forlorn,
Though I unpitied. League with you I seek,
And mutual amity, so straight, so close.

That I with you must dwell, or you with me
Henceforth. My dwelling haply may not please.
Like this fair Paradise, your sense : yet such
Accept, your Maker's work. He gave it me,
Which I as freely give : hell shall unfold,
To entertain you two, her widest gates,
And send forth all her kings; there will be room,
Not like these narrow limits, to receive
Your numerous offspring; if no better place,
Thank him who puts me loth to this revenge
On you who wrong me not, for him who wronged.
And should I at your harmless innocence
Melt, as I do, yet public reason just.
Honour and empire, with revenge enlarged
By conquering this new world, compels me now
To do what else, though damned, I should abhor.
So spake the Fiend, and with necessity,
The tyrant's plea, excused his devilish deeds.
Then from his lofty stand on that high tree
Down he alights among the sportful herd
Of those four-footed kinds, himself now one,
Now other, as their shape served best his end,
Nearer to view his prey, and unespied.
To mark what of their state he more might learn
By word or action marked. About them round
A lion now he stalks with fiery glare;
Then as a tiger, who by chance hath spied
In some purlieu two gentle fawns at play,
Straight crouches close, then rising, changes oft
His couchant watch, as one who chose his ground,
Whence rushing he might surest seize them both,
Griped in each paw; when Adam, first of men,
To first of women, Eve, thus moving speech.
Turned him, all ear to hear new utterance flow:
Sole partner, and sole part of all these joys,
Dearer thyself than all; needs must the Power

That made us, and for us this ample world,
Be infinitely good, and of his good.
As liberal, and free as infinite;
That raised us from the dust, and placed us here
In all this happiness; who at his hand
Have nothing merited, nor can perform
Aught whereof he hath need; he who requires
From us no other service than to keep
This one, this easy charge : – of all the trees
In Paradise that bear delicious fruit
So various, not to taste that only Tree
Of Knowledge, planted by the tree of Life;
So near grows death to life, whate'er death is,
Some dreadful thing no doubt; for well thou know'st
God hath pronounced it death to taste that tree,
The only sign of our obedience left
Among so many signs of power and rule
Conferred upon us, and dominion given
Over all other creatures that possess
Earth, air, and sea. Then let us not think hard
One easy prohibition, who enjoy
Free leave so large to all things else, and choice
Unlimited of manifold delights;
But let us ever praise Him, and extol
His bounty; following our delightful task,
To prune these growing plants, and tend these flowers,
Which were it toilsome, yet with thee were sweet.
To whom thus Eve replied : O thou, for whom,
And from whom, I was formed, flesh of thy flesh,
And without whom am to no end, my guide
And head ! what thou hast said is just and right.
For we to Him indeed all praises owe,
And daily thanks; I chiefly, who enjoy
So far the happier lot, enjoying thee
Pre-eminent by so much odds, while thou
Like consort to thyself canst nowhere find.

That day I oft remember, when from sleep
I first awaked, and found myself reposed,
Under a shade, on flowers, much wondering where
And what I was, whence thither brought, and how.
Not distant far from thence a murmuring sound
Of waters issued from a cave, and spread
Into a liquid plain, then stood unmoved.
Pure as the expanse of heaven. I thither went,
With unexperienced thought, and laid me down
On the green bank, to look into the clear
Smooth lake, that to me seemed another sky.
As I bent down to look, just opposite
A shape within the watery gleam appeared,
Bending to look on me : I started back.
It started back; but pleased I soon returned,
Pleased it returned as soon with answering looks
Of sympathy and love. There I had fixed
Mine eyes till now, and pined with vain desire.
Had not a voice thus warned me : What thou seest,
What there thou seest, fair creature, is thyself;
With thee it came and goes. But follow me,
And I will bring thee where no shadow stays
Thy coming, and thy soft embraces; he
Whose image thou art, him thou shalt enjoy
Inseparably thine, to him shalt bear
Multitudes like thyself, and thence be called
Mother of human race. What could I do,
But follow straight, invisibly thus led ?
Till I espied thee, fair indeed, and tall.
Under a plantane, yet methought less fair,
Less winning soft, less amiably mild,
Than that smooth watery image. Back I turned.
Thou, following, criedst aloud. Return, fair Eve;
Whom flyest thou ? whom thou flyest, of him thou art,
His flesh, his bone; to give thee being I lent
Out of my side to thee, nearest my heart,

Substantial life, to have thee by my side
Henceforth an individual solace dear;
Part of my soul, I seek thee, and thee claim,
My other half. With that thy gentle hand
Seized mine : I yielded; and from that time see
How beauty is excelled by manly grace,
And wisdom, which alone is truly fair.
    So spake our general mother; and with eyes
Of conjugal attraction unreproved,
And meek surrender, half-embracing leaned
On our first father; half her swelling breast
Naked met his, under the flowing gold
Of her loose tresses hid : he in delight
Both of her beauty and submissive charms,
Smiled with superior love, as Jupiter
On Juno smiles, when he impregns the clouds
That shed May flowers; and pressed her matron lip
With kisses pure. Aside the Devil turned
For envy; yet with jealous leer malign
Eyed them askance, and to himself thus plained:
    Sight hateful, sight tormenting ! thus these two,
Imparadised in one another's arms.
The happier Eden, shall enjoy their fill
Of bliss on bliss; while I to Hell am thrust,
Where neither joy nor love, but fierce desire,
Among our other torments not the least,
Still unfulfilled, with pain of longing pines.
Yet let me not forgret what I have grained
From their own mouths. All is not theirs, it seems
One fatal tree there stands, of Knowledge called,
Forbidden them to taste. Knowledge forbidden !
Suspicious, reasonless. Why should their Lord
Envy them that ? Can it be sin to know ?
Can it be death ? And do they only stand
By ignorance ? Is that their happy state,
The proof of their obedience and their faith ?

O fair foundation laid whereon to build
Their ruin ! Hence I will excite their minds
With more desire to know, and to reject
Envious commands, invented with design
To keep them low, whom knowledge might exalt
Equal with gods. Aspiring to be such.
They taste and die; what likelier can ensue ?
But first with narrow search I must walk round
This garden, and no corner leave unspied.
A chance but chance may lead where I may meet
Some wandering spirit of heaven by fountain side,
Or in thick shade retired, from him to draw
What further would be learned. Live while ye may,
Yet happy pair; enjoy, till I return,
Short pleasures; for long woes are to succeed.
So saying, his proud step he scornful turned,
But with sly circumspection, and began
Through wood, through waste, o'er hill, o'er dale, his roam.
Meanwhile, in utmost longitude, where heaven
With earth and ocean meets, the setting sun
Slowly descended, and with right aspect
Against the eastern gate of Paradise
Levelled his evening rays. It was a rock
Of alabaster, piled up to the clouds.
Conspicuous far, winding with one ascent
Accessible from earth, one entrance high;
The rest was craggy cliff, that overhung
Still as it rose, impossible to climb.
Betwixt these rocky pillars Gabriel sat,
Chief of the angelic guards, awaiting night.
About him exercised heroic games
The unarmed youth of Heaven, but nigh at hand
Celestial armoury, shields, helms, and spears,
Hung high, with diamond flaming, and with gold.
Thither came Uriel, gliding through the even
On a sunbeam, swift as a shooting star

In autumn, 'thwart the night, when vapours fired
Impress the air, and show the mariner
From what point of his compass to beware
Impetuous winds : he thus began in haste :
    Gabriel, to thee thy course by lot hath given
Charge and strict watch, that to this happy place
No evil thing approach or enter in.
This day at height of noon came to my sphere
A spirit, zealous, as he seemed, to know
More of the Almighty's works, and chiefly man,
God's latest image. I described his way
Bent all on speed, and marked his aery gait;
But in the mount that lies from Eden north,
Where he first lighted, soon discerned his looks
Alien from Heaven, with passions foul obscured.
Mine eye pursued him still, but under shade
Lost sight of him. One of the banished crew,
I fear, hath ventured from the deep to raise
New troubles; him thy care must be to find.
    To whom the winged warrior thus returned :
Uriel, no wonder if thy perfect sight.
Amid the sun's bright circle where thou sitt'st,
See far and wide. In at this gate none pass
The vigilance here placed, but such as come
Well known from Heaven, and since meridian hour
No creature thence. If spirit of other sort.
So minded, have o'erleaped these earthly bounds
On purpose, hard thou knowest it to exclude
Spiritual substance with corporeal bar.
But if within the circuit of these walks,
In whatsoever shape he lurk, of whom
Thou tellest, by morrow dawning I shall know.
    So promised he; and Uriel to his charge
Returned on that bright beam, whose point now raised
Bore him slope downward to the sun, now fallen

Beneath the Azores[1] whither the bright orb,
Incredible how swift, had thither rolled
Diurnal, or this less voluble earth,
By shorter flight to the east, had left him there
Arraying with reflected purple and gold
The clouds that on his western throne attend.[2]
Now came still evening on, and twilight grey
Had in her sober livery all things clad;
Silence accompanied; for beast and bird.
They to their grassy couch, these to their nests
Were slunk, all but the wakeful nightingale,
She all night long her amorous descant sung;
Silence was pleased. Now glowed the firmament
With living sapphires : . Hesperus, that led
The starry host, rode brightest; till the moon,
Rising in clouded majesty, at length.
Apparent queen, unveiled her peerless light.
And o'er the dark her silver mantle threw.
When Adam thus to Eve : Fair consort, the hour
Of night, and all things now retired to rest.
Mind us of like repose; since God hath set
Labour and rest, as day and night, to men
Successive; and the timely dew of sleep.
Now falling with soft slumbrous weight, inclines
Our eye-lids. Other creatures all day long
Rove idle, unemployed, and less need rest,
Man hath his daily work of body or mind
Appointed, which declares his dignity,
And the regard of Heaven on all his ways;
While other animals unactive range,

---

1. *Azores.*– Islands in the Western Ocean, which are sometimes confounded with the Canaries, They were due west from the seat of Paradise.

2. *His western throne attend.*—It is observable that Milton will not here say whether the Ptolemaic or the Copernican system is the true one.

And of their doings God takes no account.
To-morrow, ere fresh morning streak the east
With first approach of light, we must be risen,
And at our pleasant labour, to reform
Yon flowery arbours, yonder alleys green,
Our walk at noon, with branches overgrown,
That mock our scant manuring,[1] and require
More hands than ours to lop their wanton growth;
Those blossoms also, and those dropping gums,
That lie bestrewn, unsightly and unsmooth,
Ask riddance, if we mean to tread with ease;
Meanwhile, as Nature wills, night bids us rest.
    To whom thus Eve, with perfect beauty 'dorned :
My author and disposer, what thou bidd'st
Unargued I obey; so God ordains :
God is thy law, thou mine : to know no more
Is woman's happiest knowledge, and her praise.
With thee conversing, I forgot all time;
All seasons, and their change, all please alike.
Sweet is the breath of morn, her rising sweet,
With charm of earliest birds; pleasant the sun.
When first on this delightful land he spreads
His orient beams, on herb, tree, fruit, and flower,
Glistering with dew; fragrant the fertile earth
After soft showers; and sweet the coming on
Of grateful evening mild; then silent night.
With this her solemn bird, and this fair moon,
And these the gems of heaven, her starry train :
But neither breath of morn, when she ascends
With charm of earhest birds; nor risine sun
On this dehghtful land; nor herb, fruit, flower,
Glistering with dew; nor fragrance after showers,
Nor grateful evening mild; nor silent night,

1. *Our manuring.*–Our culture. "The manuring hand of the tiller shall root out all that burdens the soil."– *Reasons of Church Government.*

With this her solemn bird; nor walk by moon.
Or glittering starlight, without thee is sweet.
But wherefore all night long shine these ? for whom
This glorious sight, when sleep hath shut all eyes ?
　　To whom our general ancestor replied :
Daughter of God and man, accomplished Eve,
These have their course to finish round the earth
By morrow evening, and from land to land
In order, though to nations yet unborn,
Ministering light prepared, they set and rise,
Lest total darkness should by night regain
Her old possession, and extinguish life
In Nature and all things; which these soft fires
Not only enlighten, but, with kindly heat
Of various influence, foment and warm.
Temper or nourish, or in part shed down
Their stellar virtue on all kinds that grow
On Earth, made hereby apter to receive
Perfection from the sun's more potent ray.
These then, though unbeheld in deep of night,
Shine not in vain. Nor think, though men were none,
That heaven would want spectators, God want praise.
Millions of spiritual creatures walk the Earth
Unseen, both when we wake, and when we sleep.
All these with ceaseless praise His works behold
Both day and night. How often from the steep
Of echoing hill or thicket have we heard
Celestial voices to the midnight air,
Sole, or responsive each to other's note,
Singing their great Creator ! Oft in bands
While they keep watch, or nightly rounding walk,
With heavenly touch of instrumental sounds
In full harmonic number joined, their songs
Divide the night, and lift our thoughts to heaven.
　　Thus talking, hand in hand alone they passed
On to their blissful bower. It was a place

Chosen by the sovereign Planter, when he framed
All things to man's delightful use. The roof
Of thickest covert was inwoven shade.
Laurel, and myrtle, and what higher grew
Of firm and fragrant leaf; on either side
Acanthus, and each odorous bushy shrub,
Fenced up the verdant wall; each beauteous flower,
Iris all hues, roses, and jessamine,
Reared high their flourished heads between, and wrought
Mosaic; under foot the violet.
Crocus, and hyacinth, with rich inlay
Broidered the ground, more coloured than with stone
Of costliest emblem : other creature here.
Beast, bird, insect, or worm, durst enter none,
Such was their awe of man. In shadier bower
More sacred and sequestered, though but feigned,
Pan or Sylvanus[1] never slept, nor Nymph
Nor Faunus[2] haunted. Here, in close recess,
With flowers, garlands, and sweet-smelling herbs.
Espoused Eve decked first her nuptial bed;
And heavenly quires the hymenean sung,
What day the genial Angel to our sire
Brought her, in naked beauty more adorned,
More lovely than Pandora,[3] whom the gods
Endowed with all their gifts; and, O ! too like

1. *Sylvanus.* A divinity of fields and forests.

2. *Nymph nor Faunus*-Rural divinities, male and female.

3. *More lovely than Pandora.*–The story concerning Pandora is, that Prometheus, the son of Japhet, stole fire from heaven and gave it to the earth. Jupiter, to punish the theft, sent Pandora to him, endowed by the gods with all charms, as her name imports. She was brought to him by Hermes. Prometheus was not taken by the snare; but his younger brother was, and, being curious to know the contents of a casket in Pandora's possession, caused it to be opened, from which all kinds of evil came forth.

In sad event, when to the unwiser son
Of Japhet brought by Hermes, she ensnared
Mankind with her fair looks, to be avenged
On him who had stole Jove's authentic fire.
    Thus, at their shady lodge arrived, both stood,
Both turned, and under open sky adored
The God that made both sky, air, earth, and heaven,
Which they beheld, the moon's resplendent globe,
And starry pole. Thou also mad'st the night.
Maker Omnipotent, and thou the day
Which we, in our appointed work employed,
Have finished, happy in our mutual help
And mutual love, the crown of all our bliss
Ordained by thee; and this delicious place
For us too large, where thy abundance wants
Partakers, and uncropt falls to the ground.
But thou hast promised from us two a race
To fill the earth, who shall with us extol
Thy goodness infinite, both when we wake.
And when we seek, as now, thy gilted sleep.
    This said unanimous,[1] and other rites
Observing none, but adoration pure
Which God likes best, into their inmost bower
Handed they went; and, eased the putting off
These troublesome disguises which we wear,
Straight side by side were laid; nor turned, I ween,
Adam from his fair spouse, nor Eve the rites
Mysterious of connubial love refused :
Whatever hypocrites austerely talk
Of purity, and place, and innocence,
Defaming as impure what God declares
Pure, and commands to some, leaves free to all.
Our Maker bids increase; who bids abstain

1. *Unanimous.*–By both–with one heart.

But our destroyer, foe to God and man ?
Hail, wedded love, mysterious law, true source
Of human offspring, sole propriety
In Paradise, in all things common else!
By thee adulterous lust was driven from men
Among the bestial herds to range; by thee,
Founded in reason, loyal, just, and pure.
Relations dear, and all the charities
Of father, son, and brother, first were known.
Far be it, that I should write thee sin or blame,
Or think thee unbefitting holiest place;
Perpetual tountain of domestic sweets.
Whose bed is undefiled, and chaste pronounced,
Present, or past, as saints and patriarchs used.
Here Love his golden shafts employs, here lights
His constant lamp, and waves his purple wings.
Reigns here and revels; not in the bought smile
Of harlots, loveless, joyless, unendeared,
Casual fruition, nor in court amours,
Mixed dance, or wanton mask, or midnight ball,
Or serenate, which the starved lover sings
To his proud fair, best quitted with disdain.
These, lulled by nightingales, embracing slept.
And on their naked limbs the flowery roof
Showered roses, which the morn repaired. Sleep on,
Blest pair; and, O ! yet happiest, if ye seek
No happier state, and know to know no more.
Now had night measured with her shadowy cone
Half way up hill this vast sublunar vault,
And from their ivory port the cherubim,
Forth issuing at the accustomed hour, stood armed
To their night watches in warlike parade,
When Gabriel to his next in power thus spake :
Uzziel, half these draw off, and coast the south
With strictest watch; these other wheel the north;
Our circuit meets full west. As flame they part,

Half wheeling to the shield, half to the spear.
From these, two strong and subtle sp'rits he called
That near him stood, and gave them thus in charge :
    Ithuriel and Zephon, with winged speed
Search through this garden, leave unsearched no nook;
But chiefly where those two fair creatures lodge,
Now laid perhaps asleep, secure of harm.
This evening from the sun's decline arrived
Who tells of some infernal spirit seen
Hitherward bent – who could have thought ? – escaped
The bars of Hell, on errand bad no doubt:
Such, where ye find, seize fast, and hither bring.
    So saying, on he led his radiant files.
Dazzling the moon; these to the bower direct
In search of whom they sought. Him there they found,
Squat like a toad close at the ear of Eve,
Assaying by his devilish art to reach
The organs of her fancy, and with them forge
Illusions, as he list, phantasms and dreams.
Or if, inspiring venom, he might taint
The animal spirits, that from pure blood arise
Like gentle breaths from rivers pure, thence raise.
At least, distempered, discontented thoughts,
Vain hopes, vain aims, inordinate desires.
Blown up with high conceits engendering pride.
Him thus intent Ithuriel with his spear
Touched lightly; – for no falsehood can endure
Touch of celestial temper, but returns
Of force to its own likeness. Up he starts,
Discovered and surprised. As when a spark
Lights on a heap of nitrous powder, laid
Fit for the tun, some magazine to store
Against a rumoured war, the smutty grain.
With sudden blaze diffused, inflames the air;
So started up in his own shape the Fiend.
Back stept those two fair angels, half amazed

So sudden to behold the grizzly king.
Yet thus, unmoved with fear, accost him soon :
    Which of those rebel spirits adjudged to hell
Com'st thou, escaped thy prison ? and transformed,
Why satt'st thou like an enemy in wait,
Here watching at the head of these that sleep ?
    Know ye not, then, said Satan, filled with scorn.
Know ye not me ? Ye knew me once no mate
For you, there sitting where ye durst not soar:
Not to know me, argues yourselves unknown,
The lowest of your throng; or, if ye know,
Why ask ye, and superfluous begin
Your message, like to end as much in vain ?
    To whom thus Zephon, answering scorn with scorn:
Think not, revolted spirit, thy shape the same,
Or undiminished brightness to be known.
As when thou stood'st in heaven, upright and pure;
That glory then, when thou no more wast good.
Departed from thee; and thou resemblest now
Thy sin and place of doom obscure and foul.
But come; for thou, be sure, shalt give account
To him who sent us, whose charge is to keep
This place inviolable, and these from harm.
    So spake the cherub; and his grave rebuke,
Severe in youthful beauty, added grace
Invincible. Abashed the devil stood,
And felt how awful goodness is, and saw
Virtue in her shape how lovely; saw, and pined
His loss; but chiefly to find here observed
His lustre visibly impaired; yet seemed
Undaunted. If I must contend, said he,
Best with the best, the sender not the sent,
Or all at once; more glory will be won,
Or less be lost. Thy fear, said Zephon bold,
Will save us trial what the least can do
Single against thee, wicked and thence weak.

The Fiend replied not, overcome with rage;
But, like a proud steed reined, went haughty on,
Champing his iron curb : to strive or fly
He held it vain; awe from above had quelled
His heart, not else dismayed. Now drew they nigh
The western point, where those half-rounding guards
Just met, and, closing, stood in squadron joined,
Awaiting next command. To whom their chief.
Gabriel, from the front thus called aloud :
O friends ! I hear the tread of nimble feet
Hasting this way, and now by glimpse discern
Ithuriel, and Zephon, through the shade;
And with them comes a third of regal port.
But faded splendour wan, who by his gait
And fierce demeanour seems the prince of Hell,
Not likely to part hence, without contest;
Stand firm, for in his look defiance lours.
He scarce had ended, when those two approached,
And brief related whom they brought, where found.
How busied, in what form and posture couched.
To whom with stern regard thus Gabriel spake :
Why hast thou, Satan, broke the bounds prescribed
To thy transgressions, and disturbed the charge
Of others, who approve not to transgress
By thy example, but have power and right
To question thy bold entrance on this place;
Employed, it seems, to violate sleep, and those
Whose dwelling God hath planted here in bliss ?
To whom thus Satan, with contemptuous brow :
Gabriel, thou hadst m Heaven the esteem of wise,
And such I held thee; but this question asked
Puts me in doubt. Lives there who loves his pain ?
Who would not, finding way, break loose from hell,
Though thither doomed ? Thou wouldst thyself, no doubt.
And boldly venture to whatever place

Farthest from pain, where thou mightst hope to change
Torment with ease, and soonest recompense
Dole with delight, which in this place I sought;
To thee no reason, who knowest only good,
But evil hast not tried : and wilt object
His will, who bound us ? Let him surer bar
His iron gates, if he intends our stay
In that dark durance. Thus much what was asked.
The rest is true, they found me where they say;
But that implies not violence or harm.
    Thus he in scorn. The warlike Angel moved,
Disdainfully half smiling, thus replied :
O loss of one in heaven to judge of wise !
Since Satan fell, whom folly overthrew.
And now returns him from his prison 'scaped,
Gravely in doubt whether to hold them wise
Or not, who ask what boldness brought him hither
Unlicensed from his bounds in hell prescribed;
So wise he judges it to fly from pain.
However, and to 'scape his punishment!
So judge thou still, presumptuous ! till the wrath,
Which thou incurr'st by flying, meet thy flight
Sevenfold, and scourge that wisdom back to hell
Which taught thee yet no better, that no pain
Can equal anger infinite provoked.
But wherefore thou alone ? Wherefore with thee
Came not all hell broke loose ? Is pain to them
Less pain, less to be fled; or thou than they
Less hardy to endure? Courageous chief!
The first in flight from pain ! Hadst thou alleged
To thy deserted host this cause of flight,
Thou surely hadst not come sole fugitive.
    To which the Fiend thus answered, frowning stern :
Not that I less endure, or shrink from pain.
Insulting; Ange! Well thou knowest I stood
The fiercest, when in battle to thy aid

The blasting vollied thunder made all speed,
And seconded thy else not dreaded spear.
But still thy words at random as before
Argue thy inexperience, what behoves[1]
From hard assays, and ill successes past,
A faithful leader, not to hazard all
Through ways of danger by himself untried.
I therefore, I alone first undertook
To wing the desolate abyss and spy
This new-created world, whereof in hell
Fame is not silent, here in hope to find
Better abode, and my afflicted powers
To settle here on earth, or in mid air;
Though for possession put to try once more
What thou and thy gay legions dare against;
Whose easier business were to serve their Lord
High up in heaven, with songs to hymn his throne,
And practised distances to cringe, not fight.
　　To whom the warrior Angel soon replied :
To say and straight unsay, pretending first
Wise to fly pain, professing next the spy,
Argues no leader, but a liar traced,
Satan : and couldst thou faithful add ? O name,
O sacred name of faithfulness profaned !
Faithful to whom ? To thy rebellious crew ?
Army of fiends, fit body to fit head.
Was this your discipline and faith engaged.
Your military obedience, to dissolve
Allegiance to the acknowledged Power Supreme ?
And thou, sly hypocrite, who now wouldst seem
Patron of liberty, who more than thou
Once fawned, and cringed, and servilely adored
Heaven's awful monarch ? wherefore, but in hope
To dispossess him, and thyself to reign ?

1. *Inexperience, what behoves.*–As to what behoves.

But mark what I areed thee[1] now: Avaunt !
Fly thither whence thou fledd'st ! If from this hour
Within these hallowed limits thou appear.
Back to the infernal pit I drag thee chained,
And seal thee so, as henceforth not to scorn
The facile gates of hell too slightly barred.
    So threatened he; but Satan to no threats
Gave heed, but, waxing more in rage, replied :
    Then, when I am thy captive, talk of chains,
Proud limitary cherub ![2] but ere then
Far heavier load thyself expect to feel
From my prevailing arm, though heaven's king
Ride on thy wings, and thou with thy compeers,
Used to the yoke, draw'st his triumphant wheels
In progress through the road of Heaven star-paved.
    While thus he spake, the angelic squadron bright
Turned fiery red, sharpening in mooned horns
Their phalanx, and began to hem him round
With ported spears, as thick as when a field
Of Ceres, ripe for harvest, waving bends
Her bearded grove of ears, which way the wind
Sways them; the careful ploughman doubting stands
Lest on the threshing-floor his hopeful sheaves
Prove chaff. On the other side, Satan, alarmed,
Collecting all his might, dilated stood,
Like Teneriff or Atlas, unremoved :
His stature reached the sky, and on his crest
Sat horror plumed; nor wanted in his grasp
What seemed both spear and shield. Now dreadful deeds
Might have ensued; nor only Paradise,
In this commotion, but the starry cope
Of heaven perhaps, or all the elements
At least had gone to wrack, disturbed and torn

---

1. *Areed thee.*–Anglo-Saxon for counsel–admonish.
2. *Proud limitary cherub.*–One set to watch limits–to guard boundaries.

With violence of this conflict, had not soon
The Eternal, to prevent such horrid fray.
Hung forth in heaven his golden scales, yet seen
Betwixt Astrea and the Scorpion[1] sign,
Wherein all things created first He weighed.
The pendulous round earth with balanced air
In counterpoise; now ponders all events.
Battles and realms : in these he put two weights,
The sequel each of parting and of fight :
The latter quick up flew, and kicked the beam;
Which Gabriel spying, thus bespake the Fiend :
      Satan, I know thy strength, and thou know'st mine;
Neither our own, but given; what folly then
To boast what arms can do ! since thine no more
Than Heaven permits, nor mine, though doubled now
To trample thee as mire : for proof look up,
And read thy lot in yon celestial sign,
Where thou art weighed, and shown how light, how weak
If thou resist. The Fiend looked up, and knew
His mounted scale aloft: nor more;[2] but fled
Murmuring, and with him fled the shades of night.

---

1. *Betwixt Astrea and the Scorpion.*–Signs in the Zodiac.
2. *Scale aloft: nor more.*–Nor said ought more.

BOOK - V

MORNING approached, Eve relates to Adam her troublesome dream; he likes it not, yet comforts her; they come forth to their day-labours; their morning hymn at the door of their bower. God, to render man inexcusable, sends Raphael to admonish him of his obedience, of his free estate, of his enemy near at hand, who he is, and why his enemy, and whatever else may avail Adam to know. Raphael comes down to Paradise; his appearance described; his coming discerned by Adam afar off, sitting at the door of his bower; he goes out to meet him, brings him to his lodge, entertains him with the choicest fruits of Paradise, got together by Eve; their discourse at table; Raphael performs his message, minds Adam of his state and of his enemy; relates, at Adam's request, who that enemy is, and how he came to be so, beginning from the first revolt in heaven, and the occasion thereof; how he drew his legions after him to the parts of the north, and there incited them to rebel with him, persuading all but only Abdiel, a seraph, who in argument dissuades and opposes him, then forsakes him.

Now morn, her rosy steps in the eastern clime
Advancing, sowed the earth with orient pearl,
When Adam waked, so customed : for his sleep
Was aery-light, from pure digestion bred,
And temperate vapours bland, which the only sound
Of leaves and fuming rills, Aurora's fan,[1]
Lightly dispersed, and the shrill matin song
Of birds on every bough; so much the more
His wonder was to find unwakened Eve

---

1. *Aurora's fan.*–We often speak of fanning winds, and in the morning they may be described as Aurora's fan.

With tresses discomposed, and glowing cheek,
As through unquiet rest. He, on his side
Leaning, half raised, with looks of cordial love
Hung over her enamoured, and beheld
Beauty, which, whether waking or asleep.
Shot forth peculiar graces; then with voice
Mild as when Zephyrus on Flora breathes.
Her hand soft touching, whisper'd thus : – Awake,
My fairest, my espoused, my latest found.
Heaven's last, best gift, my ever-new delight !
Awake : the morning shines, and the fresh field
Calls us; we lose the prime to mark how spring
Our tender plants, how blows the citron grove,
What drops the myrrh, and what the balmy reed,
How Nature paints her colours, how the bee
Sits on the bloom extracting liquid sweet.
Such whispering waked her, but with startled eye
On Adam, whom embracing, thus she spake : –
O sole in whom my thoughts find all repose,
My glory, my perfection ! glad I see
Thy face and morn returned; for I this night –
Such night till this I never passed – have dreamed.
If dreamed, not, as I oft am wont, of thee.
Works of day past, or morrow's next design;
But of offence and trouble, which my mind
Knew never till this irksome night. Methought
Close at mine ear one called me forth to walk
With gentle voice – I thought it thine. It said,
Why sleep'st thou, Eve ? now is the pleasant time,
The cool, the silent, save where silence yields
To the night-warbling bird, that now awake
Tunes sweetest his love-laboured song; now reigns
Full-orbed the moon, and with more pleasing light
Shadowy sets off the face of things – in vain,
If none regard. Heaven wakes with all his eyes,
Whom to behold but thee, Nature's desire ?

In whose sight all things joy, with ravishment
Attracted by thy beauty still to gaze.
I rose as at thy call, but found thee not;
To find thee I directed then my walk;
And on, methought, alone I passed through ways
That brought me on a sudden to the tree
Of interdicted knowledge. Fair it seemed.
Much fairer to my fancy than by day :
And, as I wondering looked, beside it stood
One shaped and winged like one of those from heaven
By us oft seen : his dewy locks distilled
Ambrosia[1] On that tree he also gazed;
And oh, fair plant, said he, with fruit surcharged,
Deigns none to ease thy load, and taste thy sweet.
Nor God, nor man ? Is knowledge so despised ?
Or envy, or what reserve forbids to taste ?
Forbid who will, none shall from me withhold
Longer thy offered good; why else set here ?
This said, he paused not, but with venturous arm
He plucked, he tasted. Me damp horror chilled
At such bold words, vouched with a deed so bold:
But he thus, overjoyed : O fruit divine,
Sweet of thyself, but much more sweet thus cropt,
Forbidden here, it seems, as only fit
For gods, yet able to make gods of men;
And why not gods of men; since good, the more
Communicated, more abundant grows.
The author not impaired, but honoured more ?
Here, happy creature, fair angelic Eve !
Partake thou also : happy though thou art.
Happier thou mayst be, worthier canst not be,
Taste this, and be henceforth among the gods
Thyself a goddess, not to earth confined,
But sometimes in the air, as we; sometimes

1. *Ambrosia.*–Grateful odour, proper to the gods.

Ascend to Heaven, by merit thine, and see
What life the gods live there, and such live thou.
So saying, he drew nigh, and to me held.
Even to my mouth of that same fruit held part
Which he had plucked : the pleasant savoury smell
So quickened appetite, that I, methought,
Could not but taste. Forthwith up to the clouds
With him I flew, and underneath beheld
The earth outstretched immense, a prospect wide
And various; wondering at my flight and change
To this high exaltation, suddenly
My guide was gone, and I, methought, sunk down
And fell asleep; but, oh, how glad I waked
To find this but a dream. Thus Eve her night
Related, and thus Adam answered sad :
    Best image of myself, and dearer half.
The trouble of thy thoughts this night in sleep
Affects me equally; nor can I like
This uncouth dream, of evil sprung, I fear.
Yet evil whence ? in thee can harbour none,
Created pure. But know, that in the soul
Are many lesser faculties, that serve
Reason as chief Among these, Fancy next
Her office holds; of all external things,
Which the five watchful senses represent,
She forms imaginations, aery shapes,
Which reason joining or disjoining frames
All what we affirm or what deny, and call
Our knowledge or opinion; then retires
Into her private cell, when nature rests.
Oft in her absence mimic Fancy wakes
To imitate her; but misjoining shapes,
Wild work produces oft, and most in dreams;
Ill matching words and deeds long past or late,
Some such resemblances, methinks, I find
Of our last evening's talk, in this thy dream.

But with addition strange; yet be not sad.
Evil into the mind of God or Man
May come and go, so unapproved, and leave
No spot or blame behind; which gives me hope
That what in sleep thou didst abhor to dream,
Waking thou never wilt consent to do.
Be not disheartened, then, nor cloud those looks,
That wont to be more cheerful and serene.
Than when fair morning first smiles on the world;
And let us to our fresh employments rise
Among the groves, the fountains, and the flowers,
That open now their choicest bosomed smells.
Reserved from night, and kept for thee in store.
    So cheered he his fair spouse, and she was cheered,
But silently a gentle tear let fall
From either eye, and wiped them with her hair;
Two other precious drops that ready stood,
Each in their crystal sluice, he, ere they fell.
Kissed, as the gracious signs of sweet remorse
And pious awe, that feared to have offended.
    So all was cleared, and to the Held they haste.
But first from under shady arborous roof,
Soon as they forth were come to open sight
Of day-spring, and the sun, who, scarce uprisen.
With wheels yet hovering o'er the ocean-brim,
Shot parallel to the earth his dewy ray.
Discovering in wide landscape all the east
Of Paradise and Eden's happy plains,
Lowly they bowed adoring, and began
Their orisons, each morning duly paid
In various style; for neither various style
Nor holy rapture wanted they to praise
Their Maker, in fit strains pronounced, or sung
Unmeditated; such prompt eloquence
Flowed from their lips, in prose or numerous verse;

More tuneable than needed lute or harp
To add more sweetness; and they thus began :
    These are Thy glorious works. Parent of good,
Almighty ! Thine this universal frame,
Thus wondrous fair : Thyself how wondrous then !
Unspeakable, who sitt'st above these heavens
To us invisible, or dimly seen
In these thy lowest works; yet these declare
Thy goodness beyond thought, and power divine.
Speak, ye who best can tell, ye sons of light,
Angels, for ye behold Him, and with songs
And choral symphonies, day without night.
Circle his throne rejoicing; ye in heaven.
On earth join all ye creatures to extol
Him first, Him last, Him midst, and without end.
Fairest of stars, last in the train of night,
If better thou belong not to the dawn.
Sure pledge of day, that crown'st the smiling morn
With thy bright circlet, praise Him in thy sphere,
While day arises, that sweet hour of prime.
Thou Sun, of this great world both eye and soul,
Acknowledge Him thy greater; sound His praise
In thy eternal course, both when thou climb'st.
And when high noon hast gained, and when thou fall'st.
Moon, that now meet'st the orient sun, now fly'st,
With the fixed stars, fixed in their orb that flies;
And ye five other wandering fires,[1] that move
In mystic dance[2] not without song, resound
His praise, who out of darkness called up light.
Air, and ye elements, the eldest birth

1. *And ye five other wandering fires.*–The five planets known in Milton's time–Venus, Mercury, Mars, Jupiter, and Saturn.

2. *That move in mystic dance.*–The fitting action of things is often described as their music. Hence the wide application of the words harmony, concord, *&C.,* derived from music.

Of nature's womb, that in quaternion run[1]
Perpetual circle, multiform; and mix
And nourish all things; let your ceaseless change
Vary to our great Maker still new praise.
Ye mists and exhalations, that now rise
From hill or steaming lake, dusky or grey,
Till the sun paint your fleecy skirts with gold.
In honour to the world's great Author rise;
Whether to deck with clouds the uncoloured sky,
Or wet the thirsty earth with falling showers,
Rising or falling, still advance His praise.
His praise, ye winds that from four quarters blow,
Breathe soft or loud; and wave your tops, ye pines,
With every plant, in sign of worship wave.
Fountains, and ye that warble as ye flow,
Melodious murmurs, warbling tune His praise.
Join voices, all ye living souls : ye birds
That, singing, up to Heaven-gate ascend.
Bear on your wings and in your notes His praise.
Ye that in waters glide, and ye that walk
The earth, and stately tread, or lowly creep;
Witness if I be silent, morn or even,
To hill or valley, fountain or fresh shade.
Made vocal by my song, and taught His praise.
Hail, universal Lord ! be bounteous still
To give us only good; and if the night
Have gathered aught of evil, or concealed,
Disperse it, as now light dispels the dark.
        So prayed they innocent, and to their thoughts
Firm peace recovered soon, and wonted calm.
On to their morning's rural work they haste,
Among sweet dews and flowers, where any row
Of fruit-trees, over-woody, reached too far
Their pampered boughs, and needed hands to check

1. *That in quaternion run.*–A reference to the supposed four-fold influence of the first elements of things.

Fruitless embraces : or they led the vine
To wed her elm; she, spoused, about him twines
Her marriageable arms, and with her brings
Her dower, the adopted clusters, to adorn
His barren leaves. Them thus employed beheld
With pity heaven's high King, and to Him called
Raphael, the sociable spirit, that deigned
To travel with Tobias,[1] and secured
His marriage with the seven-times wedded maid.

Raphael, said he, thou hear'st what stir on Earth
Satan, from Hell 'scaped through the darksome gulf.
Hath raised in Paradise; and how disturbed
This night the human pair; how he designs
In them at once to ruin all mankind.
Go, therefore, half this day, as friend with friend.
Converse with Adam, in what bower or shade
Thou find'st him from the heat of noon retired,
To respite his day-labour with repast.
Or with repose; and such discourse bring on
As may advise him[2] of his happy state –
Happiness in his power, left free to will.
Left to his own free will, his will though free
Yet mutable; whence warn him to beware
He swerve not, too secure. Tell him withal
His danger, and from whom; what enemy
Late fallen himself from heaven, is plotting now
The fall of others from like state of bliss;
By violence ? no, for that shall be withstood;
But by deceit and lies. This let him know,
Lest, wilfully transgressing, he pretend
Surprisal, unadmonished, unforewarned.

So spake the Eternal Father, and fulfilled
All justice. Nor delayed the winged saint

1. *To travel with Tobias.*–See Book of Tobit.

2. *As may advise him.*–Make him aware of–sensible to.

After his charge received; but from among
Thousand celestial Ardours,[1] where he stood
Veiled with his gorgeous wings, up springing light,
Flew through the midst of heaven; – the angelic quires,
On each hand parting, to his speed gave way
Through all the empyreal road : till, at the gate
Of Heaven arrived, the gate self opened wide
On golden hinges turning, as by work
Divine the sov'reign Architect had framed.
From hence no cloud, or, to obstruct his sight,
Star interposed, however small – he sees,
Not unconform[2] to other shining globes,
Earth, and the garden of God, with cedars crowned
Above all hills. As when by night the glass
Of Galileo, less assured, observes
Imagined lands and regrions in the moon:
Or pilot,[3] from amidst the Cyclades,
Delos or Samos[4] first appearing, kens
A cloudy spot. Down thither prone in flight
He speeds, and through the vast ethereal sky
Sails between worlds and worlds, with steady wing,
Now on the polar winds, then with quick fan
Winnows the buxom air;[5] till, within soar
Of towering eagles, to all the fowls he seems
A phoenix, gazed by all, as that sole bird,
When, to enshrine his relics in the Sun's
Bright temple, to Egyptian Thebes he flies.
    At once on the eastern cliff of Paradise
He lights; and to his proper shape returns,

1. *Celestial Ardours.*–Seraphic powers.
2. *Not unconform.*–Sees the earth as conformed in appearance to other globes.
3. *Or pilot.*–Used by Milton for captain or commander.
4. *Cyclades, Delos or Samos.*–Greek islands.
5. *Buxom air.*–Light, yielding.

A seraph winged. Six wings he wore, to shade
His lineaments divine; the pair that clad
Each shoulder, broad, came mantling o'er his breast
With regal ornament; the middle pair
Girt like a starry zone his waist, and round
Skirted his loins and thighs with downy gold,
And colours dipt in heaven; the third his feet
Shadowed from either heel with feathered mail,
Sky-tinctured grain.[1] Like Maia's son[2] he stood.
And shook his plumes, that heavenly fragrance filled
The circuit wide. Straiijht knew him all the bands
Of Angels under watch; and to his state,
And to his message high, in honour rise;
For on some message high they guessed him bound.
Their glittering tents he passed, and now is come
Into the blissful field, through groves of myrrh.
And flowering odours, cassia, nard, and balm;
A wilderness of sweets; for Nature here
Wantoned as in her prime, and played at will
Her virgin fancies, pouring forth more sweet,
Wild above rule or art, enormous bliss.
Him through the spicy forest onward come
Adam discerned, as in the door he sat
Of his cool bower, while now the mounted sun
Shot down direct his fervid rays, to warm
Earth's inmost womb, more warmth than Adam needs;
And Eve within, due at her hour prepared
For dinner savoury fruits, of taste to please
True appetite, and not disrelish thirst
Of nectareous draughts between, from milky stream,

---

1. *Feathered mail, sky-tinctured grain.*–Beautiful colouring wrought in so as to be durable.

"Dipt in the richest tincture of the skies."

Pope, "Rape of the Lock," cant. ii.

2. *Like Maia's son.*–Like Mercury.

Berry, or grape : to whom thus Adam called :
 Haste hither. Eve, and, worth thy sight, behold.
Eastward among those trees, what glorious shape
Comes this way moving; seems[1] another morn
Risen on mid-noon. Some orreat behest from Heaven
To us perhaps he brings, and will vouchsafe
This day to be our guest. But go with speed,
And, what thy stores contain, bring forth, and pour
Abundance, fit to honour and receive
Our heavenly stranger; well we may afford
Our givers their own gifts, and large bestow
From large bestowed, where Nature multiplies
Her fertile growth, and by disburdening grows
More fruitful, which instructs us not to spare.
 To whom thus Eve : Adam, earth, hallowed mould,
Of God inspired ! small store will serve, where store,
All seasons, ripe for use hangs on the stalk;
Save what by frugal storing firmness gains
 To nourish, and superfluous moist consumes.
But I will haste, and from each bough and brake,
Each plant and juiciest gourd, will pluck such choice
To entertain our Angel-guest, as he
Beholding shall confess that here on earth
God hath dispensed his bounties as in Heaven.
 So saying, with dispatchful looks, in haste
She turns, on hospitable thoughts intent
What choice to choose for delicacy best,
What order so contrived as not to mix
Tastes not well joined, inelegant, but bring
Taste after taste upheld with kindliest change;
Bestirs her then, and from each tender stalk
Whatever Earth, all-bearing mother, yields
In India East or West, or middle shore

1. *Seems.*–It seems.

In Pontus or the Punic coast,[1] or where
Alcinous reigned;[2] fruit of all kinds, in coat
Rough, or smooth rind, or bearded husk, or shell,
She gathers, tribute large, and on the board
Heaps with unsparing hand. For drink the grape
She crushes, inoffensive must,[3] and meaths[4]
From many a berry, and from sweet kernels pressed,
She tempers dulcet creams; nor these to hold
Wants her fit vessels pure; then strews the ground
With rose and odours from the shrub unfumed.
Meanwhile our primitive great sire, to meet
His godlike guest, walks forth without more train
Accompanied than with his own complete
Perfections. In himself was all his state.
More solemn than the tedious pomp that waits
On princes, when their rich retinue long
Of horses led, and grooms besmeared with gold,
Dazzles the crowd, and sets them all agape.
Nearer his presence Adam, though not awed.
Yet with submiss approach and reverence meek,
As to a superior nature, bowing low,
Thus said : Native of Heaven, for other place
None can than Heaven such glorious shape contain;
Since by descending from the thrones above.
Those happy places thou hast deigned a while
To want, and honour these; vouchsafe with us
Two only, who yet by sovereign gift possess
This spacious ground, in yonder shady bower
To rest, and what the garden choicest bears
To sit and taste, till this meridian heat
Be over, and the sun more cool decline.

1. *Pontus or the Punic coast.–On* the northern or the southern shores of the Mediterranean.
2. *Alcinous reigned.*–He reigned over Corfu, Corcyra, &c.
3. *She crushes, inoffensive must.*–New wine, pressed from the grape, but not fermented.
4. *And meaths.*– Drinks. Anglo-Saxon.

Whom thus the angelic Virtue[1] answered mild :
Adam, I therefore came; nor art thou such
Created, or such place hast here to dwell.
As may not oft invite, though spirits of Heaven,
To visit thee. Lead on then where thy bower
O'ershades; for these mid hours, till evening rise,
I have at will. So to the sylvan lodge
They came, that like Pomona's arbour smiled,[2]
With flowerets decked, and fragrant smells. But Eve,
Undecked save with herself, more lovely fair
Than wood-nymph, or the fairest goddess feigned
Of three that in Mount Ida naked strove,[3]
Stood to entertain her guest from heaven; no veil
She needed, virtue proof; no thought infirm
Altered her cheek. On whom the angel "Hail!"
Bestowed, the holy salutation used
Long after to blest Mary, second Eve.
Hail, mother of mankind, whose fruitful womb
Shall fill the world more numerous with thy sons,
Than with these various fruits the trees of God
Have heaped this table. Raised of grassy turf
Their table was, and mossy seats had round,
And on her ample square from side to side,
All autumn piled, though spring and autumn here
Danced hand in hand. A while discourse they hold,
No fear lest dinner cool; when thus began
Our author: Heavenly stranger, please to taste
These bounties, which our Nourisher, from whom
All perfect good, unmeasured out, descends,

---

1. *Angelic Virtue.*–The Virtues were an order of their own–high in rank in the celestial hierarchy.
2. *Like Pomona's arbour smiled.*–Pomona was the goddess of fruit trees.
3. *Of three that in Mount Ida naked strove.*–Juno, Minerva, and Venus thus appealed to the judgment of Paris.

To us for food and for delight hath caused
The Earth to yield; unsavoury food perhaps
To spiritual natures; only this I know,
That one celestial Father gives to all.
    To whom the Angel: Therefore what He gives–
Whose praise be ever sung–to man in part
Spiritual, may of purest spirits be found
No ungrateful food: and food alike those pure
Intelligential substances require,
As doth your rational; and both contain
Within them every lower faculty
Of sense, whereby they hear, see, smell, touch, taste,
Tasting, concoct, digest, assimilate,
And corporeal to incorporeal turn.
For know, whatever was created needs
To be sustained and fed: of elements
The grosser feeds the purer, earth the sea.
Earth and the sea feed air, the air those fires
Ethereal, and as lowest, first the moon ;
Whence in her visage round those spots,
Vapours not yet into her substance turned.
Nor doth the moon no nourishment exhale
From her moist continent to higher orbs.
The sun, that light imparts to all, receives
From all his alimental recompense
In humid exhalations, and at even
Sups with the ocean. Though in Heaven the trees
Of life ambrosial fruitage bear, and vines
Yield nectar; though from off the boughs each morn,
We brush mellifluous dews, and find the ground
Covered with pearly grain; yet God hath here
Varied his bounty so with new delights,
As may compare with Heaven; and to taste
Think not I shall be nice. So down they sat,

And to their viands fell; nor seemingly
The Angel, nor in mist–the common gloss
Of theologians–but with keen despatch
Of real hunger[1] and concoctive heat
To transubstantiate: what redounds, transpires
Through spirits with ease; nor wonder, if by fire
Of sooty coal the empiric alchymist
Can turn, and holds it possible to turn,
Metals of drossiest ore to perfect gold.
As from the mine. Meanwhile at table Eve
Ministered naked, and their flowing cups
With pleasant liquors crowned. O innocence,
Deserving Paradise ! if ever, then.
Then[2] had the sons of God excuse to have been
Enamoured at that sight; but in those hearts
Love unlibidinous reigned, nor jealousy
Was understood, the injured lover's hell.
    Thus when with meats and drinks they had sufficed,
Not burdened nature, sudden mind arose
In Adam not to let the occasion pass.
Given him by this great conference, to know
Of things above his world, and of their being
Who dwell in heaven, whose excellence he saw
Transcend his own so far : whose radiant forms,
Divine effulgence, whose high power, so far
Exceeded human : and his wary speech
Thus to the empyreal minister he framed :
    Inhabitant with God, now know I well
Thy favour, in this honour done to man;
Under whose lowly roof thou hast vouchsafed

1. *With keen despatch of real hunger.*–This seems a confounding of spirit with matter. But Milton adheres strictly to the sacred text, and there was possibly more reality under such phenomena than is dreamt of in our philosophy.

2. *If ever, then, then.*–If the time was ever, it was then.

To enter, and these earthly fruits to taste,
Food not of Angels, yet accepted so.
As that more willingly thou couldst not seem
At heaven's high feasts to have fed : yet what compare !
To whom the winged Hierarch replied:
O Adam, one Almighty is, from whom
All things proceed, and up to Him return,
If not depraved from good, created all
Such to perfection, one first matter all,
Endued with various forms, various degrees
Of substance, and, in things that live, of life;
But more refined, more spirituous, and pure,
As nearer to Him placed, or nearer tending
Each in their several active spheres assigned,
Till body up to spirit work, in bounds
Proportioned to each kind. So from the root
Springs lighter the green stalk, from thence the leaves
More aery, last the bright consummate flower
Spirits odorous breathes : flowers and their fruit,
Man's nourishment, by gradual scale sublimed,
To vital spirits aspire, to animal,
To intellectual; give both life and sense,
Fancy and understanding; whence the soul
Reason receives, and reason is her being.
Discursive, or intuitive; discourse
If oftest yours, the latter most is ours.
Differing but in degree, of kind the same.
Wonder not, then, what God for you saw good
If I refuse not, but convert, as you.
To proper substance. Time may come when men
With angels may participate, and find
No inconvenient diet, nor too light fare;
And from these corporeal nutriments, perhaps.
Your boch'es may at last turn all to spirit,
Improved by tract of time, and winged, ascend
Ethereal, as we; or may, at choice,

Here or in heavenly paradises dwell;
If ye be found obedient, and retain
Unalterably firm, His love entire,
Whose progeny you are. Meanwhile enjoy
Your fill what happiness this happy state
Can comprehend, incapable of more.
To whom the patriarch of mankind replied :
Oh, favourable spirit, propitious guest,
Well hast thou taught the way that might direct
Our knowledge, and the scale of nature set
From centre to circumference; whereon,
In contemplation of created things.
By steps we may ascend to God. But say,
What meant that caution joined, If ye be found
Obedient ? Can we want obedience then
To Him, or possibly His love desert,
Who formed us from the dust, and placed us here
Full to the utmost measure of what bliss
Human desires can seek or apprehend ?
To whom the Angel : Son of Heaven and Earth,
Attend : that thou art happy, owe to God;
That thou continuest such, owe to thyself,
That is, to thy obedience; therein stand.
This was that caution given thee; be advised.
God made thee perfect, not immutable;
And good he made thee; but to persevere
He left it in thy power; ordained thy will
By nature free, not over-ruled by fate
Inextricable, or strict necessity. .
Our voluntary service he requires,
Not our necessitated; such with him
Finds no acceptance, nor can find; for how
Can hearts not free be tried whether they serve
Willing or no, who will but what they must
By destiny, and can no other choose ?
Myself, and all the Angelic host that stand

In sight of God, enthroned, our happy state
Hold, as you yours, while our obedience holds;
On other surety none. Freely we serve,
Because we freely love, as in our will
To love or not; in this we stand or fall.
And some are fallen, to disobedience fallen,
And so from Heaven to deepest Hell – oh, fall
From what high state of bliss into what woe !
To whom our great progenitor : Thy words
Attentive, and with more delighted ear,
Divine instructor, I have heard, than when
Cherubic songs by night from neighbouring hills
Aerial music send : nor knew I not
To be both will and deed created free.
Yet that we never shall forget to love
Our Maker, and obey him whose command
Single is yet so just, my constant thoughts
Assured me, and still assure; though what thou tell'st
Hath passed in heaven, some doubt within me move,
But more desire to hear, if thou consent,
The full relation, which must needs be strange,
Worthy of sacred silence to be heard;
And we have yet large day, for scarce the sun
Hath finished half his journey, and scarce begins
His other half in the great zone of heaven.
Thus Adam made request; and Raphael,
After short pause assenting, thus began :
High matter thou enjoinest me, oh, prime of men,
Sad task and hard : for how shall I relate
To human sense the invisible exploits
Of warring spirits ? how, without remorse,
The ruin of so many, glorious once
And perfect while they stood ? how last unfold
The secrets of another world, perhaps
Not lawful to reveal ? Yet for thy good
This is dispensed; and what surmounts the reach

Of human sense, I shall delineate so,
By likening spiritual to corporal forms,
As may express them best; though what if earth
Be but the shadow of heaven, and things therein
Each to other hke, more than on earth is thought ?
    As yet this world was not, and Chaos wild
Reigned where these heavens now roll, where earth now rests
Upon her centre poised; when on a day –
For time, though in eternity, applied
To motion, measures all things durable
By present, past, and future – on such day
As heaven's great year brings forth, the empyreal host
Of Angels, by imperial summons called.
Innumerable before the Almighty's throne
Forthwith, from all the ends of heaven, appeared
Under their Hierarchs in orders bright.
Ten thousand thousand ensigns high advanced,
Standards and gonfalons 'twixt van and rear
Stream in the air, and for distinction serve
Of Hierarchies, of Orders, and Degrees;
Or in their Hittering tissues bear imblazed
Holy memorials, acts of zeal and love.
Recorded eminent. Thus when in orbs
Of circuit inexpressible they stood.
Orb within orb, the Father infinite,
By whom in bliss embosomed sat the Son,
Amidst, as from a flaming mount, whose top
Brightness had made invisible, thus spake :
    Hear, all ye Angels, progeny of light.
Thrones, Dominations, Princedoms, Virtues, Powers;
Hear my decree, which unrevoked shall stand.
This day I have begot whom I declare
My only Son, and on this holy hill
Him have anointed, whom ye now behold
At my right hand; your head I Him appoint;

And by myself have sworn, to Him shall bow
All knees in heaven, and shall confess him Lord :
Under his great vicegerent reign abide
United, as one individual soul,
For ever happy. Him who disobeys.
Me disobeys, breaks union; and that day,
Cast out from God and blessed vision, falls
Into utter darkness, deep engulfed, his place
Ordained without redemption, without end.
So spake the Omnipotent, and with his words
All seemed well pleased – all seemed, but were not all.
That day, as other solemn days, they spent
In song and dance about the sacred hill;
Mystical dance, which yonder starry sphere
Of planets, and of fixed, in all her wheels
Resembles nearest, mazes intricate.
Eccentric, intervolved, yet regular
Then most, when most irregular they seem;
And in their motions harmony divine
So smoothes her charming tones, that God's own ear
Listens delighted. Evening now approached –
For we have also our evening and our morn,
We ours for change delectable not need –
Forthwith from dance to sweet repast they turn
Desirous. All in circles as they stood,
Tables are set, and on a sudden piled
With angels' food; and rubied nectar flows
In pearl, in diamond, and massy gold.
Fruit of delicious vines, the growth of heaven.
On flowers reposed, and with fresh flowerets crowned.
They eat, they drink; and in communion sweet
Quaff immortality and joy, secure
Of surfeit,[1] where full measure only bounds
Excess, before the all-bounteous King, who showered

1. *Secure of surfeit.*–Secure against it.

With copious hand, rejoicing in their joy.
Now when ambrosial night with clouds exhaled
From that high mount of God, whence light and shade
Spring both, the face of brightest heaven had changed
To grateful twilight, – for night comes not there
In darker veil, – and roseate dews disposed
All but the unsleeping eyes of God to rest;
Wide over all the plain, and wider far
Than all this globous earth in plain outspread, –
Such are the courts of God, – the angelic throng,
Dispersed in bands and files, their camp extend
By living streams among the trees of life,
Pavilions numberless, and sudden reared,
Celestial tabernacles, where they slept
Fanned with cool winds – save those, who in their course,
Melodious hymns about the sovereign throne
Alternate all night long. But not so waked
Satan – so call him now, his former name
Is heard no more in heaven. He of the first,
If not the first Archangel, great in power,
In favour and pre-eminence, yet fraught
With envy against the Son of God, that day
Honoured by his great Father, and proclaimed
Messiah, king anointed, could not bear
Through pride that sight, and thought himself impaired.
Deep malice thence conceiving and disdain,
Soon as midnight brought on the dusky hour
Friendliest to sleep and silence, he resolved
With all his legions to dislodge, and leave
Unworshipped, unobeyed, the throne supreme,
Contemptuous : and his next subordinate
Awakening, thus to him in secret spake :
Sleepest thou, companion dear ? What sleep can close
Thy eye-lids ? and rememberest what decree
Of yesterday, so late hath passed the lips
Of heaven's Almighty ? Thou to me thy thoughts

Was wont, I mine to thee was wont to impart;
Both waking we were one; how then can now
Thy sleep dissent ? New laws thou seest imposed;
New laws from Him who reigns, new minds may raise
In us who serve, new counsels, to debate
What doubtful may ensue – more in this place
To utter is not safe. Assemble thou.
Of all those myriads which we lead, the chief;
Tell them that by command, ere yet dim night
Her shadowy clouds withdraws, I am to haste,
And all who under me their banners wave.
Homeward, with flying march, where we possess
The quarters of the North; there to prepare
Fit entertainment to receive our king,
The great Messiah, and his new commands,
Who speedily through all the Hierarchies
Intends to pass triumphant, and give laws.
    So spake the false Archangel, and infused
Bad influence into the unwary breast
Of his associate. He together calls,
Or several one by one, the regent powers,
Under him regent; tells, as he was taught,
That the Most High commanding, now ere night,
Now ere dim night had disencumbered heaven.
The great hierarchal standard was to move;
Tells the suggested cause, and casts between
Ambiguous words and jealousies, to sound
Or taint integrity. But all obeyed
The wonted signal and superior voice
Of their great potentate; for great indeed
His name, and high was his degree in heaven.
His countenance, as the morning star that guides
The starry flock, allured them, and with lies
Drew after him the third part of heaven's host.
Meanwhile the eternal eye, whose sight discerns
Abstrusest thoughts, from forth his holy mount,

And from within the golden lamps that burn
Nightly before him, saw without their light
Rebellion rising; saw in whom, how spread
Among the sons of morn, what multitudes
Were banded to oppose his high decree;
And, smiling, to his only Son thus said :
Son, thou in whom my gloiy I behold
In full resplendence, heir of all my might,
Nearly it now concerns us to be sure
Of our omnipotence, and with what arms
We mean to hold what anciently we claim
Of deity or empire. Such a foe
Is rising, who intends to erect his throne
Equal to ours, throughout the spacious North;
Nor so content, hath in his thought to try
In battle, what our power is, or our right.
Let us advise, and to this hazard draw
With speed what force is left, and all employ
In our defence; lest unawares we lose
This our high place, our sanctuary, our hill.
To whom the Son, with calm aspect and clear,
Lightning divine, ineffable, serene,
Made answer: Mighty Father, thou thy foes
Justly hast in derision, and, secure,
Laugh'st at their vain designs and tumults vain,
Matter to me of glory, whom their hate
Illustrates, when they see all regal power
Given me to quell their pride, and in event
Know whether I be dextrous to subdue
Thy rebels, or be found the worst in heaven.
So spake the Son : but Satan, with his powers,
Far was advanced on winged speed; a host
Innumerable as the stars of night,
Or stars of morning dewdrops which the sun
Impearls on every leaf and every flower.
Regions they passed, the mighty Regencies

Of Seraphim, and Potentates, and Thrones,
In their triple degrees – regions, to which
All thy dominion, Adam, is no more
Than what this garden is to all the earth,
And all the sea, from one entire globose
Stretched into longitude – which having passed,
At length into the limits of the North
They came; and Satan to his royal seat.
High on a hill, far blazing, as a mount
Raised on a mount, with pyramids and towers
From diamond quarries hewn, and rocks of gold,
The palace of great Lucifer – so call
That structure in the dialect of men
Interpreted – which not long after, he,
Affecting all equality with God,
In imitation of that mount whereon
Messiah was declared in sight of heaven,
The Mountain of the Congregation called.
For thither he assembled all his train,
Pretending so commanded to consult
About the great reception of their king,
Thither to come; and with calumnious art
Of counterfeited truth thus held their ears.
Thrones, Dominations, Princedoms, Virtues, Powers;
If these magnific titles yet remain
Not merely titular, since by decree
Another now hath to himself engrossed
All power, and us eclipsed, under the name
Of King anointed, for whom all this haste
Of midnight march, and hurried meeting here,
This only to consult how we may best,
With what may be devised of honours new,
Receive him coming to receive from us
Knee-tribute yet unpaid, prostration vile !
Too much to one, but double how endured
To one and to his image now proclamicd ?

But what if better counsels might erect
Our minds, and teach us to cast off this yoke ?
Will ye submit your necks, and choose to bend
The supple knee ? Ye will not, if I trust
To know ye right, or if ye know yourselves
Natives and sons of heaven, possessed before
By none : and if not equal all, yet free,
Equally free; for orders and degrees
Jar not with liberty, but well consist
Who can in reason, then, or right, assume
Monarchy over such as live by right
His equals ? If in power and splendour less
In freedom equal ? Or can introduce
Law and edict on us, who without law
Err not ? much less for this to be our Lord,
And look for adoration, to the abuse
Of those imperial titles, which assert
Our being ordained to govern, not to serve.
    Thus far his bold discourse without control
Had audience : when among the seraphim
Abdiel, than whom none with more zeal adored
The Deity, and divine commands obeyed.
Stood up, and in a flame of zeal severe
The current of his fury thus opposed :
    Oh, argument blasphemous, false, and proud !
Words which no ear ever to hear in Heaven
Expected, least of all from thee, ingrate,
In place thyself so high above thy peers.
Canst thou with impious obloquy condemn
The just decree of God, pronounced and sworn
That to his only Son, by right endued
With regal sceptre, every soul in heaven
Shall bend the knee, and in that honour due
Confess him rightful king? Unjust, thou say’st,
Flatly unjust, to bind with laws the free,
And equal over equals to let reign.

One over all with unsucceeded power.
Shalt thou give law to God ? Shalt thou dispute
With Him the points of liberty, who made
Thee what thou art, and formed the Powers of heaven
Such as he pleased, and circumscribed their being ?
Yet, by experience taught, we know how good,
And of our good and of our dignity
How provident he is; how far from thought
To make us less, bent rather to exalt
Our happy state, under one head more near
United. But to grant it thee unjust,
That equal over equals monarch reign :
Thyself, though great and glorious, dost thou count,
Or all angelic nature joined in one,
Equal to Him begotten Son, by whom
As by his word, the mighty Father made
All things, even thee; and all the Spirits of heaven
By him created in their bright degrees,
Crowned them with glory, and to their glory named
Thrones. Dominations, Princedoms, Virtues, Powers,
Essential Powers; nor by his reign obscured,
But more illustrious made, since He the head.
One of our number thus reduced becomes.
His laws our laws, all honour to him done
Returns our own. Cease, then, this impious rage,
And tempt not these : but hasten to appease
The incensed Father and the incensed Son,
While pardon may be found in time besought.
    So spake the fervent Angel; but his zeal
None seconded, as out of season judged.
Or singular and rash; whereat rejoiced
The Apostate, and, more haughty, thus replied :
    That we were formed then say'st thou, and the work
Of secondary hands, by task transferred
From Father to his Son ? strange point and new !
Doctrine which we would know whence learned. Who saw

When this creation was ? Rememberest thou
Thy making, while the Maker gave thee being ?
We know no time when we were not as now;
Know none before us, self-begot, self-raised
By our own quickening power, when fatal course
Had circled his full orb, the birth mature
Of this our native Heaven, ethereal sons.
Our puissance is our own : our own right hand
Shall teach us highest deeds, by proof to try
Who is our equal. Then thou shalt behold
Whether by supplication we intend
Address, and to begirt the Almighty throne
Beseeching or besieging. This report,
These tidings carry to the anointed King;
And fly, ere evil intercept thy flight.
    He said; and, as the sound of waters deep,
Hoarse murmur echoed to his words applause
Through the infinite host : nor less for that
The flaming seraph, fearless, though alone,
Encompassed round with foes, thus answered bold;
    O alienate from God, O spirit accursed,
Forsaken of all good ! I see thy fall
Determined, and thy hapless crew involved
In this perfidious fraud, contagion spread
Both of thy crime and punishment. Henceforth
No more be troubled how to quit the yoke
Of God's Messiah. Those indulgent laws
Will not be now vouchsafed; other decrees
Against thee are grone forth without recall;
That golden sceptre which thou didst reject
Is now an iron rod to bruise and break
Thy disobedience. Well thou didst advise;
Yet not for thy advice or threats I fly
These wicked tents devoted, lest the wrath
Impendent, raging into sudden flame.
Distinguish not; for soon expect to feel

His thunder on thy head, devouring fire.
Then who created thee lamenting learn,
When who can uncreate thee thou shalt know.
  So spake the Seraph Abdiel, faithful found
Among the faithless, faithful only he;
Among innumerable false, unmoved,
Unshaken, unseduced, unterrified.
His loyalty he kept, his love, his zeal;
Nor number nor example with him wrought
To swerve from truth, or change his constant mind,
Though single. From amidst them forth he passed,
Long way through hostile scorn, which he sustained
Superior, nor of violence feared aught;
And with retorted scorn, his back he turned
On those proud towers to swift destruction doomed.

BOOK - VI

RAPHAEL continues to relate how Michael and Gabriel were sent forth to battle against Satan and his angels. The first fight described: Satan and his powers retire under night: he calls a council; invents devilish engines, which, in the second day's fight, put Michael and his angels to some disorder; but they at length pulling up mountains, overwhelm both the force and machines of Satan: yet the tumult not so ending, God, on the third day, sends Messiah his Son, for whom he had reserved the glory of that victory; He, in the power of his Father, coming to the place, and causing all his legions to stand still on either side, with his chariot and thunder driving into the midst of his enemies, pursues them, unable to resist, towards the wall of heaven; which opening, they leap down with horror and confusion into the place of punishment prepared for them in the deep: Messiah returns with triumph to his Father.

All night the dreadless angel unpursued
Through heaven's wide champain held his way; till Morn,
Waked by the circling hours, with rosy hand
Unbarred the gates of light. There is a cave
Within the mount of God, fast by his throne,
Where light and darkness in perpetual round
Lodge and dislodge by turns, which makes through heaven
Grateful vicissitude, like day and night;
Light issues forth, and at the other door
Obsequious darkness enters, till her hour
To veil the heaven, though darkness there might well
Seem twilight here : and now went forth the Morn
Such as in highest heaven, arrayed in gold
Empyreal; from before her vanished Night,

Shot through with orient beams; when all the plain,
Covered with thick embattled squadrons bright,
Chariots, and flaming arms, and fiery steeds.
Reflecting blaze on blaze first met his view :
War he perceived, war in procinct;[1] and found
Already known what he for news had thought
To have reported : gladly then he mixed
Among those friendly powers, who him received
With joy and acclamations loud, that one,
That of so many myriads fallen, yet one
Returned not lost. On to the sacred hill
They led him high applauded, and present
Before the seat supreme; from whence a voice,
From 'midst a golden cloud, thus mild was heard :
    Servant of God, well done; well hast thou fought
The better fight, who single hast maintained
Against revolted multitudes the cause
Of truth, in word mightier than they in arms;
And for the testimony of truth hast borne
Universal reproach, far worse to bear
Than violence; for this was all thy care,
To stand approved in sight of God, though worlds
Judged thee perverse. The easier conquest now
Remains thee, aided by this host of friends,
Back on thy foes more glorious to return,
Than scorned thou didst depart, and to subdue
By force, who reason for their law refuse.
Right reason for their law, and for their king
Messiah, who by right of merit reigns.
Go, Michael, of celestial armies prince.
And thou in military prowess next,
Gabriel, lead forth to battle these my sons
Invincible; lead forth my armed saints.
By thousands and by millions ranged for fight,

1. *War in procinct,*–Imminent, near.

Equal in number to that godless crew
Rebellious; them with fire and hostile arms
Fearless assault, and, to the brow of heaven
Pursuing, drive them out from God and bliss
Into their place of punishment, the gulf
Of Tartarus, which ready opens wide
His fiery chaos to receive their fall.[1]
So spake the Sovereign Voice, and clouds began
To darken all the hill, and smoke to roll
In dusky wreaths, reluctant flames, the sign
Of wrath awaked; nor with less dread the loud
Ethereal trumpet from on high 'gan blow :
At which command the powers militant.
That stood for Heaven, in mighty quadrate joined
Of union irresistible, moved on
In silence their bright legions, to the sound
Of instrumental harmony, that breathed
Heroic ardour to adventurous deeds
Under their godlike leaders, in the cause
Of God and his Messiah, On they move
Indissolubly firm; nor obvious hill.
Nor straitening vale, nor wood, nor stream, divides
Their perfect ranks; for high above the ground
Their march was, and the passive air upbore
Their nimble tread. As when the total kind
Of birds, in orderly array on wing.
Came, summoned over Eden, to receive
Their names of thee; so over many a tract
Of heaven they marched, and many a province wide,
Tenfold the length of this terrene. At last.
Far in the horizon to the North, appeared
From skirt to skirt a fiery region stretched
In battailous aspect; and, nearer view,

1. *To receive their fall.*–"And there was war in heaven: Michael and his angels fought against the Dragon; and the Dragon fought and his angels." Rev. xii, 7.

Bristled with upright beams innumerable
Of rigid spears, and helmets thronged, and shields
Various, with boastful argument portrayed.
The banded powers of Satan hasting on
With furious expedition; for they weened
That self-same day, by fight, or by surprise,
To win the mount of God, and on His throne
To set the envier of his state, the proud
Aspirer; but their thoughts proved fond and vain
In the mid-way. Though strange to us it seemed
At first, that Angel should with Angel war,
And in fierce hosting meet, who wont to meet
So oft in festivals of joy and love
Unanimous, as sons of one great Sire,
Hymning the Eternal Father. But the shout
Of battle now began, and rushing sound
Of onset ended soon each milder thought.
High in the midst, exalted as a god.
The Apostate in his sun-bright chariot sat,
Idol of majesty divine, enclosed
With flaming cherubim, and golden shields;
Then lighted from his gorgeous throne, for now
'Twixt host and host but narrow space was left,
A dreadful interval, and front to front
Presented stood in terrible array
Of hideous length. Before the cloudy van,
On the rough edge of battle ere it joined,
Satan, with vast and haughty strides advanced,
Came towering, armed in adamant and gold.
Abdiel that sight endured not, where he stood
Among the mightiest, bent on highest deeds.
And thus his own undaunted heart explores :
O Heaven! that such resemblance of the Highest
Should yet remain, where faith and realty[1]

1. *Realty*.–Realness.

Remain not ! Wherefore should not strength and might
There fail where virtue fails ? or weakest prove .
Where boldest, though to sight unconquerable ?
His puissance, trusting in the Almighty's aid,
I mean to try, whose reason I have tried
Unsound and false. Nor is it aught but just
That he, who in debate of truth hath won,
Should win m arms, in both disputes alike
Victor; though brutish that contest and foul,
When reason hath to deal with force, yet so
Most reason is that reason overcome.
　　So pondering, and from his armed peers
Forth stepping opposite, half-way he met
His daring foe, at this prevention more
Incensed, and thus securely him defied:[1]
　　Proud, art thou met ? Thy hope was to have reached
The height of thy aspiring unopposed,
The throne of God unguarded, and his side
Abandoned, at the terror of thy power
Or potent tongue. Fool ! not to think how vain
Against the Omnipotent to rise in arms;
Who out of smallest things, could, without end,
Have raised incessant armies to defeat
Thy folly; or with solitary hand
Reaching beyond all limit, at one blow,
Unaided, could have finished thee, and whelmed
Thy legions under darkness. But thou seest
All are not of thy train; there be, who faith
Prefer, and piety to God, though then
To thee not visible, when I alone
Seemed in thy world erroneous to dissent
From all; my sect thou seest.[2] Now learn too late
How few sometimes may know, when thousands err.
　　Whom the grand foe, with scornful eye askance,

---

1. *Securely him defied.*–Without fear.

2. *My sect thou seest.*–Those who are at one with me.

Thus answered : Ill for thee, but in wished hour
Of my revenge, first sought for, thou returnest
From flight, seditious Angel ! to receive
Thy merited reward, the first assay
Of this right hand provoked, since first that tongue,
Inspired with contradiction, durst oppose
A third part of the gods, in synod met
Their deities to assert; who, while they feel
Vigour divine within them, can allow
Omnipotence to none. But well thou com'st
Before thy fellows, ambitious to win
From me some plume, that thy success may show
Destruction to the rest. This pause between –
Unanswered lest thou boast – to let thee know,
At first I thought that liberty and heaven
To heavenly souls had been all one; but now
I see that most through sloth had rather serve,
Minist'ring spirits, trained up in feast and song :
Such hast thou armed, the minstrelsy of heaven.
Servility with freedom to contend,
As both their deeds compared this day shall prove.
    To whom in brief thus Abdiel stern replied :
Apostate ! still thou err'st, nor end wilt find
Of erring, from the path of truth remote.
Unjustly thou deprav'st it with the name
Of servitude, to serve whom God ordains,
Or nature. God and nature bid the same,
When he who rules is worthiest, and excels
Them whom he governs. This is servitude.
To serve the unwise, or him who hath rebelled
Against his worthier, as thine now serve thee,
Thyself not free, but to thyself inthralled;
Yet lewdly dar'st our minist'ring upbraid.
Reign thou in Hell, thy kingdom; let me serve
In Heaven God ever-blest, and His divine
Behests obey, worthiest to be obeyed.

Yet chains in hell, not realms, expect : meanwhile.
From me returned, as erst thou saidst, from flight.
This greeting on thy impious crest receive.
So saying, a noble stroke he lifted high,
Which hung not, but so swift with tempest fell
On the proud crest of Satan, that no sight,
Nor motion of swift thought, less could his shield,
Such ruin intercept. Ten paces huge
He back recoiled; the tenth on bended knee
His massy spear upstaid – as if on earth
Winds under ground, or waters forcing way,
Sidelong had pushed a mountain from his seat,
Half sunk with all his pines. Amazement seized
The rebel thrones, but greater rage, to see
Thus foiled their mightiest; ours joy filled, and shout,
Presage of victory, and fierce desire
Of battle; whereat Michael bid sound
The archangel trumpet. Through the vast of Heaven
It sounded, and the faithful armies rung
Hosanna to the Highest: nor stood at graze
The adverse legions, nor less hideous joined
The horrid shock. Now storming fury rose.
And clamour, such as heard in heaven till now
Was never; arms on armour clashing brayed
Horrible discord, and the madding wheels
Of brazen chariots raged; dire was the noise
Of conflict; overhead the dismal hiss
Of fiery darts in flaming volleys flew.
And flying vaulted either host with fire.
So under fiery cope together rushed
Both battles main,[1] with ruinous assault
And inextinguishable rage. All heaven
Resounded; and had earth been then, all earth
Had to her centre shook. What wonder ? when

1. *Both battles main.*–The mass on both sides.

Millions of fierce encountering angels fought
On either side, the least of whom could wield
These elements, and arm him with the force
Of all their regions. How much more of power
Army against army numberless to raise
Dreadful combustion warring, and disturb,
Though not destroy, their happy native seat;
Had not the Eternal King Omnipotent,
From his strong hold of heaven, high overruled
And limited their might; though numbered such,
As each divided legion might have seemed
A numerous host, in strength each armed hand.
A legion; led in fight, yet leader seemed
Each warrior, single as in chief, expert
When to advance, or stand, or turn the sway
Of battle, open when, and when to close
The ridges of grim war. No thouoht of flight,
None of retreat, no unbecoming deed
That argued fear; each on himself relied,
As only in his arm the moment lay
Of victory Deeds of eternal fame
Were done, but infinite; for wide was spread
That war, and various; sometimes on firm ground
A standing fight; then, soaring on main wing,
Tormented all the air; all air seemed then
Conflicting fire. Long time in even scale
The battle hung; till Satan, who that day
Prodigious power had shown, and met in arms
No equal, ranging through the dire attack
Of fighting seraphim confused, at length
Saw where the sword of Michael smote, and felled
Squadrons at once; with huge two-handed sway
Brandished aloft, the horrid edge came down
Wide-wasting. Such destruction to withstand
He hasted, and opposed the rocky orb
Of tenfold adamant, his ample shield.

A vast circumference. At his approach
The great Archangel from his warike toil
Surceased, and glad, as hoping here to end
Intestine war in heaven, the arch-foe subdued,
Or captive dragged in chains, with hostile frown
And visage all inflamed, first thus began :
 Author of evil unknown till thy revolt.
Unnamed in heaven, now plenteous, as thou seest
These acts of hateful strife, hateful to all,
Though heaviest, by just measure, on thyself
And thy adherents; how hast thou disturbed
Heaven's blessed peace, and into nature brought
Misery, uncreated till the crmie
Of thy rebellion ? How hast thou instilled
Thy malice into thousands, once upright
And faithful, now proved false ? But think not here
To trouble holy rest. Heaven casts thee out
From all her confines. Heaven, the seat of bliss,
Brooks not the works of violence and war.
Hence, then, and evil go with thee along.
Thy offspring, to the place of evil. Hell,
Thou and thy wicked crew – there mingle broils.
Ere this avenging sword begin thy doom,
Or some more sudden vengeance, winged from God,
Precipitate thee with augmented pain.
 So spake the prince of Angels; to whom thus
The Adversary: Nor think thou with wind
Of airy threats to awe whom yet with deeds
Thou canst not. Hast thou turned the least of these
To flight, or if to fall, but that they rise
Unvanquished, easier to transact with me,[1]
That thou shouldst hope, imperious, and with threats
To chase me hence ? Err not[2] that so shall end

1. *Easier to, &c.*–Has this failure against my followers led the to think it easier to conquer me?

2. *Err not.*–Think not, deceive not thyself by thinking, &c.

The strife which thou call'st evil, but we style
The strife of glory; which we mean to win,
Or turn this Heaven itself into the Hell
Thou fablest : here, however, to dwell free.
If not to reign. Meanwhile thy utmost force,
And join Him named Almighty to thy aid,
I fly not, but have sought thee far and nigh.
    They ended parle,[1] and both addressed for fight
Unspeakable; for who, though with the tongue
Of angels, can relate, or to what things
Liken on earth conspicuous, that may lift
Human imagination to such height
Of godlike power ? for likcst gods they seemed,
Stood they or moved, in stature, motion, arms,
Fit to decide the empire of great Heaven.
Now waved their fiery swords, and in the air
Made horrid circles : two broad suns their shields
Blazed opposite, while Expectation stood
In horror. From each hand with speed retired,
Where erst was thickest fight, the angelic throng,
And left large field,- unsafe within the wind
Of such commotion – such as, to set forth
Great things by small, if. Nature's concord broke,
Among the constellations war were sprung.
Two planets, rushing from aspect malign
Of fiercest opposition, in mid sky
Should combat, and their jarring spheres confound.
Together both, with next to almighty arm
Uplifted imminent, one stroke they aimed
That might determine, and not need repeat,
As not of power at once; nor odds appeared
In might or swift prevention. But the sword
Of Michael, from the armoury of God,
Was given him tempered so, that neither keen
Nor solid might resist that edge : it met

1. *They ended parle.*–Talk, debate.

The sword of Satan, with steep force to smite
Descending, and in half cut sheer; nor stayed,
But with swift wheel reverse, deep entering, shared[1]
All his right side; then Satan first knew pain,
And writhed him to and fro convolved; so sore
The griding sword[2] with discontinuous wound[3]
Passed through him. But the ethereal substance closed.
Not long divisible; and from the gash
A stream of nect'rous humour issuing flowed,
Sanguine, such as celestial spirits may bleed.
And all his armour stained, erewhile so bright.
Forthwith, on all sides, to his aid was run
By angels many and strong, who interposed
Defence, while others bore him on their shields
Back to his chariot, where it stood retired
From off the files of war. There they him laid
Gnashing for anguish, and despite, and shame,
To find himself not matchless, and his pride
Humbled by such rebuke, so far beneath
His confidence to equal God in power.
Yet soon he healed; for spirits that live throughout
Vital in every part, not as frail man
In entrails, heart, or head, liver or reins,
Cannot but by annihilating die;
Nor in their liquid texture mortal wound
Receive, no more than can the fluid air.
All heart they live, all head, all eye, all ear,
All intellect, all sense; and, as they please.
They limb themselves, and colour, shape, or size,
Assume, as likes them best, condense or rare.
    Meanwhile, in other parts, like deeds, deserved

1. *Shared.*–Ploughed down.
2. *Griding sword.*–Old English for cutting, severing.
3. *With discontinuous wound.*–A wound severing the proper continuity of parts.

Memorial, where the might of Gabriel fought,
And with fierce ensigns pierced the deep array
Of Moloch, furious king, who him defied.
And at his chariot-wheels to drag him bound
Threatened, nor from the Holy One of heaven
Refrained his tongue blasphemous; but anon,
Down cloven to the waist, with shattered arms.
And uncouth pain,[1] fled bellowing. On each wing,
Uriel and Raphael, his vaunting foe,
Though huge, and in a rock of diamond armed,
Vanquished Adramelech and Asmadai,
Two potent thrones, that to be less than gods
Disdained, but meaner thoughts learned in their flight
Mangled with ghastly wounds through plate and mail.
Nor stood unmindful Abdiel to annoy
The atheist crew, but with redoubled blow,
Ariel, and Arioch, and the violence
Of Ramiel, scorched and blasted, overthrew.
I might relate of thousands, and their names
Eternise here on Earth; but those elect
Angels, contented with their fame in Heaven,
Seek not the praise of men; the other sort.
In might though wondrous, and in acts of war,
Nor of renown less eager, yet by doom
Cancelled from Heaven and sacred memory.
Nameless in dark oblivion let them dwell.
For strength from truth divided, and from just,
Illaudable, nought merits but dispraise
And ignominy; yet to glory aspires,
Vain-glorious, and through ignominy seeks fame;
Therefore eternal silence be their doom.
And now, their mightiest quelled, the battle swerved,
With many an inroad gored; deformed rout
Entered, and foul disorder; all the ground

1. *Uncouth pain.*–Disfiguring, strange.

With shivered armour strown, and on a heap
Chariot and charioteer lay overturned.
And fiery-foaming steeds; what stood, recoiled,
O'er- wearied, through the faint Satanic host,
Defensive scarce, or with pale fear surprised,
Then first with fear surprised, and sense of pain,
Fled ignominious, to such evil brought
By sin of disobedience; till that hour
Not liable to fear, or flight, or pain.
Far otherwise the inviolable Saints,
In cubic phalanx firm advanced entire,
Invulnerable, impenetrably armed.
Such high advantages their innocence
Gave them above their foes; not to have sinned,
Not to have disobeyed; in fight they stood
Unwearied, unobnoxious to be pained
By wound, though from their place by violence moved.
    Now Night her course began, and, over heaven
Inducing darkness, grateful truce[1] imposed.
And silence on the odious din of war.
Under her cloudy covert both retired,
Victor and vanquished. On the foughten field
Michael and his angels, prevalent
Encamping, placed in guard their watches round
Cherubic waving fires : on the other part,
Satan with his rebellious disappeared,
Far in the dark dislodged; and, void of rest,
His potentates to council called by night,
And in the midst thus undismayed began :
    Oh now in danger tried, now known in arms
Not to be overpowered, companions dear,
Found worthy not of liberty alone,
Too mean pretence ! but, what we more affect,
Honour, dominion, glory, and renown :

1. *Grateful truce.*–Welcome truce.

Who have sustained one day, in doubtful fight –
And if one day, why not eternal days ? –
What heaven's Lord had powerfulest to send
Against us from about his throne, and judged
Sufficient to subdue us to his will.
But proves not so : then fallible, it seems,
Of future[1] we may deem him, though, till now,
Omniscient thought. True is,[2] less firmly armed,
Some disadvantage we endured, and pain,
Till now not known, but, known, as soon contenmed;
Since now we find this our empyreal form
Incapable of mortal injury,
Imperishable, and, though pierced with wound,
Soon closing, and by native vigour healed.
Of evil, then, so small, as easy think
The remedy. Perhaps more valid arms.
Weapons more violent, when next we meet,
May serve to better us, and worse our foes.
Or equal what between us made the odds,
In nature none. If other hidden cause
Left them superior, while we can preserve
Unhurt our minds, and understanding sound,
Due search and consultation will disclose.
He sat; and in the assembly next upstood
Nisroch, of principalities the prime.
As one he stood escaped from cruel fight,
Sore toiled, his riven arms to havoc hewn,
And, cloudy in aspect, thus answering spake :
Deliverer from new Lords, leader to free
Enjoyment of our rights as Gods; yet hard
For Gods, and too unequal work we find.
Against unequal arms, to fight in pain,
Against unpained, impassive; from which evil
Ruin must needs ensue. For what avails

1. *Fallible of future.* – Not knowing the future.

2. *True is.* – True it is.

Valour or strength, though matchless, quelled with pain
Which all subdues, and makes remiss the hands
Of mightiest ? Sense of pleasure we may well
Spare out of life, perhaps, and not repine.
But live content, which is the calmest life;
But pain is perfect misery, the worst
Of evils, and, excessive, overturns
All patience. He who, therefore, can invent
With what more forcible we may offend
Our yet unwounded enemies, or arm
Ourselves with like defence, to me deserves
No less than for deliverance what we owe.
Whereto, with look composed, Satan replied :
Not uninvented that, which thou aright
Believest so main to our success, I bring.
Which of us who beholds the brioht surface
Of this ethereous mould whereon we stand,
This continent of spacious heaven, adorned
With plant, fruit, flower ambrosial, gems, and gold;
Whose eye so superficially surveys
These things, as not to mind from whence they grow,
Deep under ground, materials dark and crude.
Of spiritous and fiery spume; till touched
With heaven's ray, and tempered, they shoot forth
So beauteous, opening to the ambient light ?
These, in their dark nativity, the deep
Shall yield us, pregnant with infernal flame;
Which, into hollow[1] engines, long and round,
Thick-rammed, at the other bore with touch of .fire
Dilated and infuriate, shall send forth
From far, with thundering noise, among our foes,
Such implements of mischief, as shall dash
To pieces, and o'erwhelm, whatever stands
Adverse, that they shall fear we have disarmed
The Thunderer of His only dreaded bolt.

1. *Which, into hollow*, &c.–That which in, &c.

Nor long shall be our labour : yet, ere dawn.
Effect shall end our wish. Meanwhile revive;
Abandon fear; to strength and counsel joined
Think nothing hard, much less to be despaired.
He ended; and his words their drooping cheer
Enlightened, and their languished hope revived :
The invention all admired, and each how he
To be the inventor missed; so easy it seemed
Once found, which yet unfound most would have thought
Impossible. Yet, haply, of thy race.
In future days, if malice should abound.
Some one, intent on mischief, or inspired
With devilish machination, might devise
Like instrument to plague the sons of men
For sin, on war and mutual slaughter bent.
Forthwith from council to the work they flew;
None arguing stood; innumerable hands
Were ready; in a moment up they turned
Wide the celestial soil, and saw beneath
The originals of nature in their crude
Conception; sulphurous and nitrous foam
They found; they mingled, and, with subtle art,
Concocted and adusted,[1] they reduced
To blackest grain, and into store conveyed.
Part hidden veins digged up (nor hath this earth
Entrails unlike) of mineral and stone,
Whereof to found their engines and their balls
Of missive ruin; part incentive reed
Provide, pernicious with one touch to fire.
So all, ere day-spring, under conscious night,
Secret they finished, and in order set.
With silent circumspection, unespied.
Now when fair Morn orient in heaven appeared,
Up rose the victor-angels, and to arms

1. *And adusted.*–Adustus, made to be as dust by fire.

The matin trumpet sung; in arms they stood
Of golden panoply, refulgent host.
Soon banded; others from the dawning hills
Looked round, and scouts each coast, light-armed, scour
Each quarter, to descry the distant foe,
Where lodged, or whither fled; or if for fight
In motion of in halt. Him soon they met,
Under spread ensigns, moving nigh, in slow
But firm battalion. Back, with speediest sail,
Zophiel, of cherubim the swiftest wing.
Came flying, and, in mid air, aloud thus cried :
  Arm, warriors, arm for fight. The foe at hand,
Whom fled we thought, will save us long pursuit.
This day, fear not his flight; so thick a cloud
He comes, and settled in his face I see
Sad[1] resolution, and secure.[2] Let each
His adamantine coat gird well, and each
Fit well his helm, gripe fast his orbed shield.
Borne even or high; for this day will pour down,
If I conjecture aught, no drizzling shower,
But rattling storm of arrows barbed with fire.
  So warned he them, aware themselves, and soon
In order, quit of all impediment.
Instant, without disturb,[3] they took alarm,[4]
And onward moved embattled : when, behold !
Not distant far, with heavy pace, the foe
Approaching gross and huge, in hollow cube,
Training his devilish enginery, impaled
On every side with shadowing squadrons deep,
To hide the fraud. At interview both stood
Awhile; but suddenly at head appeared

1. *Sad.*–Grave, thoughtful.

2. *Secure.*–Confident.

3. *Disturb.*– Disturbance.

4. *They look alarm.* – Took the warning.

Satan, and thus was heard commanding loud :
Vanguard, to right and left the front unfold,
That all may see who hate us, how we seek
Peace and composure, and with open breast
Stand ready to receive them, if they like
Our overture, and turn not back perverse :
But that I doubt. However, witness heaven !
Heaven, witness thou anon, while we discharge
Freely our part. Ye, who appointed stand.
Do as you have in charge, and briefly touch
What we propound, and loud, that all may hear.
So scoffing in ambiguous words, he scarce
Had ended, when to right and left the front
Divided, and to either flank retired :
Which to our eyes discovered, new and strange,
A triple mounted row of pillars, laid
On wheels (for like to pillars most they seemed.
Or hollowed bodies made of oak or fir.
With branches lopt, in wood or mountain felled).
Brass, iron, stony mould, had not their mouths
With hideous orifice gaped on us wide.
Portending hollow truce. At each, behind.
A seraph stood, and in his hand a reed
Stood waving, tipt with fire; while we, suspense,[1]
Collected stood, within our thoughts amused,[2]
Not long, for sudden, all at once, their reeds
Put forth, and to a narrow vent applied
With nicest touch. Immediate, in a flame,
But soon obscured with smoke, all heaven appeared,
From those deep-throated engines belched, whose roar
Embowelled with outrageous noise the air,
And all her entrails tore, disgorging foul
Their devilish glut, chained thunderbolts and hail
Of iron globes; which, on the victor host

1. *Suspense.*–In suspense.

2. *Within our thoughts amused.*–Musing, wondering.

Levelled, with such impetuous fury smote.
That whom they hit, none on their feet might stand,
Though standing else as rocks, but down they fell
By thousands. Angel on Archangel rolled.
The sooner for their arms; unarmed, they might
Have easily, as spirits, evaded swift
By quick contraction or remove; but now
Foul dissipation followed, and forced rout;
Nor served it to relax their serried files.
What should they do ? If on they rushed, repulse
Repeated, and indecent overthrow
Doubled, would render them yet more despised.
And to their foes a laughter; for in view
Stood ranked of seraphim another row.
In posture to displode their second tire
Of thunder : back defeated to return
They worse abhorred. Satan beheld their plight.
And to his mates thus in derision called :

O friends ! why come not on these victors proud
Erewhile they fierce were coming; and when we,
To entertain them fair with open front
And breast, – what could we more ? – propounded terms
Of composition, straight they changed their minds,
Flew off, and into strange vagaries fell.
As they would dance. Yet for a dance they seemed
Somewhat extravagant and wild; perhaps,
For joy of offered peace. But I suppose,
If our proposals once again were heard,
We should compel them to a quick result.

To whom thus Belial, in like gamesome mood :
Leader, the terms we sent were terms of weight.
Of hard contents, and full of force urged home;
Such as we might perceive amused them all.
And stumbled many. Who receives them right,
Had need from head to foot well understand;
Not understood, this gift they have besides.

They show us when our foes walk not upright.
　　So they among themselves in pleasant vein
Stood scoffing, heightened in their thoughts beyond
All doubt of victory; Eternal Might
To match with their inventions they presumed
So easy, and of his thunder made a scorn.
And all his host derided, while they stood
Awhile in trouble. But they stood not long.
Rage prompted them at length, and found them arms
Against such hellish mischief fit to oppose.
Forthwith – behold the excellence, the power,
Which God hath in his mighty angels placed !
Their arms away they threw, and to the hills –
For earth hath this variety from heaven
Of pleasure situate in hill and dale, –
Light as the lightning glimpse, they ran, they flew;
From their foundations loosening to and fro,
They plucked the seated hills, with all their load,
Rocks, waters, woods, and by the shaggy tops
Uplifting, bore them in their hands. Amaze,
Be sure, and terror, seized the rebel host.
When coming towards them so dread they saw
The bottom of the mountains upward turned.
Till on those cursed engines' triple row
They saw them whelmed, and all their confidence
Under the weight of mountains buried deep;
Themselves invaded next, and on their heads
Main promontories flung, which in the air
Came shadowing, and oppressed whole legions armed.
Their armour helped their harm, crushed in and bruised
Into their substance pent, which wrought them pain
Implacable,[1] and many a dolorous groan.
Long struggling underneath, ere they could wind
Out of such prison, though spirits of purest light,
Purest at first, now gross by sinning grown.

1. *Implacable.*–Not to be assuaged.

The rest, in imitation, to like arms
Betook them, and the neighbouring hills uptore :
So hills amid the air encountered hills,
Hurled to and fro with jaculation dire,
That under ground they fought in dismal shade.
Infernal noise! war seemed a civil game
To this uproar : horrid confusion heaped
Upon confusion rose. And now all heaven
Had gone to wrack, with ruin overspread.
Had not the Almighty Father, where He sits
Shrined in his sanctuary of heaven secure,
Consulting on the sum of things, foreseen
This tumult, and permitted all, advised;
That his great purpose he might so fulfil.
To honour his anointed Son avenged
Upon his enemies, and to declare
All power on Him transferred. Whence to his Son,
The assessor of his throne, he thus began :
    Effulgence of my glory, Son beloved,
Son, in whose face invisible is beheld
Visibly what by Deity I am,
And in whose hand what by decree I do,
Second Omnipotence ! two days are past.
Two days, as we compute the days of heaven.
Since Michael and his powers went forth to tame
These disobedient. Sore hath been their fight,
As likeliest was, when two such foes met armed :
For to themselves I left them; and thou knowest,
Equal in their creation they were formed.
Save what sin hath impaired, which yet hath wrought
Insensibly, for I suspend their doom;
Whence in perpetual fight they needs must last
Endless, and no solution will be found.
War wearied hath performed what war can do.
And to disordered rage let loose the reins.
With mountains, as with weapons, armed; which makes

Wild work in heaven, and dangerous to the main.[1]
Two days are therefore past, the third is Thine;
For thee I have ordained it; and thus far
Have suffered, that the glory may be thine
Of ending this great war, since none but Thou
Can end it. Into thee such virtue and grace
Immense I have transfused, that all may know
In Heaven and Hell thy power above compare;
And this perverse commotion governed thus.
To manifest Thee worthiest to be Heir
Of all things; to be Heir and to be King
By sacred unction, thy deserved right.
Go, then, thou Mightiest, in thy Father's might;
Ascend my chariot, guide the rapid wheels
That shake heaven's basis, bring forth all my war,
My bow and thunder; my almighty arms
Gird on, and sword upon thy puissant thigh;
Pursue these sons of darkness, drive them out
From all heaven's bounds into the utter deep;
There let them learn, as likes them, to despise
God, and Messiah, his anointed King.
He said, and on his Son with rays direct
Shone full; He all his Father full expressed.
Ineffably into his face received;
And thus the filial Godhead answering spake :
O Father, O Supreme of heavenly Thrones,
First, Highest, Holiest, Best, thou always seek'st
To glorify thy Son; I always Thee,
As is most just. This I my glory account,
My exaltation, and my whole delight,
That thou, in me well pleased, declarest thy will
Fulfilled, which to fulfil is all my bliss.
Sceptre and power, thy giving, I assume.
And gladlier shall resign, when in the end
Thou shalt be all in all, and I in Thee

1. *To the main–To heaven itself–as a whole.*

For ever, and in me all whom thou lovest :
But whom thou hatest, I hate, and can put on
Thy terrors, as I put thy mildness on,
Image of Thee in all things; and shall soon,
Armed with thy might, rid heaven of these rebelled,[1]
To their prepared ill mansion driven down,
To chains of darkness, and the undying worm.
That from thy just obedience could revolt.
Whom to obey is happiness entire.
Then shall thy saints, unmixed, and from the Impure
Far separate, circling thy holy mount.
Unfeigned hallelujahs to Thee sing,
Hymns of high praise, and I among them chief
  So said. He, o'er his sceptre bowing, rose
From the right hand of glory where he sat;
And the third sacred morn began to shine,
Dawning through heaven. Forth rushed with whirlwind sound
The chariot of Paternal Deity,
Flashing thick flames, wheel within wheel undrawn.
Itself instinct with spirit, but convoyed
By four cherubic shapes. Four faces each
Had wondrous; as with stars, their bodies all,
And wings, were set with eyes; with eyes the wheels
Of beryl, and careering fires between;
Over their heads a crystal firmament,
Whereon a sapphire throne, inlaid with pure
Amber, and colours of the showery arch.
He, in celestial panoply' all armed
Of radiant Urim,[2] work divinely wrought,
Ascended; at his right hand Victory
Sat, eagle-winged; beside him hung his bow
And quiver with three-bolted thunder stored;
And from about him fierce effusion rolled

1. *These rebelled.* – Who have rebelled.
2. *Of radiant Urim.*–Aaron's breastplate was so called. The word means " brilliancy."

Of smoke, and bickering flame, and sparkles dire :
Attended with ten thousand thousand saints,
He onward came. Far off His coming shone;
And twenty thousand – I their number heard –
Chariots of God, half on each hand, were seen.
He on the wings of cherub rode sublime.
On the crystalline sky, in sapphire throned,
Illustrious far and wide, but by his own
First seen; them unexpected joy surprised,
When the fjreat ensign of Messiah blazed
Aloft, by angels borne, His sign in heaven;
Under whose conduct Michael soon reduced
His army, circumfused on either wing.
Under their Head embodied all in one.
Before him Power Divine his way prepared;
At his command the uprooted hills retired
Each to his place; they heard His voice, and went
Obsequious : Heaven its wonted face renewed.
And with fresh flow'rets hill and valley smiled.
This saw his hapless foes, but stood obdured,
And to rebellious fight rallied their powers,
Insensate, hope conceiving from despair !
In heavenly spirits could such perverseness dwell ?
But to convince the proud what signs avail,
Or wonders move, the obdurate to relent ?
They, hardened more by what might most reclaim,
Grieving to see His glory, at the sight
Took envy, and, aspiring to His height.
Stood re-embattled fierce, by force or fraud
Weening to prosper, and at length prevail
Against God and Messiah, or to fall
In universal ruin last : and now
To final battle drew, disdaining flight.
Or faint retreat; when the great Son of God
To all his host on either hand thus spake :
Stand still in bright array, ye saints; here stand,
Ye angels armed; this day from battle rest.

Faithful hath been your warfare, and of God
Accepted, fearless in his righteous cause;
And as ye have received, so have ye done,
Invincibly. But of this cursed crew
The punishment to other hand belongs;
Vengeance is His, or whose He sole appoints.
Number to this day's work is not ordained.
Nor multitude; stand only, and behold
God's indignation on these godless poured
By me; not you, but me, they have despised,
Yet envied; against me is all their rage,
Because the Father, to whom, in heaven supreme,
Kingdom, and power, and glory, appertain.
Hath honoured me, according to his will.
Therefore to me their doom He hath assigned :
That they may have their wish, to try with me
In battle which the stronger proves; they all.
Or I alone against them; since by strength
They measure all, of other excellence
Not emulous, nor care who them excels;
Nor other strife with them do I vouchsafe.
So spake the Son, and into terror changed
His countenance, too severe to be beheld,
And full of wrath bent on his enemies.
At once the four spread out their starry wings
With dreadful shade contiguous, and the orbs
Of his fierce chariot rolled, as with the sound
Of torrent floods, or, of a numerous host.
He on his impious foes right onward drove,
Gloomy as night. Under his burning wheels
The steadfast Empyrean shook throughout,
All but the throne itself of God. Full soon
Among them he arrived, in his right hand
Grasping ten thousand thunders, which he sent
Before him, such as in their souls infixed
Plagues. They, astonished, all resistance lost,

All courage; down their idle weapons dropt.
O'er shields, and helms, and helmed heads He rode –
Of Thrones and mighty Seraphim prostrate;
That wished the mountains now micrht be again
Thrown on them, as a shelter from His ire.
Nor less on either side tempestuous fell
His arrows, from the fourfold-visaged four
Distinct with eyes, and from the living wheels
Distinct alike with multitude of eyes;
One spirit in them ruled, and every eye
Glared lightning, and shot forth pernicious fire
Among the accursed, that withered all their strength,
And of their wonted vigour left them drained,
Exhausted, spiritless, afflicted, fallen.
Yet half his strength he put not forth, but checked
His thunder in mid volley; for he meant
Not to destroy, but root them out of heaven.
The overthrown he raised, and as a herd
Of goats or timorous flock together thronged,
Drove them before him, thunderstruck, pursued
With terrors, and with furies, to the bounds
And crystal wall of Heaven; which, opening wide,
Rolled inward, and a spacious gap disclosed
Into the wasteful Deep. The monstrous sight
Struck them with horror backward, but far worse
Urged them behind – headlong themselves they threw
Down from the verge of Heaven; eternal wrath
Burnt after them to the bottomless pit.
Hell heard the unsufferable noise; Hell saw
Heaven ruinino;; from Heaven, and would have fled
Affrighted; but strict Fate had cast too deep
Her dark foundations, and too fast had bound.
Nine days they fell; confounded Chaos roared,
And felt tenfold confusion in their fall
Through his wild anarchy; so huge a rout
Encumbered him with ruin. Hell at last,
Yawning, received them whole, and on them closed;

Hell, their fit habitation, fraught with fire
Unquenchable, the house of woe and pain.
Disburdened Heaven rejoiced, and soon repaired
Her mural breach, returning whence it rolled.
  Sole Victor, from the expulsion of his foes,
Messiah his triumphal chariot turned.
To meet Him, all his saints, who silent stood
Eye-witnesses of his almighty acts,
With jubilee advanced; and, as they went,
Shaded with branching palm, each order bright
Sung triumph, and Him sung victorious King,
Son, Heir, and Lord, to Him dominion given,
Worthiest to reign. He, celebrated, rode
Triumphant through mid heaven, into the courts
And temple of his mighty Father throned
On high; who into glory Him received.
Where now he sits at the riijht hand of bliss.
  Thus measuring things in heaven by things on earth.
At thy request, and that thou may'st beware
By what is past, to thee I have revealed
What might have else to human race been hid :
The discord which befell, and war in heaven
Among the angelic powers, and the deep fall
Of those, too high aspiring, who rebelled
With Satan; he who envies now thy state,
Who now is plotting how he may seduce
Thee also froiti obedience, that with him,
Bereaved of happiness, thou mayest partake
His punishment, eternal misery;
Which would be all his solace and revenge,
As a despite done against the Most High,
Thee once to gain companion of his woe.
But listen not to his temptations, warn
Thy weaker; let it profit thee to have heard,
By terrible example, the reward
Of disobedience; firm they might have stood.
Yet fell; remember, and fear to transgress.

BOOK - VII

Raphael, at the request of Adam, relates how and wherefore this world was first created; that God, after the expelling of Satan and His angels out of heaven, declared His pleasure to create another world, and other creatures to dwell therein; sends His Son with glory, and attendance of angels, to perform the work of creation in six days : the angels celebrate with hymns the performance thereof, and His re-ascension into Heaven.

Descend from heaven,[1] Urania – by that name
If rightly thou art called – whose voice divine
Following, above the Olympian hill I soar,
Above the flight of Pegasean wing
The meaning, not the name, I call; for thou
Nor of the Muses nine, nor on the top
Of old Olympus dwellest, but, heavenly-born,
Before the hills appeared, or fountain flowed,
Thou with Eternal Wisdom[2] didst converse.
Wisdom thy sister, and with her didst play
In presence of the Almighty Father, pleased
With thy celestial song. Up led by thee,
Into the Heaven of Heavens I have presumed.

---

1. *Descend from Heaven.*–The theme of the poet now descends from heaven to earth, and he prays that the Muse, or inspiration, which has hitherto been his guide, may descend with him. Urania was one of the Greek muses, dwelling in Olympus, and Milton means to say that under that doubtful name he has sought aid that might enable him to treat of matters which Olympian inspiration could never reveal, and to soar beyond the flight of Pegasus–the horse from whose back liellerbphon fell in his attempted flight towards heaven.
2. *Eternal Wisdom.*–Such was the inspiration the poet sought–that of the Eternal Word.

An earthly guest, and drawn Empyreal air.
Thy tempering. With like safety guided down,
Return me to my native element;
Lest from this flying steed unreined – as once
Bellerophon, though from a lower clime –
Dismounted, on the Aleian[1] field I fall.
Erroneous there to wander, and forlorn.
Half yet remains unsung, but narrower bound
Within the visible diurnal sphere :
Standing on earth, not rapt above the pole,
More safe I sing with mortal voice unchanged
To hoarse or mute, though fallen on evil days,
On evil days though fallen, and evil tongues;
In darkness, and with dangers compassed round,
And solitude; yet not alone, while thou
Visit'st my slumbers nightly, or when Morn
Purples the east. Still govern thou my song,
Urania, and fit audience find, though few.
But drive far off the barbarous dissonance
Of Bacchus and his revellers, the race
Of that wild rout that tore the Thracian bard[2]
In Rodope, where woods and rocks had ears
To rapture, till the savage clamour drowned
Both harp and voice; nor could the muse defend
Her son. So fail not thou, who thee implores;
For thou art heavenly, she an empty dream.
　　Say, goddess, what ensued when Raphael,
The affable Archangel, had forewarned
Adam, by dire example, to beware

---

1. *The Aleian field.*–The field of wandering, in which Bellerophon roamed after his fall.

2. *The Thracian bard.*–The Thracians were said to have torn the poet Orpheus, the son of the Muse Calliope, to pieces. Milton here refers to the riotous cavaliers and courtiers of the time of Charles II., from whose hands he seems to have thought it possible that a similar fate might befall himself.

Apostasy, by what befell in heaven
To those apostates, lest the like befall
In Paradise to Adam or his race.
Charged not to touch the interdicted tree.
If they transgress, and slight that sole command.
So easily obeyed amid the choice
Of all tastes else to please their appetite
Though wandering. He, with his consorted Eve,
The story heard attentive, and was filled
With admiration and deep muse,[1] to hear
Of things so high and strange; things to their thought
So unimaginable as hate in heaven,
And war so near the peace of God in bliss,
With such confusion : but the evil, soon
Driven back, redounded as a flood on those
From whom it sprung, impossible to mix
With blessedness. Whence Adam soon repealed[2]
The doubts that in his heart arose; and now
Led on, yet sinless, with desire to know
What nearer might concern him, how this world
Of heaven and earth conspicuous[3] first began;
When, and whereof created; for what cause;
What within Eden, or without, was done
Before his memory, as one, whose drought
Yet scarce allayed, still eyes the current stream,
Whose liquid murmur heard, new thirst excites,
Proceeded thus to ask his heavenly guest :
    Great things, and full of wonder in our ears,
Far differing from this world, thou hast revealed,
Divine interpreter ! by favour sent
Down from the Empyrean, to forewarn
Us timely of what might else have been our loss,

1. *With admiration and deep muse.*–With wonder and deep thought.
2. *Repealed.*–Possibly the word should be "repelled." That is certainly the idea intended to be conveyed.
3. *Conspicuous.*–Visible, present to the senses.

Unknown, which human knowledge could not reach;
For which, to the infinitely Good we owe
Immortal thanks, and His admonishment
Receive, with solemn purpose to observe
Immutably his sovereign will, the end
Of what we are. But since thou hast vouchsafed
Gently, for our instruction, to impart
Things above earthly thought, which yet concerned
Our knowing, as to highest Wisdom seemed,
Deign to descend now lower, and relate
What may no less, perhaps, avail us known :
How first began this heaven which we behold
Distant so high, with moving fires adorned
Innumerable; and this which yields or fills
All space, the ambient air wide interfused,
Embracing round this florid earth : what cause
Moved the Creator, in his holy rest
Through all eternity, so late to build
In Chaos; and the work begun, how soon
Absolved; if unforbid thou mayest unfold
What we, not to explore the secrets, ask
Of His eternal empire, but the more
To magnify his works, the more we know.
And the great light of day yet wants to run
Much of his race, though steep. Suspense in heaven,
Held by thy voice, thy potent voice, he hears,
And longer will delay, to hear thee tell
His generation, and the rising birth
Of nature from the unapparent deep;
Or if the star of evening and the moon
Haste to thy audience, night with her will bring
Silence; and sleep, listening to thee, will watch;
Or we can bid his absence, till thy song
End, and dismiss thee ere the morning shine.
    Thus Adam his illustrious guest besought;
And thus the godlike Angel answered mild :

This also thy request, with caution asked.
Obtain; though, to recount almighty works.
What words or tongue of Seraph can suffice.
Or heart of man suffice to comprehend ?
Yet what thou canst attain, which best may serve
To glorify the Maker, and infer
Thee[1] also happier, shall not be withheld
Thy hearing; such commission from above
I have received, to answer thy desire
Of knowledge within bounds; beyond, abstain
To ask; nor let thine own inventions hope
Things not revealed, which the invisible King,
Only Omniscient, hath suppressed in night.
To none communicable in Earth or Heaven.
Enough is left besides to search and know;
But knowledge is as food, and needs no less
Her temperance over appetite, to know
In measure what the mind may well contain;
Oppresses else with surfeit, and soon turns
Wisdom to folly, as nourishment to wind.
Know then, that, after Lucifer from Heaven –
So call him, brighter once amidst the host
Of Angels, than that star the stars among –
Fell with his flaming legions through the Deep
Into his place, and the great Son returned
Victorious with his saints, the Omnipotent
Eternal Father from his throne beheld
Their multitude, and to his Son thus spake :
At least our envious foe hath failed, who thought
All like himself rebellious; by whose aid
This inaccessible high strength, the seat
Of Deity supreme, us dispossessed,
He trusted to have seized, and into fraud
Drew many, whom their place knows here no more,
Yet far the greater part have kept, I see,

1. *Infer thee.*–Make thee–help thee to be.

Their station; Heaven, yet populous, retains
Number sufficient to possess her realms
Though wide, and this high temple to frequent
With ministeries due, and solemn rites.
But, lest his heart exalt him in the harm
Already done, to have dispeopled heaven,
My damage fondly deemed, I can repair
That detriment, if such it be, to lose
Self-lost; and in a moment will create
Another world, out of one man a race
Of men innumerable, there to dwell;
Not here, till by degrees of merit raised,
They open to themselves at length the way
Up hither, under long obedience tried.
And Earth be changed to Heaven, and Heaven to Earth,
One kingdom, joy and union without end.
Meanwhile, inhabit lax,[1] ye Powers of Heaven;
And thou, my Word, begotten Son, by thee
This I perform; speak Thou, and be it done !
My overshadowing Spirit and might with thee
I send along; ride forth, and bid the deep
Within appointed bounds be Heaven and Earth;
Boundless the Deep, because I Am, who fill
Infinitude; nor vacuous the space,
Though I, uncircumscribed myself, retire,
And put not forth my goodness, which is free
To act or not; necessity and chance
Approach not me, and what I will is fate.
So spake the Almighty, and to what he spake,
His Word, the filial Godhead, gave effect.
Immediate are the acts of God, more swift
Than time or motion; but to human ears
Cannot without process of speech be told.
So told as earthly notion can receive.
Great triumph and rejoicing were in Heaven,

1. *Inhabit lax.*–With ample space.

When such was heard declared the Almighty's will;
Glory they sung to the Most High, good-will
To future men, and in their dwellings peace :
Glory to Him, whose just avenging ire
Had driven out the ungodly from his sight
And the habitations of the just; to Him
Glory and praise, whose wisdom had ordained
Good out of evil to create; instead
Of spirits malign, a better race to bring
Into their vacant room, and thence diffuse
His good to worlds and ages infinite.
So sang the Hierarchies. Meanwhile the Son
On his great expedition now appeared,
Girt with omnipotence, with radiance crowned
Of majesty divine, sapience and love
Immense, and all His Father in him shone.
About His chariot numberless were poured
Cherub and Seraph, Potentates and Thrones,
And Virtues, winged Spirits, and Chariots winged
From the armoury of God; where stand of old
Myriads, between two brazen mountains lodged
Against a solemn day, harnessed at hand.
Celestial equipage; and now come forth,
Spontaneous, for within them spirit lived.
Attendant on their Lord. Heaven opened wide
Her ever-during gates, harmonious sound.
On golden hinges moving, to let forth
The King of Glory in his powerful Word
And Spirit, coming to create new worlds.
On heavenly ground they stood; and from the shore
They viewed the vast immeasurable Abyss
Outrageous as a sea, dark, wasteful, wild
Up from the bottom turned by furious winds
And surging waves, as mountains, to assault
Heaven's height, and with the centre mix the pole.
Silence, ye troubled waves, and thou Deep, peace,

Said then the omnific Word, your discord end!
Nor stayed; but on the wings of cherubim
Uplifted, in paternal glory rode
Far into Chaos, and the World unborn;
For Chaos heard his voice. Him all his train
Followed in bright procession, to behold
Creation, and the wonders of his might.
Then stayed the fervid wheels, and in his hand
He took the golden compasses, prepared
In God's eternal store, to circumscribe
This Universe, and all created things.
One foot he centred, and the other turned
Round through the vast profundity obscure.
And said – Thus far extend, thus far thy bounds,
This be thy just circumference, O world !
    Thus God the heaven created, thus the earth,
Matter unformed and void. Darkness profound
Covered the abyss; but on the watery calm
His brooding wings the Spirit of God outspread.
And vital virtue infused, and vital warmth.
Throughout the fluid mass; but downward purged
The black, tartareous, cold, infernal dregs,
Adverse to life : then founded, then conglobed
Like things to like; the rest to several place
Disparted, and between spun out the air;
And earth, self-balanced, on her centre hung.
    Let there be light, said God; and forthwith light
Ethereal, first of things, quintessence pure,
Sprung from the deep; and from her native east
To journey through the aery gloom began.
Sphered in a radiant cloud – for yet the sun
Was not – she in a cloudy tabernacle
Sojourned the while. God saw the light was good;
And light from darkness by the hemisphere
Divided. Light, the Day, and darkness, Night,
He named. Thus was the first day even and morn;

Nor passed uncelebrated, nor unsung
By the celestial choirs, when orient light
Exhaling first from darkness they beheld,
Birth-day of heaven and earth, with joy and shout
The hollow universal orb they filled.
And touched their golden harps, and hymning praised
God and his works: Creator Him they sung.
Both when first evening was, and when first morn.
Again, God said : – Let there be firmament
Amid the waters, and let it divide
The waters from the waters; and God made
The firmament, expanse of liquid pure,
Transparent, elemental air, diffused
In circuit to the uttermost convex
Of this great round; partition firm and sure,
The waters underneath from those above
Dividing : for as earth, so He the world
Built on circumfluous waters, calm, in wide
Crystalline ocean, and the loud misrule
Of Chaos far removed, lest fierce extremes
Contiguous might distemper the whole frame.
And heaven He named the firmament. So even
And morning chorus sung the second day.
The earth was formed, but in the womb as yet
Of waters, embryon immature involved.
Appeared not; over all the face of earth
Main ocean flowed, not idle, but with warm
Prolific humour softening all her globe,
Fermented the great mother to conceive.
Satiate with genial moisture; when God said,
Be gathered now, ye waters under heaven,
Into one place, and let dry land appear.
Immediately the mountains huge appear
Emergent, and their broad bare backs upheave
Into the clouds; their tops ascend the sky.
So high as heaved the tumid hills, so low

Down sunk a hollow bottom broad and deep,
Capacious bed of waters. Thither they
Hasted with glad precipitance, uprolled.
As drops on dust conglobing from the dry;
Part rise in crystal wall, or ridge direct,
For haste; such flight the great command impressed
On the swift floods; as armies at the call
Of trumpet – for of armies thou hast heard –
Troop to their standard, so the watery throng,
Wave rolling after wave, where way they found;
If steep, with torrent rapture;[1] if through plain,
Soft ebbing : nor withstood them rock or hill;
But they, or under ground, or circuit wide
With serpent error wandering,[2] found their way.
And on the washy ooze deep channels wore;
Easy, ere God had bid the ground be dry,
All but within those banks, where rivers now
Stream, and perpetual draw their humid train.
The dry land, Earth, and the great receptacle
Of congregated waters. He called Seas;
And saw that it was good; and said : – Let the earth
Put forth the verdant grass, herb yielding seed.
And fruit-tree yielding fruit after her kind,
Whose seed is in herself upon the earth.
He scarce had said, when the bare earth, till then
Desert and bare, unsightly, unadorned,
Brought forth the tender grass, whose verdure clad
Her universal face with pleasant green;
Then herbs of every leaf, that sudden flowered,
Opening their various colours, and made gay
Her bosom, smelling sweet; and, these scarce blown,

---

1. *With torrent rapture.*–Torrent which forces everything from its path.
2. *With serpent error wandering.*–An obscure expression. A winding path might be described as serpentine, but why is it said to be erroneous? Perhaps because it seems to suppose action and reaction, which itself supposes imperfect knowledge.

Forth flourished thick the clustering vine, forth crept
The swelling gourd, up stood the corny reed
Embattled in her field, and the humble shrub,
And bush with frizzled hair implicit[1] last
Rose, as in dance, the stately trees, and spread
Their branches, hung with copious fruit, or gemmed
Their blossoms. With high woods the hills were crowned.
With tufts the valleys, and each fountain side;
With borders long the rivers; that Earth now
Seemed like to Heaven, a seat where Gods might dwell,
Or wander with delight, and love to haunt
Her sacred shades; though God had yet not rained
Upon the earth, and man to till the ground
None was, but from the earth a dewy mist
Went up, and watered all the ground, and each
Plant of the field; which, ere it was in the earth,
God made, and every herb, before it grew
On the green stem. God saw that it was good :
So even and morn recorded the third day.
Again the Almighty spake : – Let there be lights
High in the expanse of heaven, to divide
The day from night; and let them be for signs,
For seasons, and for days, and circling years;
And let them be for lights, as I ordain
Their office in the firmament of heaven.
To give light on the earth; and it was so.
And God made two great lights, great for their use
To man, the greater to have rule by day,
The less by night, altern;[2] and made the stars,
And set them in the firmament of heaven
To illuminate the earth, and rule the day
In their vicissitude, and rule the night.
And light from darkness to divide. God saw,
Surveying his great work, that it was good :

1. *Frizzled hair implicit.–Implicitus*–entangled. (Latin.)
2. *Altern.*–Alternately.

For, of celestial bodies, first the sun,
A mighty sphere, he framed, unlightsome[1] first,
Though of ethereal mould; then formed the moon
Globose, and every magnitude of Stars,
And. sowed with stars the heaven, thick as a field.
Of light by far the greater part he took.
Transplanted from her cloudy shrine, and placed
In the sun's orb, made porous to receive
And drink the liquid light; firm to retain
Her gathered beams, great palace now of light.
Hither, as to their fountain, other stars
Repairing, in their golden urns draw light,
And hence the morning planet gilds her horns;
By tincture or reflection they augment[2]
Their small peculiar, though from human sight
So far remote, with diminution seen.
First in his east the glorious lamp was seen,
Regent of day, and all the horizon round
Invested with bright rays, jocund to run
His longitude through heaven's high road; the grey
Dawn, and the Pleiades, before him danced.
Shedding sweet influence. Less bright the moon,
But opposite in levelled west was set,
His mirror, with full face borrowing her light
From him; for other light she needed none
In that aspect, and still that distance keeps
Till night; then in the east her turn she shines,
Revolved on heaven's great axle, and her reign
With thousand lesser lights dividual holds,
With thousand thousand stars, that then appeared
Spangling the hemisphere. Then first adorned
With her bright luminaries, that set and rose,

---

1. *Unlightsome.*–Not luminous.
2. *By tincture or reflection they augment.* – The horns of Venus, which are tinged and magnified by the solar light.

Glad evening and glad morn crowned the fourth day.
 And God said : – Let the waters generate
Reptile with spawn abundant, living soul;
And let fowl fly above the earth, with wings
Displayed on the open firmament of heaven.
And God created the great whales, and each
Soul living, each that crept, which plenteously
The waters generated by their kinds.
And every bird of wing after his kind,
And saw that it was good, and blessed them, saying : –
Be fruitful, multiply, and in the seas.
And lakes, and running streams, the waters fill,
And let the fowl be multiplied on the earth.
Forthwith the sounds and seas, each creek and bay.
With fry innumerable swarm, and shoals
Of fish that, with their fins, and shining scales,
Glide under the green wave, in sculls that oft
Bank the mid-sea. Part single, or with mate,
Graze the sea-weed their pasture, and through groves
Of coral stray; or, sporting with quick glance,
Show to the sun their waved coats, dropt with gold;
Or, in their pearly shells at ease, attend
Moist nutriment; or under rocks their food.
In jointed armour, watch; on smooth, the seal
And bended dolphins play; part, huge of bulk,
Wallowing unwieldy, enormous in their gait.
Tempest the ocean.[1] There leviathan,[2]
Hugest of living creatures, on the deep
Stretched like a promontory, sleeps or swims,
And seems a moving land; and at his gills
Draws in, and at his trunk spouts out, a sea.
Meanwhile the tepid caves, and fens, and shores,

1. *Tempest the ocean.*–From the Italian *tempestare*–bring tempest to it.
"The huge dolphin tempesting the wave."–*Pope.*
2. *Leviathan.*–The *whale* seems to be intended.

Their brood as numerous hatch from the egg that soon,
Bursting with kindly rupture, forth disclosed
Their callow young ;[1] but feathered soon and fledge
They summed their pens,[2] and, soaring the air sublime,
With clang despised the ground, under a cloud
In prospect. There the eagle and the stork
On cliffs and cedar-tops their eyries build :
Part loosely wing the region; part, more wise,
In common, ranged in figure, wedge their way,
Intelligent of seasons, and set forth
Their aery caravan, high over seas
Flying, and over lands, with mutual wing
Easing their flight – so steers the prudent crane
Her annual voyage, borne on winds – the air
Floats as they pass, fanned with unnumbered plumes;
From branch to branch the smaller birds with song
Solaced the woods, and spread their painted wings
Till even; nor then the solemn nightingale
Ceased warbling, but all night tuned her soft lays.
Others, on silver lakes and rivers, bathed
Their downy breast; the swan with arched neck,
Between her white wings, mantling proudly,[3] rows
Her state with oary feet;[4] yet oft they quit.
The dank, and, rising on stiff pennons, tower
The mid aerial sky. Others on ground
Walked firm; the crested cock, whose clarion sounds
The silent hours, and the other, whose gay train
Adorns him, coloured with[5] the florid hue
Of rainbows and starry eyes. The waters thus

1. *Their callow young.*–Young resembling birds unfledged.
2. *They summed their pens.*–Summed is a word from falconry. The sense here is–put on their wing feathers.
3. *Mantling proudly.*–A term in falconry for spreading the wings like a mantle.
4. *Oary feet.*–Feet which act like oars.
5. *Coloured with the florid hue of rainbows.*–The peacock.

With fish replenished, and the air with fowl.
Evening and morn solemnised the fifth day.
The sixth, and of creation last, arose
With evening harps and matin; when God said.
Let the earth bring forth soul living in her kind,
Cattle, and creeping things, and beast of the earth.
Each in their kind. The earth obeyed, and straight
Opening her fertile womb, teemed at a birth
Innumerous living creatures, perfect forms,
Limbed and full-grown. Out of the ground up rose,
As from his lair, the wild beast, where he wons[1]
In forest wild, in thicket, brake, or den;
Among the trees in pairs they rose, they walked;
The cattle in the fields and meadows green :
Those rare and solitary, these in flocks
Pasturing at once, and in broad herds upsprung.
The grassy clods now calved;[2] now half appeared
The tawny lion, pawing to get free
His hinder parts, then springs, as broke from bonds,
And rampant shakes his brinded main; the ounce.
The libbard, and the tiger, as the mole.
Rising, the crumbled earth above them threw
In hillocks; the swift stag from underground
Bore up his branching head; scarce from his mould
Behemoth, biggest born of earth,[3] upheaved
His vastness; fleeced the flocks and bleating rose,
As plants; ambiguous between sea and land,
The river-horse, and scaly crocodile.
At once came forth whatever creeps the ground,

1. *Where he wons.*–Anglo-Saxon for dwells.
2. *The grassy clods now calved.*–*Calved* is an old English expression for bringing forth generally. Thus the hinds are said to calve. (Job xxxix.; Psalm xxix.) We read also of the *calves* of the lips. (Hosea xiv.)
3. *Behemoth, biggest born of earth.*–Behemoth in Job is the hippopotamus, the river-horse–here it means the elephant.

Insect or worm. Those waved their limber fans
For wings, and smallest lineaments exact
In all the liveries decked of summer's pride,
With spots of gold and purple, azure and green :
These, as a line, their long dimension drew,
Streaking the ground with sinuous trace : not all
Minims of nature; some of serpent kind.
Wondrous in length and corpulence, involved
Their snaky folds, and added wings. First crept
The parsimonious emmet, provident
Of future; in small room large heart enclosed;
Pattern of just equality, perhaps.
Hereafter joined in her popular tribes
Of commonalty. Swarming, next appeared
The female bee, that feeds her husband drone
Deliciously, and builds her waxen cells
With honey stored. The rest are nurnberless.
And thou their natures know'st, and gavest them names.
Needless to thee repeated; nor unknown
The serpent, subdest beast of all the field,
Of huge extent sometimes, with brazen eyes
And airy mane terrific, though to thee
Not noxious, but obedient at thy call.
  Now heaven in all her glory shone, and rolled
Her motions, as the great first Mover's hand
First wheeled their course; earth in her rich attire
Consummate lovely smiled; air, water, earth,
By fowl, fish, beast, was flown, was swam, was walked,
Frequent; and of the sixth day yet remained.
There wanted yet the master-work, the end
Of all yet done; a creature, who, not prone
And brute, as other creatures, but endued
With sanctity of reason, might erect
His stature, and upright, with front serene.
Govern the rest, self-knowing; and from thence
Magnanimous, to correspond with Heaven;

But grateful to acknowledge whence his good
Descends; thither, with heart, and voice, and eyes,
Directed in devotion, to adore
And worship God supreme, who made him chief
Of all his works : therefore the Omnipotent
Eternal Father – for where is not He
Present ? – thus to his Son audibly spake :
    Let us make now Man in our image, man
In our similitude, and let them rule
Over the fish and fowl of sea and air,
Beast of the field, and over all the earth.
And every creeping thing that creeps the ground.
This said, he formed thee, Adam, thee, O man,
Dust of the ground, and in thy nostrils breathed
The breath of life; in His own image he
Created thee, in the image of God
Express, and thou becamest a living soul.
Male he created thee; but thy consort.
Female, for race; then blessed mankind, and said,
Be fruitful, multiply, and fill the Earth,
Subdue it, and throughout dominion hold
Over fish of the sea, and fowl of the air.
And every living thing that moves on the earth.
Wherever thus created, for no place
Is yet distinct by name, thence, as thou know'st,
He brought thee into this delicious grove.
This garden planted with the trees of God,
Delectable both to behold and taste;
And freely all their pleasant fruit for food
Gave thee. All sorts are here that all the earth yields,
Variety without end. But of the tree,
Which, tasted, works knowledge of good and evil,
Thou mayest not; in the day thou eat'st thou diest,
Death is the penalty imposed. Beware,
And govern well thy appetite; lest Sin
Surprise thee, and her black attendant, Death.

Here finished He, and all that he had made
Viewed, and behold all was entirely good.
So even and morn accomplished the sixth day.
Yet not till the Creator, from his work
Desisting, though unwearied, up returned.
Up to the Heaven of Heavens, his high abode,
Thence to behold this new created world.
The addition of his empire, how it shewed
In prospect from his throne, how good, how fair,
Answering His great idea. Up he rode.
Followed with acclamation, and the sound
Symphonious of ten thousand harps, that tuned
Angelic harmonies. The earth, the air
Resounded – thou remember'st, for thou heardst –
The heavens and all the constellations rung,
The planets in their station listening stood.
While the bright pomp ascended jubilant.
Open, ye everlasting gates ! they sung,
Open, ye heavens ! your living doors; let in
The great Creator, from his work returned
Magnificent, his six days' work, a world;
Open, and henceforth oft; for God will deign
To visit oft the dwellings of just men,
Delighted, and with frequent intercourse
Thither will send his winged messengers
On errands of supernal grace. So sung
The glorious train ascending. He, through heaven,
That opened wide her blazing portals, led
To God's eternal house direct the way –
A broad and ample road, whose dust is gold,
And pavement stars, as stars to thee appear,
Seen in the galaxy, that milky way.
Which nightly, as a circling zone, thou seest
Powdered with stars. And now on earth the seventh
Evening arose in Eden, for the sun
Was set, and twilight from the east came on,

Forerunning night; when at the holy mount
Of heaven's high-seated top, the imperial throne
Of Godhead fixed for ever firm and sure,
The Filial Power arrived, and sat him down
With his great Father, for He also went
.Invisible, yet stayed – such privilege
Hath Omnipresence – and the work ordained.
Author and end of all things : and, from work
Now resting, blessed and hallowed the seventh day.
As resting on that day from all his work.
But not in silence holy kept : the harp
Had work, and rested not; the solemn pipe,
And dulcimer, all organs of sweet stop.
All sounds on fret by string or golden wire.
Tempered soft tunings, intermixed with voice
Choral or unison : of incense clouds.
Fuming from golden censers, hid the mount.
Creation and the six days' acts they sung :
Great are thy works, Jehovah ! infinite
Thy power ! what thought can measure Thee, or tongue
Relate Thee ? Greater now in thy return
Than from the giant Angels. Thee that day
Thy thunders magnified; but to create
Is greater than, created, to destroy.
Who can impair Thee, Mighty King, or bound
Thy empire ? Easily the proud attempt
Of spirits apostate, and their counsels vain,
Thou hast repelled; while impiously they thought
Thee to diminish, and from thee withdraw
The number of thy worshippers. Who seeks
To lessen Thee, against his purpose serves
To manifest the more thy might : his evil
Thou usest, and from thence createst more good.
Witness this new-made world, another heaven,
From Heaven-gate not far, founded, in view,

On the clear hyaline, the glassy sea;
Of amplitude almost immense, with stars
Numerous, and every star, perhaps, a world
Of destined habitation; but thou know'st
Their seasons. Among these the seat of men,
Earth with her nether ocean circumfused,
Their pleasant dwelling-place. Thrice happy men
And sons of men, whom God hath thus advanced
Created in His image there to dwell
And worship him; and in reward to rule
Over his works, on earth, in sea, or air,
And multiply a race of worshippers
Holy and just; thrice happy, if they know
Their happiness, and persevere upright !
So sung they, and the Empyrean rung
With hallelujahs : thus was Sabbath kept.
And thy request think now fulfilled, that asked
How first this world and face of things began.
And what before thy memory was done
From the beginning, that posterity,
Informed by thee, might know – if else thou seek'st
Aught not surpassing human measure, say.

BOOK - VIII

Adam inquires concerning celestial motions; is doubtfully answered, and exhorted to search rather things more worthy of knowledge; Adam assents; and, still desirous to detain Raphael, relates to him what he remembered since his own creation; his placing in Paradise; his talk with God concerning solitude and fit society; his first meeting and nuptials with Eve; his discourse with the angel thereupon, who, after admonitions repeated, departs.

The angel ended, and in Adam's ear
　　So charming left his voice, that he awhile
Thought him still speaking, still stood fixed to hear;[1]
Then, as new-waked, thus gratefully replied :
　　What thanks sufficient, or what recompense
Equal, have I to render thee, divine
Historian, who thus largely hast allayed
The thirst I had of knowledge, and vouchsafed
This friendly condescension, to relate
Things else by me unsearchable; now heard
With wonder, but delight, and, as is due,
With glory attributed to the high
Creator ? Something yet of doubt remains,
Which only thy solution can resolve.
When I behold this goodly frame, this world.
Of Heaven and Earth consisting, and compute
Their magnitudes; this earth, a spot, a grain,
An atom, with the firmament compared
And all her numbered stars, that seem to roll

1. *Stood fixed to hear.*–"Stood" here should evidently have been "sat." The first three lines of this book were introduced in the second edition, in which the poem was made to consist of twelve books instead of ten.

Spaces incomprehensible – for such
Their distance argues, and their swift return
Diurnal – merely to officiate light
Round this opacous earth, this punctual spot,[1]
One day and night; in all their vast survey
Useless besides; reasoning, I oft admire,
How nature, wise and frugal, could commit
Such disproportions, with superfluous hand
So many nobler bodies to create.
Greater, so manifold, to this one use,
For aught appears, and on their orbs impose
Such restless revolution, day by day
Repeated; while the sedentary earth,
That better might with far less compass move,
Served by more noble than herself, attains
Her end without least motion, and receives.
As tribute, such a sumless journey brought
Of incorporeal speed, her warmth and light –
Speed, to describe whose swiftness number fails.
So spake our sire, and by his countenance seemed
Entering on studious thoughts abstruse; which Eve
Perceiving, where she sat retired in sight,
With lowliness majestic from her seat.
And grace that won who saw to wish her stay.
Rose, and went forth among her fruits and flowers,
To visit how they prospered, bud and bloom.
Her nursery; they at her coming sprung.
And, touched by her fair tendance, gladlier grew.
Yet went she not, as not with such discourse
Delighted, or not capable her ear
Of what was high : such pleasure she reserved,
Adam relating, she sole auditress;
Her husband the relater she preferred
Before the angel, and of him to ask

1. *This punctual spot.–Punctum,* a mere point in comparison with the universe.

Chose rather; he, she knew, would intermix
Grateful digressions, and solve high dispute
With conjugal caresses from his lip.
Not words alone pfeased her. O ! when meet now
Such pairs, in love and mutual honour joined ?
With goddess-like demeanour forth she went,
Not unattended, for on her, as queen,
A pomp of winning graces waited still.
And from about her shot darts of desire
Into all eyes, to wish her still in sight.
And Raphael now, to Adam's doubt proposed,
Benevolent and facile thus replied :
    To ask or search, I blame thee not; for heaven
Is as the book of God before thee set,
Wherein to read his wondrous works, and learn
His seasons, hours, or days, or months, or years.
This to attain, whether heaven move or earth,
Imports not, if thou reckon right; the rest
From man or angel the great Architect
Did wisely to conceal, and not divulge
His secrets, to be scanned by them who ought
Rather admire; or, if they list to try
Conjecture, he his fabric of the heavens
Hath left to their disputes – perhaps to move
His laughter at their quaint opinions wide
Hereafter, when they come to model heaven
And calculate the stars, how they will wield
The mighty frame, how build, unbuild, contrive,
To save appearances, how gird the sphere
With centric and eccentric scribbled o'er.
Cycle and epicyle, orb in orb.
Already by thy reasoning this I guess.
Who art to lead thy offspring, and supposest
That bodies bright and greater should not serve
The less, not bright; nor heaven such journeys run,
Earth sitting still, when she alone receives

The benefit. Consider first, that great
Or bright infeis not excellence : the earth,
Though, in comparison of heaven, so small.
Nor glistering, may of solid good contain
More plenty than the sun that barren shines;
Whose virtue on itself works no effect.
But in the fruitful earth, there first received,
His beams, inactive else, their vigour find.
Yet not to earth are those bright luminaries
Officious, but to thee, earth's habitant.
And for the heaven's wide circuit, let it speak
The Maker's high magnificence, who built
So spacious, and his line stretched out so far,
That man may know he dwells not in his own,
An edifice too large for him to fill.
Lodged in a small partition, and the rest
Ordained for uses to his Lord best known.
The swiftness of those circles attribute,
Though numberless, to his omnipotence,
That to corporeal substances could add
Speed almost spiritual. Me thou think'st not slow,
Who since the morning hour set out from Heaven,
Where God resides, and ere mid-day arrived
In Eden – distance inexpressible
By numbers that have name. But this I urge.
Admitting motion in the heavens, to shew
Invalid that which thee to doubt it moved;
Not that I so affirm, though so it seem
To thee who hast thy dwelling here on earth.
God, to remove his ways from human sense.
Placed heaven from earth so far, that earthly sight.
If it presume, might err in things too high.
And no advantage gain. What if the sun
Be centre to the world, and other stars,
By his attractive virtue and their own
Incited, dance about him various rounds !

Their wandering course, now high, now low, then hid,
Progressive, retrograde, or standing still.
In six thou seest; and what if seventh to these.
The planet Earth, so steadfast though she seem,
Insensibly three different motions move ?
Which else to several spheres thou must ascribe,
Moved contrary with thwart obliquities;
Or save the sun his labour, and that swift
Nocturnal and diurnal rhomb[1] supposed.
Invisible else above all stars, the wheel
Of day and night; which needs not thy belief,
If earth, industrious of herself, fetch day
Travelling east, and with her part averse
From the sun's beam meet night, her other part
Still luminous by his ray. What if that light.
Sent from her through the wide transpicuous air,
To the terrestrial moon be as a star,
Enlightening her by day, as she by night
This earth ? reciprocal, if land be there,
Fields and inhabitants. Her spots thou seest
As clouds, and clouds may rain, and rain produce
Fruits in her softened soil, for some to eat
Allotted there; and other suns, perhaps.
With their attendant moons, thou wilt descry.
Communicating male and female light,
Which two great sexes animate the world,
Stored in each orb, perhaps, with some that live.
For such vast room in nature[2] unpossessed
By living soul, desert and desolate,
Only to shine, yet scarce to contribute
Each orb a glimpse of light, conveyed so far
Down to this habitable, which returns
Light back to them, is obvious to dispute.
But whether thus these things, or whether not;

1. *Diurnal rhomb.*–A term in geometry denoting obliqueness.
2. *For such vast room in nature.*–For that such vast room there is in nature.

Whether the sun, predominant in heaven,
Rise on the earth, or earth rise on the sun,
He from the east his flaming road begin.
Or she from west her silent course advance,
With inoffensive pace that spinning sleeps
On her soft axle, while she paces even,
And bears thee soft with the smooth air along.
Solicit not thy thoughts with matters hid.
Leave them to God above. Him serve and fear.
Of other creatures, as Him pleases best,
Wherever placed, let Him dispose; joy thou
In what he gives to thee, this Paradise
And thy fair Eve; heaven is for thee too high
To know what passes there; be lowly wise :
Think only what concerns thee, and thy being;
Dream not of other worlds, what creatures there
Live, in what state, condition, or degree.
Contented that thus far hath been revealed.
Not of earth only, but of Highest Heaven.
To whom thus Adam, cleared of doubt, replied :
How fully hast thou satisfied me, pure
Litelligence of heaven. Angel serene !
And, freed from intricacies, taught to live
The easiest way, nor with perplexing thoughts
To interrupt the sweet of life, from which
God hath bid dwell far off all anxious cares.
And not molest us, unless we ourselves
Seek them with wandering thoughts, and notions vain.
But apt the mind or fancy is to rove
Unchecked, and of her roving is no end;
Till warned, or by experience taught, she learn,
That not to know at large of thinors remote
From use, obscure and subtle, but to know
That which before us lies in daily life.
Is the prime wisdom : what is more, is fume,
Or emptiness, or fond impertinence,

And renders us, in things that most concern,
Unpractised, unprepared, and still to seek.
Therefore from this high pitch let us descend
A lower flight, and speak of things at hand,
Useful, whence, haply, mention may arise
Of something not unseasonable to ask.
By sufferance, and thy wonted favour, deigned.
Thee I have heard relating what was done
Ere my remembrance. Now, hear me relate
My story, which, perhaps, thou hast not heard;
And day is yet not spent, till then thou seest
How subtly to detain thee I devise.
Inviting thee to hear while I relate;
Fond,[1] were it not in hope of thy reply.
For, while I sit with thee, I seem in heaven;
And sweeter thy discourse is to my ear
Than fruits of palm-tree pleasantest to thirst
And hunger both, from labour, at the hour
Of sweet repast; they satiate, and soon fill.
Though pleasant; but thy words, with grace divine
Imbued, bring to their sweetness no satiety.
To whom thus Raphael answered heavenly meek :
Nor are thy lips ungraceful, sire of men.
Nor tongue ineloquent; for God on thee
Abundantly his gifts hath also poured.
Inward and outward both, his image fair :
Speaking, or mute, all comeliness and grace
Attends thee, and each word, each motion, forms.
Nor less think we in heaven of thee on earth
Than of our fellow-servant, and inquire
Gladly into the ways of God with Man;
For God, we see, hath honoured thee, and set
On man his equal love. Say therefore on;
For I that day was absent, as befell.
Bound on a voyage uncouth and obscure,

1. *Fond.*–Foolish.

Far on excursion toward the gates of hell;
Squared in full legion – such command we had –
To see that none thence issued forth a spy,
Or enemy, while God was in his work;
Lest he, incensed at such eruption bold,
Destruction with creation might have mixed.
Not that they durst without his leave attempt;
But us he sends upon his high behests
For state, as sovereign King, and to inure
Our prompt obedience. Fast we found, fast shut,
The dismal gates, and barricadoed strong.
But, long ere our approaching, heard within
Noise, other than the sound of dance or song;
Torment, and loud lament, and furious rage.
Glad we returned up to the coasts of light
Ere Sabbath evening. So we had in charge.
But thy relation now for I attend,
Pleased with thy words no less than thou with mine.
　　So spake the godlike Power, and thus our Sire
For man to tell how human life began
Is hard; for who himself beginning knew ?
Desire with thee still longer to converse
Induced me. As new waked from soundest sleep
Soft on the flowery herb I found me laid.
In balmy sweat, which with his beams the sun
Soon dried, and on the reeking moisture fed.
Straight toward heaven my wondering eyes I turned.
And gazed awhile the ample sky; till, raised
By quick instinctive motion, up I sprung,
As thitherward endeavouring, and upright .
Stood on my feet. About me round I saw
Hill, dale, and shady woods, and sunny plains,
And liquid lapse of murmuring streams; by these,
Creatures that lived and moved, and walked or flew;
Birds on the branches warbling; all things smiled;
With fragrance and with joy my heart o'erflowed.

Myself I then perused,[1] and limb by limb
Surveyed, and sometimes went, and sometimes ran
With supple joints, as lively vigour led.
But who I was, or where, or from what cause.
Knew not. To speak I tried, and forthwith spake;
My tongue obeyed, and readily could name
Whatever I saw. Thou Sun, said I, fair light,
And thou enlightened Earth, so fresh and gay,
Ye hills, and dales, ye rivers, woods, and plains,
And ye that live and move, fair creatures, tell,
Tell if ye saw, how came I thus, how here ?
Not of myself; by some great Maker then,
In goodness and in power pre-eminent.
Tell me how may I know Him, how adore;
From whom I have that thus I move and live,
And feel that I am happier than I know ?
While thus I called, and strayed I knew not whither,
From where I first drew air, and first beheld
This happy light; when answer none returned,
On a green shady bank, profuse of flowers.
Pensive I sat me down : there gentle sleep
First found me, and with soft oppression seized
My drowsed sense, untroubled, though I thought
I then was passing to my former state
Insensible, and forthwith to dissolve.
When suddenly stood at my head a dream,
Whose inward apparition gently moved
My fancy to believe I yet had being,
And lived. One came, me thought, of shape divine,
And said. Thy mansion wants thee, Adam; rise,
First man, of men innumerable ordained
First father ! Called by thee, I come thy guide
To the garden of bliss, thy seat prepared.
So saying, by the hand he took me, raised.
And over fields and waters, as in air

1. *Perused.*–Examined.

Smooth sliding without step, last led me up
A woody mountain, whose high top was plain,
A circuit wide enclosed, with goodliest trees
Planted, with walks and bowers; that what I saw
Of earth before scarce pleasant seemed. Each tree,
Loaden with fairest fruit, that hung to the eye
Tempting, stirred in me sudden appetite
To pluck and eat; whereat I waked, and found
Before mine eyes all real, as the dream
Had lively shadowed. Here had new begun
My wandering, had not He, who was my guide
Up hither, from among the trees appeared,
Presence Divine. Rejoicing, but with awe,
In adoration at His feet I fell
Submiss.[1] He reared me, and. Whom thou sought'st I am,
Said mildly. Author of all this thou seest
Above, or round about thee, or beneath.
This Paradise I give thee; count it thine
To till and keep, and of the fruit to eat.
Of every tree that in the garden grows
Eat freely with glad heart; fear here no dearth.
But of the tree, whose operation brings
Knowledge of good and ill, which I have set
The pledge of thy obedience and thy faith,
Amid the garden by the tree of life –
Remember what I warn thee – shun to taste,
And shun the bitter consequence; for know,
The day thou eat'st thereof, my sole command
Transgressed, inevitably thou shalt die,
From that day mortal, and this happy state
Shalt lose, expelled from hence into a world
Of woe and sorrow. Sternly He pronounced
The rigid interdiction, which resounds
Yet dreadful in mine ear, though in my choice
Not to incur; but soon His clear aspect

1. *Submiss.*–Bowing down, submissive.

Returned, and gracious purpose thus renewed :
Not only these fair bounds, but all the earth
To thee and to thy race I give; as lords
Possess it, and all things that therein live,
Or live in sea, or air; beast, fish, and fowl.
In sign whereof, each bird and beast behold
After their kinds, I bring them to receive
From thee their names,[1] and pay thee fealty
With low subjection. Understand the same
Of fish within her watery residence,
Not hither summoned, since they cannot change
Their element to draw the thinner air.
As thus he spake, each bird and beast behold.
Approaching two and two; these cowering low
With blandishment, each bird stooped on his wing
I named them as they passed, and understood
Their nature; with such knowledge God endued
My sudden apprehension. But in these
I found not what me thought I wanted still;
And to the heavenly vision thus presumed :
Oh, by what name, for Thou above all these,
Above mankind, or aught than mankind higher,
Surpassest far my naming; how may I
Adore thee, Author of this universe.
And all this good to man ? for whose well-being
So amply, and with hands so liberal,
Thou hast provided all things. But with me
I see not who partakes. In solitude
What happiness ? Who can enjoy alone,
Or, all enjoying, what contentment find ?
Thus I, presumptuous; and the Vision bright,
As with a smile more brightened, thus replied :
What call'st thou solitude ? Is not the Earth

1. *From thee their names.*–"The Lord God formed every beast of the field, and every fowl of the air, and brought them unto Adam to see what he would call them : and whatsoever Adam called every living creature, that was the name thereof." (Gen. ii. 19.)

With various living creatures, and the air.
Replenished, and all these at thy command
To come and play before thee ? Know'st thou not
Their language and their ways ? They also know,
And reason not contemptibly; with these
Find pastime, and bear rule; thy realm is large.
So spake the Universal Lord, and seemed
So ordering. I, with leave of speech implored.
And humble deprecation, thus replied :
    Let not my words offend thee, heavenly Power;
My Maker, be propitious while I speak.
Hast thou not made me here thy substitute.
And these inferior far beneath me set ?
Among unequals what society
Can sort, what harmony, or true delight ?
Which must be mutual, in proportion due
Given and received; but, in disparity,
The one intense, the other still remiss,
Cannot well suit with either, but soon prove
Tedious alike. Of fellowship I speak
Such as I seek, fit to participate
All rational delight, wherein the brute
Cannot be human consort. They rejoice
Each, with their kind, lion with lioness;
So fitly them in pairs thou hast combined;
Much less can bird with beast, or fish with fowl,
So well converse, nor with the ox the ape;
Worse, then, can man with beast, and least of all.
    Whereto the Almighty answered, not displeased
A nice and subtle happiness, I see
Thou to thyself proposest, in the choice
Of thy associates, Adam, and wilt taste
No pleasure, though in pleasure, solitary.
What think'st thou, then, of me, and this my state ?
Seem I to thee sufficiently possessed
Of happiness, or not, who am alone

From all eternity ? for none I know
Second to me, or like, equal much less.
How have I, then, with whom to hold converse,
Save with the creatures which I made, and those
To me inferior, infinite descents
Beneath what other creatures are to thee ?
He ceased; I lowly answered : To attain
The height and depth of Thy eternal ways
All human thoughts come short. Supreme of things !
Thou in Thyself art perfect, and in Thee
Is no deficience found : not so is Man,
But in degree, the cause of his desire,
By conversation with his like, to help
Or solace his defects. No need that Thou
Shouldst propagate, already infinite,
And through all numbers absolute, though one.
But man by number is to manifest
His single imperfection, and beget
Like of his like, his image multiplied,
In unity defective; which requires
Collateral love, and dearest amity.
Thou in thy secrecy, although alone.
Best with Thyself accompanied, seek'st not
Social communication; yet, so pleased,
Canst raise thy creature to what height thou wilt
Of union or communion, deified :
I, by conversing, cannot these erect
From prone, nor in their ways complacence find.
Thus I, emboldened, spake, and freedom used
Permissive, and acceptance found; which gained
This answer from the gracious Voice divine :
Thus far to try thee, Adam, I was pleased;
And find thee knowing, not ol beasts alone.
Which thou hast rightly named, but of thyself;
Expressing well the spirit within thee free.
My image, not imparted to the brute;

Whose fellowship, therefore, unmeet for thee,
Good reason was thou freely shouldst dislike.
And be so minded still. I, ere thou spakest,
Knew it not good for man to be alone;
And no such company as then thou saw'st
Intended thee; for trial only brought,
To see how thou couldst judge of fit and meet.
What next I bring shall please thee, be assured,
Thy likeness, thy fit help, thy other self,
Thy wish exactly to thy heart's desire.
He ended, or I heard no more; for now
My earthly by His heavenly overpowered,
Which it had long stood under, strained to the height
In that celestial colloquy sublime,
As with an object that excels the sense,
Dazzled and spent, sunk down, and sought repair
Of sleep, which instantly fell on me, called
By nature as in aid, and closed mine eyes.
Mine eyes he closed, but open left the cell
Of fancy, my internal sight; by which,
Abstract, as in a trance, methought I saw.
Though sleeping, where I lay, and saw the shape
Still glorious before whom awake I stood.
Who, stooping, opened my left side, and took
From thence a rib, with cordial spirits warm.
And life-blood streaming fresh. Wide was the wound
But suddenly with flesh filled up and healed.
The rib he formed and fashioned with his hands;
Under His forming hands a creature grew,
Man-like, but different sex; so lovely fair,
That what seemed fair in all the world, seemed now
Mean, or in her summed up, in her contained.
And in her looks, which, from that time, infused
Sweetness unto my heart unfelt before.
And into all things, from her air, inspired
The spirit of love and amorous delight.

She disappeared, and left me dark; I waked
To find her, or for ever to deplore
Her loss, and other pleasures all abjure;
When out of hope, behold her, not far off,
Such as I saw her in my dream, adorned
With what all earth or heaven could bestow
To make her amiable. On she came.
Led by her heavenly Maker, though unseen,
And guided by his voice; nor uninformed
Of nuptial sanctity and marriage rites.
Grace was in all her steps, heaven in her eye,
In every gesture dignity and love.
I, overjoyed, could not forbear aloud:
This turn hath made amends : thou hast fulfilled
Thy words, Creator bounteous and benign,
Giver of all things fair ! but fairest this
Of all thy gifts ! nor enviest. I now see
Bone of my bone, flesh of my flesh, myself
Before me. Woman is her name; of man
Extracted : for this cause he shall forego
Father and mother, and to his wife adhere;
And they shall be one flesh, one heart, one soul.
She heard me thus : and, though divinely brought,
Yet innocence and virgin modesty.
Her virtue and the conscience of her worth,[1]
That would be wooed, and not unsought be won,
Not obvious, not obtrusive, but, retired.
The more desirable; or, to say all,
Nature herself, though pure of smful thought.
Wrought in her so, that, seeing me, she turned;
I followed her; she what was honour knew.
And with obsequious majesty approved
My pleaded reason. To the nuptial bower
I led her, blushing like the morn : all heaven,
And happy constellations, on that hour

1. *Conscience of her worth.*– Conscious of knowing it.

Shed their selectest influence : the earth
Gave sign of gratulation, and each hill;
Joyous the birds; fresh gales and gentle airs
Whispered it to the woods, and from their wings
Flung rose, flung odours from the spicy shrub.
Disporting, till the amorous bird of night
Sung spousal, and bid haste the evening star,
On his hill-top, to light the bridal lamp.
Thus have I told thee all my state, and brought
My story to the sum of earthly bliss
Which I enjoy; and must confess to find
In all things else delight indeed, but such
As, used or not, works in the mind no change,
Nor vehement desire; these delicacies
I mean of taste, sight, smell, herbs, fruits, and flowers,
Walks, and the melody of birds. But here
Far otherwise, transported I behold,
Transported touch; here passion first I felt,
Commotion strange ! in all enjoyments else
Superior and unmoved; here only weak
Against the charm of beauty's powerful glance,
Or nature failed in me, and left some part
Not proof enough such object to sustain;
Or, from my side subducting, took, perhaps,
More than enough; at least on her bestowed
Too much of ornament, in outward show
Elaborate, of inward less exact.
For well I understand, in the prime end
Of nature, her the inferior in the mind
And inward faculties, which most excel;
In outward, also, her resembling less
His image who made both, and less expressing
The character of that dominion given
O'er other creatures. Yet, when I approach
Her loveliness, so absolute she seems.
And in herself complete, so well to know

Her own, that what she wills to do or say
Seems wisest, virtuousest, discreetest, best.
All higher knowledge in her presence falls
Degraded. Wisdom in discourse with her
Loses, discountenanced, and like folly shews.
Authority and reason on her wait.
As one intended first, not after made
Occasionally; and, to consummate all,
Greatness of mind, and nobleness, their seat
Build in her loveliest, and create an awe
About her, as a guard angelic placed.
    To whom the Angel, with contracted brow :
Accuse not Nature, she hath done her part;
Do thou but thine, and be not diffident
Of wisdom; she deserts thee not, if thou
Dismiss not her, when most thou need'st her nigh,
By attributing overmuch to things
Less excellent, as thou thyself perceivest.
For, what admirest thou, what transports thee so ?
An outside; fair, no doubt, and worthy well
Thy cherishing, thy honouring, and thy love;
Not thy subjection; weigh with her thyself;
Then value. Ofttimes nothing profits more
Than self-esteem, grounded on just and right
Well managed. Of that skill, the more thou knowst,
The more she will acknowledge thee her head,
And to realities yield all her shows :
Made so adorn[1] for thy delight the more,
So awful, that with honour thou may'st love
Thy mate, who sees when thou art seen least wise.
But if the sense of touch, whereby mankind
Is propagated, seem such dear delight
Beyond all other, think the same vouchsafed
To cattle and each beast; which would not be
To them made common and divulged, if aught

1. *Made so adorn.*–Adorned.

Therein enjoyed were worthy to subdue
The soul of man, or passion in him move.
What higher in her society thou find'st
Attractive, human, rational, love still;
In loving thou dost well, in passion not.
Wherein true love consists not. Love refines
The thoughts, and heart enlarges; hath his seat
In reason, and is judicious; is the scale
By which to heavenly love thou may'st ascend,
Not sunk in carnal pleasure; for which cause.
Among the beasts no mate for thee was found.
    To whom thus, half abashed, Adam replied:
Neither her outside, formed so fair, nor aught
In procreation, common to all kinds –
Though higher of the genial bed by far,
And with mysterious reverence I deem –
So much delights me, as those graceful acts,
Those thousand decencies, that daily flow
From all her words and actions, mixed with love
And sweet compliance, which declare unfeigned
Union of mind, or in us both one soul :
Harmony to behold in wedded pair
More grateful than harmonious sound to the ear.
Yet these subject not; I to thee disclose
What inward thence I feel, not therefore foiled,
Who meet with various objects, from the sense
Variously representing; yet, still free.
Approve the best, and follow what I approve.
To love thou blamest me not; for love, thou say'st,
Leads up to heaven, is both the way and guide.
Bear with me, then, if lawful what I ask :
Love not the heavenly Spirits, and how their love
Express they, by looks only, or do they mix
Irradiance, virtual or immediate touch ?
    To whom the angel, with a smile that glowed
Celestial rosy red, love's proper hue.

Answered : Let it suffice thee that thou knowest
Us happy, and without love no happiness.
Whatever pure thou in the body enjoyest –
And pure thou wert created – we enjoy
In eminence, and obstacle find none
Of membrane, joint, or limb, exclusive bars.
Easier than air with air, if Spirits embrace,
Total they mix, union of pure with pure
Desiring, nor restrained conveyance need.
As flesh to mix with flesh, or soul with soul.
But I can now no more; the parting Sun,
Beyond the Earth's green cape and verdant isles
Hesperian, sets; my signal to depart.
Be strong, live happy, and love; but, first of all,
Him, whom to love is to obey; and keep
His great command. Take heed lest passion sway
Thy judgment to do aught which, else, free-will
Would not admit : thine, and of all thy sons,
The weal or woe in thee is placed; beware !
I in thy persevering shall rejoice,
And all the blest. Stand fast; to stand or fall
Free in thine own arbitrement it lies.
Perfect within, no outward aid require;
And all temptation to transgress repel.
    So saying, he arose, whom Adam thus
Followed with benediction : Since to part,
Go, heavenly guest, ethereal messenger.
Sent from whose sovereign goodness I adore !
Gentle to me and affable hath been
Thy condescension, and shall be honoured ever
With grateful memory; thou to mankind
Be good and friendly still, and oft return !
    So parted they : the Angel up to heaven
From the thick shade, and Adam to his bower

BOOK - IX

Satan, having compassed the earth, with meditated guile returns, as a mist, by night, into Paradise; enters into the serpent sleeping. Adam and Eve in the morning go forth to their labours, which Eve proposes to divide in several places, each labouring apart: Adam consents not, alleging the danger lest that enemy of whom they were forewarned, should attempt her, found alone: Eve, loth to be thought not circumspect or firm enough, urges her going apart, the rather desirous to make trial of her strength; Adam at last yields; the serpent finds her alone: his subtle approach, first gazing, then speaking; with much flattery extolling Eve above all other creatures. Eve, wondering to hear the serpent speak, asks how he attained to human speech, and such understanding, not till now : the serpent answers that, by tasting of a certain tree in the garden, he attained both to speech and reason, till then void of both. Eve requires him to bring her to that tree, and finds it to be the tree of knowledge, forbidden : the serpent, now grown bolder, with many wiles and arguments induces her at length to eat; she, pleased with the taste, deliberates awhile whether to impart thereof to Adam or not; at last brings him of the fruit: relates what persuaded her to cat thereof. Adam, at first amazed, but perceiving her lost, resolves, through vehemence of love, to perish with her; and, extenuating the trespass, eats also of the fruit : the effects thereof in them both; they seek to cover their nakedness; then fall to variance and accusation ot one another.

No more of talk where God, or Angel guest.
With Man, as with his friend, familiar used
To sit indulgent, and with him partake
Rural repast; permitting him the while
Venial discourse[1] unblamed. I now must change
Those notes to tragic; foul distrust, and breach
Disloyal, on the part of Man, revolt

1. *Venial discourse.*–Pardonable, allowable.

And disobedience; on the part of Heaven,
Now alienated, distance, and distaste,
Anger and just rebuke, and judgment given.
That brought into this world a world of woe,
Sin and her shadow death, and misery
Death's harbinger. Sad task ! yet argument
Not less, but more heroic than the wrath
Of stern Achilles[1] on his foe pursued.
Thrice fugitive, about Troy wall; or rage
Of Turnus for Lavinia[2] disespoused;
Or Neptune's ire, or Juno's,[3] that so long
Perplexed the Greek, and Cytherea's[4] son;
If answerable style I can obtain
Of my celestial patroness, who deigns
Her nightly visitation unimplored.
And dictates to me slumbering, or inspires
Easy my unpremeditated verse.
Since first this subject for heroic song
Pleased me, long choosing and beginning late,
Not sedulous by nature to indite
Wars, hitherto the only argument
Heroic deemed, chief mastery to dissect,
With long and tedious havoc, fabled knights,
In battles feigned – the better fortitude
Of patience and heroic martyrdom
Unsung – or to describe races and games,
Or tilting furniture, emblazoned shields.
Impresses quaint, caparisons and steeds.

1. *Stern Achilles.*–The principal hero in the "Iliad," described as the most handsome and brave of all the Greeks.

2. *Of Turnus far Lavinia.*–A Latin prince who tought against Æneas, because King Latinus had given his daughter Lavinia to him in marriage.

3. *Neptune's ire, or Juno's.*–Neptune was hostile to Ulysses, Juno to Æneas.

4. *Cytherea.*–One of the names of Venus.

Bases and tinsel trappings, gorgeous knights
At joust and tournament, then marshalled feast
Served up in hall with sewers and seneschals,
The skill of artifice or office mean.
Not that which justly gives heroic name
To person or to poem. Me, of these
Nor skilled nor studious, higher argument
Remains; sufficient of itself to raise
That name, unless an age too late, or cold
Climate, or years, damp my intended wing
Depressed; and much they may if all be mine,
Not hers, who brings it nightly to my ear.[1]
    The sun was sunk, and after him the star
Of Hesperus, whose office is to bring
Twilight upon the earth, short arbiter
'Twixt day and night; and now, from end to end,
Night's hemisphere had veiled the horizon round,
When Satan, who late fled before the threats
Of Gabriel out of Eden, now improved
In meditated fraud and malice, bent
On Man's destruction, maugre what might hap
Of heavier on himself, fearless returned.
By night he fled, and at midnight returned
From compassing the earth; cautious of day.
Since Uriel, regent of the sun, descried
His entrance, and forewarned the cherubim
That kept their watch. Thence, full of anguish, driven.
The space of seven continued nights he rode
With darkness : thrice the equinoctial line
He circled, four times crossed the car of Night
From pole to pole, traversing each colure;[2]

1. *Nightly to my ear.*–These personal episodes have been censured by critics as displaced in such a poem., and perhaps not without reason. But as they come from Milton, the reader, we doubt not, will give them a cordial and sympathetic welcome.

2. *Each colure.*–The colures are two great circles intersecting each other

On the eighth returned, and, on the coast averse
From entrance or cherubic watch, by stealth
Found unsuspected way. There was a place,
Now not, though sin, not time, first wrought the change,
Where Tigris, at the foot of Paradise,
Into a gulf shot under ground, till part
Rose up a fountain by the tree of life :
In with the river sunk, and with it rose,
Satan, involved in rising mist, then sought
Where to lie hid. Sea he had searched, and land
From Eden over Pontus, and the pool
Mæotis, up beyond the river Ob;
Downward as far antarctic; and, in length.
West from Orontes to the ocean barred
At Darien, thence to the land where flows
Ganges and Indus. Thus the orb he roamed
With narrow search, and, with inspection deep,
Considered every creature, which of all
Most opportune might serve his wiles, and found
The serpent subtlest beast of all the field.
Him, after long debate, irresolute,
Of thoughts revolved, his final sentence chose,
Fit vessel, fittest imp of fraud, in whom
To enter, and his dark suggestions hide
From sharpest sight; for, in the wily snake,
Whatever sleights, none would suspicious mark,
As from his wit and native subtlety
Proceeding, which, in other beasts observed,
Doubt might beget of diabolic power
Active within, beyond the sense of brute.
Thus he resolved, but first, from inward grief,
His bursting passion into plaints thus poured:
O Earth, how like to Heaven, if not preferred

at right angles in the poles, and encompassing the earth from north to south, and from south to north again, so that to traverse these was to traverse the whole globe.

More justly, seat worthier of gods, as built
With second thoughts, reforming what was old !
For what god, after better, worse would build ?
Terrestrial Heaven, danced round by other heavens
That shine, yet bear their bright officious lamps,
Light above light, for thee alone, as seems,
In thee concentring all their precious beams
Of sacred influence ! As God in Heaven
Is centre, yet extends to all; so thou.
Centring, receivest from all those orbs; in thee.
Not in themselves, all their known virtue appears
Productive in herb, plant, and nobler birth
Of creatures animate with gradual life
Of growth, sense, reason, all summed up in Man.
With what delight could I have walked thee round,
If I could joy in aught ! Sweet interchange
Of hill, and valley, rivers, woods, and plains,
Now land, now sea, and shores with forest crowned.
Rocks, dens, and caves ! But I in none of these
Find place or refuge; and the more I see
Pleasures about me, so much more I feel
Torment within me, as from the hateful siege
Of contraries. All good to me becomes
Bane, and in heaven much worse would be my state.
But neither here seek I, no, nor in Heaven,
To dwell, unless by mastering heaven's Supreme.
Nor hope to be myself less miserable
By what I seek, but others to make such
As I, though thereby worse to me redound.
For only in destroying I find ease
To my relentless thoughts; and, him destroyed,
Or won to what may work his utter loss,
For whom all this was made, all this will soon
Follow, as to him linked in weal or woe;
In woe then; that destruction wide may range.
To me shall be the glory sole among

The infernal Powers, in one day to have marred
What He, Almighty styled, six nights and days
Continued making, and who knows how long
Before had been contriving, though, perhaps,
Not longer than since I, in one night, freed,
From servitude inglorious, well-nigh half
The angelic name, and thinner left the throng
Of his adorers. He, to be avenged,
And to repair his numbers thus impaired,
Whether such virtue, spent of old, now failed
More Angels to create – if they at least
Are His created – or, to spite us more,
Determined to advance into our room
A creature formed of earth, and him endow,
Exalted from so base original,
With heavenly spoils, our spoils. What he decreed,
He effected; man he made, and for him built,
Magnificent, this world, and Earth his seat,
Him lord pronounced, and, O indignity!
Subjected to his service. Angel-wings,
And framing ministers, to watch and tend
Their earthly charge. Of these the vigilance
I dread; and, to elude, thus wrapt in mist
Of midnight vapour, glide obscure, and pry
In every bush and brake, where hap may find
The serpent sleeping, in whose mazy folds
To hide me, and the dark intent I bring.
O foul descent! that I, who erst contended
With gods to sit the highest, am now constrained
Into a beast; and, mixed with beastial slime.
This essence to incarnate and imbrute.
That to the height of Deity aspired !
But what will not ambition and revenge
Descend to ? Who aspires, must down as low
As high he soared, obnoxious, first or last,
To basest things. Revenge, at first so sweet,

Bitter ere long, back on itself recoils.
Let it – I reck not, so it light well-aimed,
Since higher I fall short, on him who next
Provokes my envy, this new favourite
Of Heaven, this man of clay, son of despite;
Whom, us the more to spite, his Maker raised
From dust. Spite then with spite is best repaid.
So saying, through each thicket, dank or dry,
Like a black mist, low creeping, he held on
His midnight search, where soonest he might find
The serpent. Him, fast sleeping, soon he found
In labyrinth of many a round, self-rolled,
His head the midst, well stored with subtle wiles,
Not yet in horrid shade or dismal den.
Nor nocent yet; but, on the grassy herb,
Fearless, unfeared, he slept. In at his mouth
The devil entered, and his brutal sense.
In heart or head, possessing, soon inspired
With act intelligential; but his sleep
Disturbed not, waiting close the approach of morn.
Now, when as sacred light began to dawn
In Eden on the humid flowers, that breathed
Their morning incense, when all things that breathe,
From the earth's great altar, sent up silent praise
To the Creator, and His nostrils fill
With grateful smell, forth came the human pair,
And joined their vocal worship to the quire
Of creatures wanting voice; that done, partake
The season, prime for sweetest scents and airs :
Then commune how that day they best may ply
Their growing work; for much their work outgrew
The hands' dispatch of two, gardening so wide;
And Eve first to her husband thus began :
Adam, well may we labour still to dress
This garden, still to tend plant, herb, and flower,
Our pleasant task enjoined; but till more hands

Aid us, the work under our labour grows.
Luxurious by restraint; what we by day
Lop, overgrown, or prune, or prop, or bind,
One night or two with wanton growth derides.
Tending to wild. Thou, therefore, now advise,
Or hear what to my mind first thoughts present :
Let us divide our labours; thou, where choice
Leads thee, or where most needs, whether to wind
The woodbine round this arbour, or direct
The clasping ivy where to climb; while I,
In yonder spring of roses intermixed
With myrtle, find what to redress till noon :
For, while so near each other thus all day
Our task we choose, what wonder if, so near,
Looks intervene, and smiles, or object new
Casual discourse draw on, which intermits
Our day's work, brought to little, though begun
Early, and the hour of supper comes unearned ?
    To whom mild answer Adam thus returned :
Sole Eve, associate sole, to me, beyond
Compare, above all living creatures dear !
Well hast thou motioned, well thy thoughts employed,
How we micrht best fulfil the work which here
God hath assigned us; nor of me shalt pass
Unpraised; for nothing lovelier can be found
In woman, than to study household good,
And good works in her husband to promote.
Yet not so strictly hath our Lord imposed
Labour, as to debar us when we need
Refreshment, whether food, or talk between,
Food of the mind, or this sweet intercourse
Of looks and smiles, – for smiles from reason flow,
To brute denied, and are of love the food,
Love, not the lowest end of human life.
For not to irksome toil, but to delight.
He made us, and delight to reason joined.

These paths and bowers doubt not but our joint hands
Will keep from wilderness with ease, as wide
As we need walk, till younger hands ere long
Assist us. But if much converse, perhaps,
Thee satiate, to short absence I could yield;
For solitude sometimes is best society,
And short retirement urees sweet return.
But other doubt possesses me, lest harm
Befall thee, severed from me; for thou know'st
What hath been warned us; what malicious foe,
Envying our happiness, and of his own
Despairing, seeks to work us woe and shame
By sly assault; and somewhere, nigh at hand.
Watches, no doubt, with greedy hope to find
His wish and best advantage, us asunder;
Hopeless to circumvent us joined, where each
To other speedy aid might lend at need.
Whether his first design be to withdraw
Our fealty from God, or to disturb
Conjugal love, than which, perhaps, no bliss
Enjoyed by us excites his envy more;
Or this, or worse, leave not the faithful side
That gave thee being, still shades thee, and protects.
The wife, where danger or dishonour lurks.
Safest and seemliest by her husband stays.
Who guards her, or with her the worst endures.
    To whom the virgin majesty of Eve,
As one who loves, and some unkindness meets.
With sweet austere composure thus replied :
    Offspring of heaven and earth, and all earth's lord
That such an enemy we have, who seeks
Our ruin, both by thee informed I learn.
And from the parting Angel overheard,
As in a shady nook I stood behind, .
Just then returned at shut of evening flowers.
But that thou shouldst my firmness therefore doubt

To God or thee, because we have a foe
May tempt it, I expected not to hear.
His violence thou fearest not; being such
As we, not capable of death or pain,
Can either not receive, or can repel.
His fraud is, then, thy fear; which plain infers
Thy equal fear, that my firm faith and love
Can by his fraud be shaken or seduced :
Thoughts, which how found they harbour in thy breast,
Adam, misthought of her to thee so dear ?
To whom, with healing words, Adam replied :
Daughter of God and Man, immortal Eve !
For such thou art, from sin and blame entire;
Not diffident of thee do I dissuade
Thy absence from my sight, but to avoid
The attempt itself, intended by our foe.
For he who tempts, though in vain, at least asperses
The tempted with dishonour foul, supposed
Not incorruptible of faith, not proof
Against temptation. Thou thyself, with scorn
And anger wouldst resent the offered wrong.
Though ineffectual found; misdeem not, then,
If such affront I labour to avert
From thee alone, which on us both at once
The enemy, though bold, will hardly dare.
Or daring, first on me the assault shall light.
Nor thou his malice and false guile contemn;
Subtle he needs must be, who could seduce
Angels. Nor think superfluous others' aid.
I, from the influence of thy looks, receive
Access in every virtue. In thy sight
More wise, more watchful, stronger, if need were
Of outward strength; while shame, thou looking on.
Shame to be overcome or over-reached,
Would utmost vigour raise, and raised, unite.
Why shouldst not thou like sense within thee feel

When I am present, and thy trial choose
With me, best witness of thy virtue tried ?
So spake domestic Adam in his care,
And matrimonial love. But Eve, who thought
Less attributed to her faith sincere,
Thus her reply with accent sweet renewed :
If this be our condition, thus to dwell
In narrow circuit straitened by a foe,
Subtle or violent, we not endued
Single with like defence, wherever met,
How are we happy, still in fear of harm ?
But harm precedes not sin. Only our foe,
Tempting, affronts us with his foul esteem
Of our integrity: his foul esteem
Sticks no dishonour on our front, but turns
Foul on himself; then wherefore shunned or feared
By us, who rather double honour gain
From his surmise proved false, find peace within,
Favour from Heaven, our witness, from the event.
And what is faith, love, virtue, unassayed
Alone, without exterior help sustained ?
Let us not, then, suspect our happy state
Left so imperfect by the Maker wise,
As not secure to single or combined.
Frail is our happiness, if this be so;
And Eden were no Eden, thus exposed.
To whom thus Adam fervently replied :
O woman, best are all things as the will
Of God ordained them. His creating hand
Nothing imperfect, or deficient, left
Of all that he created, much less man.
Or aught that might his happy state secure,
Secure from outward force. Within himself
The danger lies, yet lies within his power :
Against his will he can receive no harm.
But God left free the will, for what obeys

Reason is free; and reason he made right,
But bid her well be ware, and still erect,
Lest, by some fair-appearing good surprised,
She dictate false, and misinform the will
To do what God expressly hath forbid.
Not then mistrust, but tender love, enjoins,
That I should mind thee oft, and mind thou me.
Firm we subsist, yet possible to swerve.
Since reason not impossibly may meet
Some specious object by the foe suborned.
And fall into deception unaware,
Not keeping strictest watch, as she was warned.
Seek not temptation, then, which to avoid
Were better, and most likely if from me
Thou sever not; trial will come unsought.
Wouldst thou approve thy constancy, approve
First thy obedience; the other who can know ?
Not seeing thee attempted, who attest ?
But, it thou think trial unsought may find
Us both securer than thus warned thou seemest,
Go; for thy stay, not free, absents thee more;
Go in thy native innocence, rely
On what thou hast of virtue; summon all :
For God towards thee hath done His part, do thine.
  So spake the patriarch of mankind; but Eve
Persisted; yet subm.iss, though last, replied :
  With thy permission, then, and thus forewarned
Chiefly by what thy own last reasoning words
Touched only, that our trial, when least sought,
May find us both, perhaps, far less prepared,
The willinger I go, nor much expect
A foe so proud will first the weaker seek;
So bent, the more shall shame him his repulse
  Thus saying, from her husband's hand her hand
Soft she withdrew, and, like a wood-nymph light,

Oread, or Dryad, or of Delia's train,[1]
Betook her to the groves – but Delia's self,
In gait surpassed, and goddess-like deport,
Though not as she with bow and quiver armed,
But with such gardening tools as art, yet rude.
Guiltless of fire, had formed, or Angels brought.
To Pales,[2] or Pomona,[3] thus adorned,
Likest she seemed – Pomona, when she fled
Vertumnus, or to Ceres in her prime.
Yet virgin of Proserpina from Jove.
Her long, with ardent look, his eye pursued
Delighted, but desiring more her stay.
Oft he to her his charge of quick return
Repeated; she to him as oft engaged
To be returned by noon amid the bower,
And all things in best order to invite
Noontide repast, or afternoon's repose.
O much deceived, much failing, hapless Eve,
Of thy presumed return ! event perverse!
Thou never from that hour in Paradise
Found'st either sweet repast, or sound repose !
Such ambush, hid among sweet flowers and shades
Waited, with hellish rancour imminent,
To intercept thy way, or send thee back
Despoiled of innocence, of faith, of bliss !
For now, and since first break of dawn, the Fiend,
Mere serpent in appearance, forth was come.
And on his quest, where likeliest he might find
The only two of mankind, but in them
The whole included race, his purposed prey.
In bower and field he sought where any tuft

1. *Oread, or Dryad, or of Delia's train.*–Female divinities with which the Greeks peopled the neighbourhood of their rivers, woods, and mountains.

2. *Pales.*–The Roman goddess of flocks–shepherds.

3. *Pomona.*–The female guardian of fruit trees.

Of grove or garden-plot more pleasant lay,
Their tendance, or plantation for deliglit;
By fountain or by shady rivulet
He sought them both, but wished his hap might find
Eve separate; he wished, but not with hope
Of what so seldom chanced; when to his wish,
Beyond his hope. Eve, separate he spies.
Veiled in a cloud of fragrance, where she stood,
Half spied, so thick the roses blushing round
About her glowed, oft stooping to support
Each flower of tender stalk, whose head, though gay
Carnation, purple, azure, or specked with gold.
Hung drooping, unsustained; then she upstays
Gently with myrtle band, mindless the while
Herself, though fairest unsupported flower.
From her best prop so far, and storm so nigh.
Nearer he drew, and many a walk traversed
Of stateliest covert, cedar, pine, or palm;
Then voluble and bold;[1] now hid, now seen
Among thick woven arborets, and flowers
Imbordered on each bank, the hand of Eve :
Spot more delicious than those gardens feigned
Or of revived Adonis,[2] or renowned
Alcinous,[3] host of old Laertes' son.
Or that, not mystic,[4] where the sapient king
Held dalliance with his fair Egyptian spouse.
Much he the place admired, the person more:
As one who, long in populous city pent,
Where houses thick, and sewers, annoy the air,
Forth issuing on a summer's morn, to breathe

1. *Voluble and bold.*–Curved and confident.
2. *Adonis.*–Tradition made Adonis to delight in a beautiful garden.
3. *Alcinous*- Alcinous was a son of Neptune, happy in his rule over a portion of the island of Scheria
4. *Not mystc*–This reference shows the sense in which Milton understood the Song of Solomon.

Among the pleasant villages and farms
Adjoined, from each thing met conceives delight;
The smell of grain, or tedded grass[1] or kine,
Or daily, each rural sight, each rural sound;
If chance, with nymph-like step, fair virgin pass,
What pleasing seemed, for her now pleases more.
She most, and in her look sums all delight.
Such pleasure took the serpent to behold
This flowery plat, the sweet recess of Eve
Thus early, thus alone; her heavenly form
Angelic, but more soft, and feminine,
Her graceful innocence, her every air
Of gesture, or least action, overawed
His malice, and with rapine sweet bereaved
His fierceness of the fierce intent it brought.
That space the evil one abstracted stood
From his own evil, and for the time remained
Stupidly good; of enmity disarmed,
Of guile, of hate, of envy, of revenge.
But the hot hell that always in him burns,
Though in mid heaven, soon ended his delight,
And tortures him now more, the more he sees
Of pleasure, not for him ordained : then soon
Fierce hate he recollects,[2] and all his thoughts
Of mischief, gratulating,[3] thus excites :
Thoughts, whither have ye led me ! With what sweet
Compulsion thus transported, to forget
What hither brought us ? Hate, not love; nor hope
Of Paradise for Hell, hope here to taste
Of pleasure, but all pleasure to destroy.
Save what is in destroying; other joy
To me is lost. Then, let me not let pass
Occasion which now smiles; behold alone

1. *Tedded grass.* – Grass cast about newly cut.
2. *Fierce hate he recollects.* –Recalls, rallies.
3. *Gratulating.* –Rejoicing in.

The woman, opportune to all attempts,
Her husband, for I view far round, not nigh.
Whose higher intellectual more I shun,
And strength, of courage haughty, and of limb
Heroic built, though of terrestrial mould;
Foe not informidable, exempt from wound,
I not; so much hath hell debased, and pain
Enfeebled me, to what I was in heaven.
She fair, divinely fair, fit love for gods !
Not terrible, though terror be in love
And beauty, not approached by stronger hate.
Hate stronger, under show of love well feigned,
The way which to her ruin now I tend.
 So spake the enemy of mankind enclosed
In serpent, inmate bad, and toward Eve
Addressed his way : not with indented wave,
Prone on the ground, as since; but on his rear,
Circular base of rising folds, that towered
Fold above fold, a surging maze; his head
Crested aloft, and carbuncle his eyes;
With burnished neck of verdant gold, erect
Amidst his circling spires, that on the grass
Floated redundant. . Pleasing was his shape.
And lovely; never since of serpent-kind
Lovelier; not those that in Illyria changed
Hermione and Cadmus,[1] or the god
In Epidaurus;[2] nor to which transformed
Ammonian Jove,[3] or Capitoline was seen;
He, with Olympias, this, with her who bore
Scipio, the height of Rome. With tract oblique

1. *Hermione and Cadmus.*–Fabled as changed into serpents.
2. *Epidaurus.*–Another name for Æsculapius, the god of physic, who, being sent for to Rome in the time of a plague was said to have entered the city in the form of a serpent.
3. *Ammonian Jove.*–Said to have conversed with his mother Olympia in the form of a serpent–the matron who, as the mother of Scipio Africanus, raised Rome to its height of greatness.

At first, as one who sought access, but feared
To interrupt, sidelong he works his way.
As when a ship, by skilful steersman wrought,
Nigh river's mouth or foreland, where the wind
Veers oft, as oft so steers, and shifts her sail :
So varied he, and of his tortuous train
Curled many a wanton wreath in sight of Eve,
To lure her eye. She, busied, heard the sound
Of rustling leaves, but minded not, as used
To such disport before her through the field.
From every beast, more duteous at her call,
Than at Circean call the herd disguised.[1]
He, bolder now, uncalled before her stood,
But as in gaze admiring : oft he bowed
His turret crest, and sleek enamelled neck.
Fawning; and licked the ground whereon she trod.
His gentle dumb expression turned at length
The eye of Eve to mark his play; he, glad
Of her attention gained, with serpent tongue
Organic, or impulse of vocal air,
His fraudulent temptation thus began:
Wonder not, sovereign mistress, if, perhaps.
Thou canst, who art sole wonder; much less arm
Thy looks, the heaven of mildness, with disdain.
Displeased that I approach thee thus, and gaze
Insatiate, I thus single, nor have feared
Thy awful brow, more awful thus retired.
Fairest resemblance of thy Maker fair.
Thee all things living gaze on, all things thine
By gift, and thy celestial beauty adore,
With ravishment beheld ! there best beheld,
Where universally admired. But here.
In this enclosure wild, these beasts among,
Beholders rude, and shallow to discern

1. *At Circean call the herd disguised.*–In allusion to Circe, who was said to have turned men into beasts. (Ovid. "Met." xiv. 45.)

Half what in thee is fair, one man except,
Who sees thee ? – and what is one ? – who shouldst be seen
A goddess among gods, adored and served
By Angels numberless, thy daily train.
So glozed the tempter, and his proem tuned;
Into the heart of Eve his words made way.
Though at the voice much marvelling : at length.
Not unamazed, she thus in answer spake :
What may this mean ? language of man, pronounced
By tongue of brute, and human sense expressed !
The first, at least, of these, I thought denied
To beasts, whom God, on their creation-day,
Created mute to all articulate sound;
The latter I demur;[1] for in their looks
Much reason, and in their actions, oft appears.
Thee, serpent, subtlest beast of all the field
I knew, but not with human voice endued;
Redouble, then, this miracle, and say,
How earnest thou speakable of mute, and how
To me so friendly grown, above the rest
Of brutal kind, that daily are in sight ?
Say, for such wonder claims attention due.
To whom the guileful tempter thus replied :
Empress of this fair world, resplendent Eve !
Easy to me it is to tell thee all
What thou commandest, and right thou shouldst be obeyed.
I was at first as other beasts that graze
The trodden herb, of abject thoughts and low,
As was my food; nor aught but food discerned,
Or sex, and apprehended nothing high :
Till, on a day roving the field, I chanced
A goodly tree far distant to behold,
Loaden with fruit of fairest colours mixed.
Ruddy and gold. I nearer drew to gaze;
When from the boughs a savoury odour blown,

1. *The latter I demur.*–Question, doubt.

Grateful to appetite, more pleased my sense
Than smell of sweetest fennel, or the teats
Of ewe or goat dropping with milk at even,
Unsucked of lamb or kid, that tend their play.
To satisfy the sharp desire I had
Of tasting those fair apples, I resolved
Not to defer; hunger and thirst at once.
Powerful persuaders, quickened at the scent
Of that allurinor fruit, urged me so keen.
About the mossy trunk I wound me soon;
For, high from ground, the branches would require
Thy utmost reach, or Adam's : round the tree,
All other beasts that saw, with like desire
Longing and envying stood, but could not reach.
Amid the tree now got, where plenty hung
Tempting, so nigh, to pluck and eat my fill
I spared not; for such pleasure, till that hour,
At feed or fountain, never had I found.
Sated at length, ere long I might perceive
Strange alteration in me, to degree
Of reason in my inward powers, and speech
Wanted not long, though to this shape retained.
Thenceforth to speculations high or deep
I turned my thoughts, and with capacious mind
Considered all things visible in heaven.
Or earth, or middle; all things fair and good.
But all that fair and good in thy divine
Semblance, and in thy beauty's heavenly ray,
United I beheld : no fair to thine
Equivalent or second ! which compelled
Me thus, though importune perhaps, to come
And gaze, and worship thee, of right declared
Sovereign of creatures, universal dame !
　　So talked the spirited sly snake, and Eve,
Yet more amazed, unwary thus replied :
　　Serpent, thy overpraising leaves in doubt

The virtue of that fruit, in thee first proved.
But say, where grows the tree ? from hence how far ?
For many are the trees of God that grow
In Paradise, and various yet unknown
To us; in such abundance lies our choice.
As leaves a greater store of fruit untouched,
Still hanging incorruptible, till men
Grow up to their provision, and more hands
Help to disburden nature of her birth.
    To whom the wily adder, blithe and glad :
Empress, the way is ready, and not long;
Beyond a row of myrtles, on a flat,
Fast by a fountain, one small thicket past
Of blowing myrrh and balm : if thou accept
My conduct, I can bring thee thither soon.
    Lead, then, said Eve. He, leading, swiftly rolled
In tangles, and made intricate seem straight.
To mischief swift. Hope elevates, and joy
Brightens his crest. As when a wandering fire,
Compact of unctuous vapour, which the night
Condenses, and the cold environs round.
Kindled through agitation to a flame.
Which oft, they say, some evil spirit attends.
Hovering and blazing with delusive light.
Misleads the amazed night-wanderer from his way
To bogs and mires, and oft through pond or pool,
There swallowed up and lost, from succour far :
So glistered the dire snake, and into fraud
Led Eve, our credulous mother, to the tree
Of prohibition, root of all our woe;
Which, when she saw, thus to her guide she spake :
    Serpent, we might have spared our coming hither,
Fruitless to me, though fruit be here to excess,
The credit of whose virtue rest with thee;
Wondrous, indeed, if cause of such effects !
But of this tree we may not taste nor touch;

God so commanded, and left that command
Sole daughter of his voice : the rest, we live
Law to ourselves; our reason is our law.
    To whom the tempter guilefully replied :
Indeed ! hath God then said that of the fruit
Of all these garden-trees ye shall not eat,
Yet lords declared of all in earth or air ?
    To whom thus Eve, yet sinless : Of the fruit
Of each tree in the garden we may eat :
But of the fruit of this fair tree amidst
The garden, God hath said. Ye shall not eat
Thereof, nor shall ye touch it, lest ye die.
    She scarce had said, though brief, when now more bold
The tempter, but, with show of zeal and love
To man, and indignation at his wrong.
New part puts on; and, as to passion moved,
Fluctuates disturbed, yet comely, and in act
Raised, as of some great matter to begin.
As when, of old, some orator renowned.
In Athens, or free Rome, where eloquence
Flourished, since mute, to some great cause addressed,
Stood in himself collected; while each part.
Motion, each act, won audience ere the tongue,
Sometimes in height began, as no delay
Of preface brooking, through his zeal of right :
So standing, moving, or to height up-grown,
The tempter, all impassioned, thus began
    Oh, sacred, wise, and wisdom giving plant,
Mother of science ! now I feel thy power
Within me clear; not only to discern
Things in their causes, but to trace the ways
Of highest agents, deemed however wise.
Queen of this universe ! do not believe
Those rigid threats of death. Ye shall not die.
How should ye ? By the fruit ? It gives you life
To knowledge. By the Threatener ? Look on me,

Me, who have touched and tasted, yet both live,
And life more perfect have attained than fate
Meant me, by venturing higher than my lot.
Shall that be shut to Man, which to the beast
Is open ? Or will God incense his ire
For such a petty trespass, and not praise
Rather your dauntless virtue, whom the pain
Of death denounced, whatever thing death be,
Deterred not from achieving what might lead
To happier life, knowledge of good and evil;
Of good, how just ? of evil, if what is evil
Be real, why not known, since easier shunned ?
God, therefore, cannot hurt ye, and be just;
Not just, not God; not feared then, nor obeyed :
Your fear itself of death removes the fear.
Why, then, was this forbid ? Why, but to awe;
Why, but to keep ye low and ignorant.
His worshippers. He knows that in the day
Ye eat thereof, your eyes, that seem so clear.
Yet are but dim, shall presently be then
Opened and cleared, and ye shall be as gods,
Knowing both good and evil, as they know.
That ye shall be as gods, since I as man.
Internal man, is but proportion meet;
I, of brute, human; ye, of human, gods.
So ye shall die, perhaps, by putting off
Human, to put on gods; death to be wished,
Though threatened, which no worse than this can bring
And what are gods, that man may not become
As they, participating godlike food ?
The gods are first, and that advantage use
On our belief, that all from them proceeds.
I question it; for this fair earth I see.
Warmed by the sun, producing every kind;
Them, nothing. If they all things, who enclosed
Knowledge of good and evil in this tree,

That whoso eats thereof, forthwith attains
Wisdom without their leave ? And wherein lies
The offence, that man should thus attain to know ?
What can your knowledge hurt Him, or this tree
Impart against His will, if all be His ?
Or is it envy ? and can envy dwell
In heavenly breasts ? These, these, and many more
Causes import your need of this fair fruit.
Goddess humane, reach, then, and freely taste.
He ended; and his words, replete with guile,
Into her heart too easy entrance won :
Fixed on the fruit she gazed, which to behold
Might tempt alone; and in her ears the sound
Yet rung of his persuasive words, impregned
With reason, to her seeming, and with truth :
Meanwhile the hour of noon drew on, and waked
An eager appetite, raised by the smell
So savoury of that fruit, which, with desire,
Inclinable now grown to touch or taste.
Solicited her longing eye. Yet first.
Pausing awhile, thus to herself she mused :
Great are thy virtues, doubtless, best of fruits.
Though kept from Man, and worthy to be admired;
Whose taste, too long forborne, at first assay
Gave elocution to the mute, and taught
The tongue, not made for speech, to speak thy praise.
Thy praise He also, who forbids thy use,
Conceals not from us, naming thee the tree
Of knowledge, knowledge both of good and evil;
Forbids us, then, to taste : but His forbidding
Commends thee more, while it infers the good
By thee communicated, and our want :
For good unknown sure is not had; or, had,
And yet unknown, is as not had at all.
In plain, then, what forbids He but to know,
Forbids us good, forbids us to be wise ?

Such prohibitions bind not. But, if death
Bind us with after-bands, what profits, then,
Our inward freedom ? In the day we eat
Of this fair fruit, our doom is, we shall die !
How dies the serpent ? He hath eaten, and lives.
And knows, and speaks, and reasons, and discerns,
Irrational till then. For us alone
Was death invented ? Or to us denied
This intellectual food, for beasts reserved ?
For beasts it seems; yet that one beast which first
Hath tasted envies not, but brings with joy
The good befallen him, author unsuspect,
Friendly to man, far from deceit or guile.
What fear I, then ? Rather, what know to fear
Under this ignorance of good or evil,
Of God or death, of law or penalty ?
Here grows the cure of all, this fruit divine.
Fair to the eye, inviting to the taste,
Of virtue to make wise : what hinders, then,
To reach, and feed at once both body and mind ?
So saying, her rash hand, in evil hour,
Forth reaching to the fruit, she plucked, she ate !
Earth felt the wound, and Nature, from her seat,
Sighing through all her works, gave signs of woe,
That all was lost. Back to the thicket slunk
The guilty serpent; and well might, for Eve,
Intent now only on her taste, nought else
Regarded; such delight till then, as seemed.
In fruit she never tasted, whether true
Or fancied so, through expectation high
Of knowledge; nor was godhead from her thought.
Greedily she engorged without restraint.
And knew not eating death. Satiate at length,
And heightened as with wine, jocund and boon,
Thus to herself she pleasingly began :
O sovereign, virtuous, precious of all trees

In Paradise ! of operation blest
To sapience, hitherto obscured, infamed,
And thy fair fruit let hang, as to no end
Created; but henceforth my early care,
Not without song, each morning, and due praise,
Shall tend thee, and the fertile burden case
Of thy full branches, offered free to all;
Till, dieted by thee, I grow mature
In knowledge, as the gods, who all things know;
Though others envy what they cannot give :
For, had the gift been theirs, it had not here
Thus grown. Experience, next, to thee I owe.
Best guide : not following thee, I had remained
In ignorance; thou openest wisdom's way,
And givest access, though secret she retire.
And I, perhaps, am secret. Heaven is high,
High, and remote to see from thence distinct
Each thing on earth; and other care, perhaps.
May have diverted from continual watch
Our great Forbidder, safe with all his spies
About him. But to Adam in what sort
Shall I appear ? Shall I to him make known
As yet my change, and give him to partake
Full happiness with me, or rather not,
But keep the odds of knowledge in my power,
Without copartner ? so to add what wants
In female sex, the more to draw his love,
And render me more equal, and, perhaps,
A thing not undesirable, sometimes
Superior; for, inferior, who is free ?
This may be well. But what if God have seen.
And death ensue ? Then I shall be no more !
And Adam, wedded to another Eve,
Shall live with her, enjoying; I extinct :
A death to think ! Confirmed, "then, I resolve,
Adam shall share with me in bliss or woe;

So dear I love him, that with him all deaths
I could endure – without him live no life.
　　So saying, from the tree her step she turned,
But first low reverence done, as to the power
That dwelt within, whose presence had infused
Into the plant sciential sap, derived
From nectar, drink of gods. Adam, the while,
Waiting, desirous her return, had wove
Of choicest flowers a garland, to adorn
Her tresses, and her rural labours crown.
As reapers oft are wont their harvest queen.
Great joy he promised to his thoughts, and new
Solace in her return, so long delayed :
Yet oft his heart, divine of something ill.
Misgave him; he the faltering measure felt,
And forth to meet her went, the way she took
That morn when first they parted. By the tree
Of knowledge he must pass, there he her met,
Scarce from the tree returning; in her hand
A bough of fairest fruit, that downy smiled.
New gathered, and ambrosial smell diffused.
To him she hasted; in her face excuse
Came prologue, and apology too prompt;
Which, with bland words at will, she thus addressed :
　　Hast thou not wondered, Adam, at my stay ?
Thee I have missed, and thought it long, deprived
Thy presence; agony of love till now
Not felt, nor shall be twice; for never more
Mean I to try, what rash untried I sought.
The pain of absence from thy sight. But strange
Hath been the cause, and wonderful to hear.
This tree is not, as we are told, a tree
Of danger tasted, nor to evil unknown
Opening the way, but of divine effect
To open eyes, and make them gods who taste;
And hath been tasted such. The serpent, wise,

Or not restrained as we, or not obeying.
Hath eaten of the fruit, and is become,
Not dead, as we are threatened, but thenceforth
Endued with human voice and human sense,
Reasoning to admiration, and with me
Persuasively hath so prevailed, that I
Have also tasted, and have also found
The effects to correspond; opener mine eyes
Dimerst, dilated spirits, ampler heart.
And growing up to Godhead; which for thee
Chiefly I sought; without thee can despise.
For bliss, as thou hast part, to me is bliss;
Tedious, unshared with thee, and odious soon.
Thou, therefore, also taste, that equal lot
May join us – equal joy as equal love;
Lest, thou not tasting, different degree
Disjoin us, and I then too late renounce
Deity for thee, when fate will not permit.
    Thus Eve, with countenance blithe, her story told;
But in her cheek distemper flushing glowed.
On the other side, Adam, soon as he heard
The fatal trespass done by Eve, amazed,
Astonied stood and blank, while horror chill
Ran through his veins, and all his joints relaxed;
From his slack hand the garland, wreathed for Eve,
Down dropt, and all the faded roses shed;
Speechless he stood and pale; till thus, at length,
First to himself, he inward silence broke :
    Oh, fairest of creation, last and best
Of all God's works ! creature, in whom excelled
Whatever can to sight or thought be formed,
Holy, divine, good, amiable, or sweet !
How art thou lost ! how on a sudden lost.
Defaced, deflowered, and now to death devote !
Rather, how hast thou yielded to transgress
The strict forbiddance – how to violate

The sacred fruit forbidden ? Some cursed fraud
Of enemy hath beguiled thee, yet unknown.
And me with thee hath ruined; for with thee
Certain my resolution is to die.
How can I live without thee ? How forego
Thy sweet converse, and love so dearly joined,
To live again in these wild woods forlorn ?
Should God create another Eve, and I
Another rib afford, yet loss of thee
Would never from my heart : no, no ! I feel
The link of nature draw me, flesh of flesh.
Bone of my bone thou art, and from thy state
Mine never shall be parted, bliss or woe.
　　So having said, as one from sad dismay
Recomforted, and after thoughts disturbed,
Submitting to what seemed remediless,
Thus, in calm mood, his words to Eve he turned :
　　Bold deed thou hast presumed, adventurous Eve,
And peril great provoked, who thus hast dared,
Had it been only coveting to eye
That sacred fruit, sacred to abstinence.
Much more to taste it, under ban to touch.
But past, who can recall, or done, undo ?
Not God omnipotent, nor fate. Yet so
Perhaps thou shalt not die, perhaps the fact
Is not so heinous now, foretasted fruit.
Profaned first by the serpent, by him first
Made common, and unhallowed, ere our taste.
Nor yet on him found deadly; he yet lives;
Lives, as thou saidst, and gains to live, as Man,
Higher degree of life; inducement strong
To us, as likely, tasting, to attain
Proportional ascent; which cannot be
But to be gods, or angels, demi-gods.
Nor can I think that God, Creator wise,
Though threatening, will in earnest so destroy

Us, his prime creatures, dignified so high,
Set over all his works; which, in our fall.
For us created, needs with us must fail.
Dependent made; so God shall uncreate.
Be frustrate, do, undo, and labour lose :
Not well conceived of God, who, though his power
Creation could repeat, yet would be loth
Us to abolish, lest the Adversary
Triumph and say : Fickle their state, whom God
Most favours; who can please Him long ? Me first
He ruined, now mankind; whom will he next ?
Matter of scorn, not to be given the Foe.
However, I with thee have fixed my lot,
Certain to undergo like doom : if death
Consort with thee death is to me as life :
So forcible within my heart I feel
The bond of nature draw me to my own;
My own in thee, for what thou art is mine;
Our state cannot be severed; we are one.
One flesh; to lose thee were to lose myself.
So Adam; and thus Eve to him replied :
Oh, glorious trial of exceeding love,
Illustrious evidence, example high !
Engaging me to emulate; but, short
Of thy perfection, how shall I attain ?
Adam ! from whose dear side I boast me sprung,
And gladly of our union hear thee speak,
One heart, one soul in both; whereof good proof
This day affords, declaring thee resolved,
Rather than death, or aught than death more dread,
Shall separate us, linked in love so dear,
To undergo with me one guilt, one crime,
If any be, of tasting this fair fruit.
Whose virtue – for of good still good proceeds,
Direct, or by occasion – hath presented
This happy trial of thy love, which else

So eminently never had been known.
Were it I thought death menaced would ensue
This my attempt, I would sustain alone
The worst, and not persuade thee; rather die
Deserted, than oblige thee with a fact
Pernicious to thy peace, chiefly assured
Remarkably so late of thy so true.
So faithful love, unequalled; but I feel
Far otherwise the event; not death, but life
Augmented, opened eyes, new hopes, new joys,
Taste so divine, that what of sweet before
Hath touched my sense, flat seems to this, and harsh.
On my experience, Adam, freely taste,
And fear of death deliver to the winds.
So saying, she embraced him, and for joy
Tenderly wept; much won, that he his love
Had so ennobled, as of choice to incur
Divine displeasure for her sake, or death.
In recompense – for such compliance bad
Such recompense best merits, – from the bough
She gave him of that fair enticing fruit
With liberal hand : he scrupled not to eat.
Against his better knowledge : not deceived,
But fondly overcome with female charm.
Earth trembled from her entrails, as again
In pangs; and nature gave a second groan;
Sky loured, and, muttering thunder, some sad drops
Wept at completing of the mortal sin
Original; while Adam took no thought
Eating his fill; nor Eve to iterate
Her former trespass feared, the more to soothe
Him with her loved society; that now,
As with new wine intoxicated both.
They swim in mirth, and fancy that they feel
Divinity within them breeding wings.
Wherewith to scorn the earth. But that false fruit

Far other operation first displayed,
Carnal desire inflaminor : he on Eve
Began to cast lascivious eyes; she him
As wantonly repaid; in lust they burn.
Till Adam thus 'gan Eve to dalliance move :
    Eve, now I see thou art exact of taste.
And elegant, of sapience no small part;
Since to each meaning savour we apply,
And palate call judicious; I the praise
Yield thee, so well this day thou hast purveyed.
Much pleasure we have lost, while we abstained
From this delightful fruit, nor known till now
True relish, tasting. If such pleasure be
In things to us forbidden, it might be wished,
For this one tree had been forbidden ten.
But come, so well refreshed, now let us play,
As meet is, after such delicious fare;
For never did thy beauty, since the day
I saw thee first, and wedded thee, adorned
With all perfections, so inflame my sense
With ardour to enjoy thee, fairer now
Than ever; bounty of this virtuous tree !
    So said he, and forbore not glance or toy
Of amorous intent, well understood
Of Eve, whose eye darted contagious fire.
Her hand he seized; and to a shady bank.
Thick overhead with verdant roof embowered.
He led her, nothing loth; flowers were the couch,
Pansies, and violets, and asphodel.
And hyacinth; earth's freshest, softest lap.
There they their fill of love and love's disport
Took largely, of their mutual guilt the seal,
The solace of their sin; till dewy sleep
Oppressed them, wearied with their amorous play.
    Soon as the force of that fallacious fruit,
That with exhilarating vapour bland,

About their spirits had played, and inmost powers
Made err, was now exhaled; and grosser sleep.
Bred of unkindly fumes, with conscious dreams
Encumbered, now had left them; up they rose
As from unrest, and, each the other viewing,
Soon found their eyes how opened, and their minds
How darkened. Innocence, that, as a veil.
Had shadowed them from knowing ill, was gone;
Just confidence, and native righteousness.
And honour, from about them, naked left
To guilty shame : he covered, but his robe
Uncovered more. So rose the Danite strong,
Herculean Samson, from the harlot-lap
Of Philistean Dalilah, and waked
Shorn of his strength; they, destitute and bare
Of all their virtue, silent, and in face
Confounded; long they sat, as stricken mute;
Till Adam, though not less than Eve abashed.
At length gave utterance to these words constrained:
O Eve, in evil hour thou didst give ear
To that false worm, of whomsoever taught
To counterfeit man's voice; true in our fall,
False in our promised rising; since our eyes
Opened we find, indeed, and find we know
Both good and evil; good lost, and evil got;
Bad fruit of knowledge, if this be to know,
Which leaves us naked thus, of honour void.
Of innocence, of faith, of purity,
Our wonted ornaments now soiled and stained,
And in our faces evident the signs
Of foul concupiscence; whence evil store;
Even shame, the last of evils; of the first
Be sure then. How shall I behold the face
Henceforth of God or Angel, erst with joy
And rapture so oft beheld ? Those heavenly shapes
Will dazzle now this earthly, with their blaze

Insufferably bright. O ! might I here
In solitude live savage, in some glade
Obscured, where highest woods, impenetrable
To star or sun light, spread their umbrage broad
And brown as evening ! Cover me, ye pines !
Ye cedars, with innumerable boughs
Hide me, where I may never see them more !
But let us now, as in bad plight, devise
What best may, for the present, serve to hide
The parts of each from other, that seem most
To shame obnoxious, and unseemliest seen.
Some tree, whose broad smooth leaves, together sewed,
And girded on our loins, may cover round
Those middle parts; that this new-comer. Shame,
There sit not, and reproach us as unclean.
So counselled he, and both together went
Into the thickest wood; there soon they chose
The fig-tree, not that kind for fruit renowned.
But such as, at this day, to Indians known,
In Malabar or Decan spreads her arms,
Branching so broad and long, that in the ground
The bended twigs take root, and daughters grow
About the mother-tree, a pillared shade,
High over-arched, and echoing walks between;
There oft the Indian herdsman, shunning heat,
Shelters in cool, and tends his pasturing herds
At loop-holes cut through thickest shade. Those leave
They gathered, broad as Amazonian targe,
And, with what skill they had, together sewed,
To gird their waist : vain covering, if to hide
Their guilt and dreaded shame ! Oh, how unlike
To that first naked glory ! Such, of late,
Columbus found the American, so girt
With feather'd cincture; naked else, and wild
Among the trees on isles and woody shores.
Thus fenced, and, as they thought, their shame in part

Covered, but not at rest or ease of mind,
They sat them down to weep. Nor only tears
Rained at their eyes, but high winds worse within
Began to rise; high passions, anger, hate,
Mistrust, suspicion, discord, and shook sore
Their inward state of mind, calm region once.
And full of peace, now tost and turbulent.
For understanding ruled not, and the will
Heard not her lore; both in subjection now
To sensual appetite, who, from beneath,
Usurping over sovereign reason, claimed
Superior sway. From thus distempered breast,
Adam, estranged in look and altered style,
Speech intermitted thus to Eve renewed :

Would thou hadst hearkened to my words, and stayed
With me, as I besought thee, when that strange
Desire of wandering, this unhappy morn,
I know not whence possessed thee; we had then
Remained still happy; not as now, despoiled
Of all our good; shamed, naked, miserable!
Let none henceforth seek needless cause to approve
The faith they owe; when earnestly they seek
Such proof, conclude they then begin to fail.

To whom, soon moved with touch of blame, thus Eve:
What words have passed thy lips, Adam, severe ?
Imputest thou that to my default, or will
Of wandering, as thou callest it, which who knows
But might as ill have happened thou being by.
Or to thyself, perhaps? Hadst thou been there,.
Or here the attempt, thou couldst not have discerned
Fraud in the serpent, speaking as he spake;
No ground of enmity between us known,
Why he should mean me ill, or seek to harm.
Was I to have never parted from thy side ?
As good have grown there still, a lifeless rib.
Being as I am, why didst not thou, the head,

Command me absolutely not to go.
Going into such danger, as thou saidst ?
Too facile, then, thou didst not much gainsay :
Nay, didst permit, approve, and fair dismiss.
Hadst thou been firm and fixed in thy dissent,
Neither had I transgressed, nor thou with me.
    To whom, then first incensed, Adam replied
Is this the love, is this the recompense
Of mine to thee, ingrateful Eve, expressed
Immutable when thou wert lost, not I;
Who might have lived, and joyed immortal bliss.
Yet willingly chose rather death with thee ?
And am I now upbraided as the cause
Of thy transgressing ? Not enough severe,
It seems, in my restraint : what could I more ?
I warned thee, I admonished thee, foretold
The danger, and the lurking Enemy
That lay in wait; beyond this had been force,
And force upon free-will hath here no place.
But confidence then bore thee on; secure
Either to meet no danger, or to find
Matter of glorious trial; and, perhaps,
I also erred in overmuch admiring
What seemed in thee so perfect, that I thought
No evil durst attempt thee. But I rue
That error now, which is become my crime,
And thou the accuser. Thus it shall befall
Him who, to worth in woman overtrusting.
Lets her will rule : restraint she will not brook :
And left to herself, if evil thence ensue.
She first his weak indulgence will accuse.
    Thus they in mutual accusation spent
The fruitless hours, but neither self-condemning;
And of their vain contest appeared no end.

BOOK - X

Man's transgression known, the guardian angels forsake Paradise, and return up to heaven to approve their vigilance, and are approved; God declaring that the entrance of Satan could not be by them prevented. He sends His Son to judge the transgressors; who descends, and gives sentence accordingly; then, in pity, clothes them both, and re-ascends. Sin and Death, sitting till then at the gates of hell, by wondrous sympathy feeling the success of Satan in this new world, and the sin by man there committed, resolve to sit no longer confined in hell, but to follow Satan, Sheir sire, up to the place of man. To make the way easier from hell to this world to and fro, they pave a broad highway or bridge over Chaos, according to the track that Satan first made; then, preparing for earth, they meet him, proud of his success, returning to hell; their mutual gratulation. Satan arrives at Pandemonium; in full assembly relates, with boasting, his success against man; instead of applause is entertained wilh a general hiss by all his audience, transformed, with himself also, suddenly into serpents, according to his doom given in Paradise; then, deluded with a show of the forbidden tree springing up before them, they, greedily reaching to take of the fruit, chew dust and bitter ashes. The proceedings of Sin and Death; God foretells the final victory of His Son over them, and the renewing of all things; but, for the present, commands His angels to make several alterations in the heavens and elements. Adam, more and more perceiving his fallen condition, heavily bewails, rejects the condolement of Eve; she persists, and at length appeases him : then, to evade the curse likely to fall on their offspring, proposes to Adam violent ways, which he approves not; but, conceiving better hope, puts her in mind of the late promise made them, that her seed should be revenged on the serpent; and exhorts her, with him, to seek peace of the offended Deity, by renpntance and supplication.

Meanwhile the heinous and despiteful act
Of Satan done in Paradise; and how
He, in the serpent, had perverted Eve,
Her husband she, to taste the fatal fruit.

Was known in heaven – for what can 'scape the eye
Of God all-seeing, or deceive His heart
Omniscient ? who, in all things wise and just,
Hindered not Satan to attempt the mind
Of man, widi strength entire, and free-will armed
Complete to have discovered and repulsed
Whatever wiles of foe or seeming friend.
For still they knew, and ought to have still remembered.
The high injunction, not to taste that fruit.
Whoever tempted; which they, not obeying,
Incurred – what could they less? – the penalty;
And manifold in sin, deserved to fall.
Up into heaven from Paradise, in haste,
The Angelic guards ascended, mute and sad,
For Man; for of his state by this they knew,
Much wondering how the subtle Fiend had stolen
Entrance unseen. Soon as the unwelcome news
From earth arrived at heaven-gate, displeased
All were who heard; dim sadness did not spare
That time celestial visages, yet, mixed
With pity, violated not their bliss.
About the new-arrived, in multitudes,
The ethereal people ran, to hear and know
How all befell. They, towards the throne supreme,
Accountable, made haste, to make appear.
With righteous plea, their utmost vigilance.
And easily approved; when the Most High,
Eternal Father, from his secret cloud
Amidst, in thunder uttered thus his voice :

Assembled Angels, and ye Powers returned
From unsuccessful charge, be not dismayed.
Nor troubled at these tidings from the Earth,
Which your sincerest care could not prevent;
Foretold so lately what would come to pass,
When first this tempter crossed the gulf from hell.
I told ye then he should prevail, and speed

On his bad errand; man should be seduced.
And flattered out of all, believing lies
Against his Maker; no decree of mine
Concurring to necessitate his fall,
Or touch with lightest moment of impulse
His free-will, to her own inclining left
In even scale. But fallen he is; and now
What rests, but that the mortal sentence pass
On his transgression, death denounced that day?
Which he presumes already vain and void,
Because not yet inflicted, as he feared,
By some immediate stroke; but soon shall find
Forbearance no acquittance, ere day end.
Justice shall not return, as bounty, scorned.
But whom send I to judge them ? Whom but Thee,
Vicegerent Son ? To thee I have transferred
All judgment, whether in Heaven, or Earth, or Hell.
Easy it may be seen that I intend
Mercy colleague with justice, sending Thee,
Man's Friend, his Mediator, his designed
Both Ransom and Redeemer voluntary,
And, destined Man himself, to judge man fallen.
 So spake the Father; and, unfolding bright
Toward the right hand his glory, on the Son
Blazed forth unclouded deity : He full
Resplendent all his Father manifest
Expressed, and thus divinely answered mild :
 Father Eternal, thine is to decree;
Mine, both in heaven and earth, to do thy will
Supreme; that thou in me, thy Son beloved,
Mayest ever rest well pleased. I go to judge
On earth these thy transgressors; but thou knowst,
Whoever judged, the worst on me must light,
When time shall be; for so I undertook
Before Thee; and, not repenting, this obtain
Of right, that I may mitigate their doom

On me derived; yet I shall temper so
Justice with mercy, as may illustrate most
Them fully satisfied, and thee appease.
Attendance none shall need, nor train, where none
Are to behold the judgment, but the judged.
Those two : the third, best absent, is condemned.
Convict by flight, and rebel to all law :
Conviction to the serpent none belongs.
Thus saying, from his radiant seat he rose
Of high collateral glory. Him, Thrones and Powers,
Princedoms, and Dominations ministrant,
Accompanied to Heaven-gate; from whence
Eden, and all the coast, in prospect lay.
Down he descended straight; the speed of Gods
Time counts not, though with swiftest minutes winged.
Now was the sun in western cadence low
From noon and gentle airs, due at their hour,
To fan the earth, now waked, and usher in
The evening cool; when He, from wrath more cool,
Came, the mild judge and intercessor both,
To sentence Man. The voice of God they heard
Now walking in the garden, by soft winds
Brought to their ears, while day declined. They heard,
And from His presence hid themselves among
The thickest trees, both man and wife; till God,
Approachmg, thus to Adam called aloud :
Where art thou, Adam, wont with joy to meet
My coming, seen far off ? I miss thee here,
Not pleased, thus entertained with solitude.
Where obvious duty erewhile appeared unsought :
Or come I less conspicuous, or what change
Absents thee, or what chance detains ? Come forth !
He came, and with him. Eve, more loath, though first
To offend; discountenanced both, and discomposed;
Love was not in their looks, either to God,
Or to each other; but apparent guilt,

And shame, and perturbation, and despair;
Anger, and obstinacy, and hate, and guile.
Whence Adam, faltering long, thus answered brief:
I heard thee in the garden, and of thy voice
Afraid, being naked, hid myself To whom
The gracious judge, without revile, replied :
My voice thou oft hast heard, and hast not feared,
But still rejoiced; how is it now become
So dreadful to thee ? That thou art naked, who
Hath told thee ? Hast thou eaten of the tree
Whereof I gave thee charge thou shouldst not eat ?
To whom thus Adam, sore beset, replied :
O Heaven! in evil strait this day I stand
Before my judge; either to undergo
Myself the total crime, or to accuse
My other self, the partner of my life;
Whose failing, while her faith to me remains,
I should conceal, and not expose to blame.
By my complaint; but strict necessity
Subdues me, and calamitous constraint,
Lest on my head both sin and punishment,
However insupportable, be all
Devolved; though, should I hold my peace, yet thou
Wouldst easily detect what I conceal.
This woman, whom thou madest to be my help.
And gavest me as thy perfect gift, so good,
So fit, so acceptable, so divine,
That from her hand I could suspect no ill,
And what she did, whatever in itself,
Her doing seemed to justify the deed;
She gave me of the tree, and I did eat.
To whom the sovereign Presence thus replied:
Was she thy God, that her thou didst obey
Before His voice ? Or was she made thy guide,
Superior, or but equal, that to her
Thou didst resign thy manhood, and the place

Wherein God set thee above her, made of thee,
And for thee, whose perfection far excelled
Hers in all real dignity ? Adorned
She was, indeed, and lovely, to attract
Thy love, not thy subjection; and her gifts
Were such as under government well seemed.
Unseemly to bear rule, which was thy part
And person, hadst thou known thyself aright.
So having said, he thus to Eve in few:[1]
Say, woman, what is this which thou hast done ?
To whom sad Eve, with shame nigh overwhelmed,
Confessing soon, yet not before her judge
Bold or loquacious, thus abashed replied :
The serpent me beguiled, and I did eat.
Which when the Lord God heard, without delay
To judgment he proceeded on the accused
Serpent, though brute, unable to transfer
The guilt on him who made him instrument
Of mischief, and polluted from the end
Of his creation; justly then accursed,
As vitiated in nature. More to know
Concerned not man – since he no further knew –
Nor altered his offence. Yet God at last
To Satan, first in sin, his doom applied,
Though in mysterious terms, judged as then best;
And on the serpent thus his curse let fall :
Because thou hast[2] done this, thou art accursed
Above all cattle, each beast of the field;
Upon thy belly grovelling thou shalt go,
And dust shalt eat all the days of thy life.
Between thee and the woman I will put
Enmity, and between thine and her seed;
Her seed shall bruise thy head, thou bruise his heel.
So spake this oracle, then verified.

1. *Thus to Eve in few.*– In few words.

2. *Because thou hast.*–Gen iii. 14, 15.

When Jesus, Son of Mary, second Eve,
Saw Satan fall, like lightning down from heaven,
Prince of the air; then, rising from his grave,
Spoiled Principalities and Powers, triumphed
In open show; and, with ascension bright,
Captivity led captive through the air,
The realm itself of Satan, long usurped;
Whom He shall tread at last under our feet,
Even He, who now foretold his fatal bruise.
And to the woman thus his sentence turned :
    Thy sorrow I will greatly multiply
By thy conception; children thou shalt bring
In sorrow forth; and to thy husband's will
Thine shall submit, he over thee shall rule.
    On Adam last thus judgment he pronounced :
Because thou hast hearkened to the voice of thy wife,
And eaten of the tree concerning which
I charged thee, saying, Thou shalt not eat thereof.
Cursed is the ground for thy sake; thou in sorrow
Shalt eat thereof all the days of thy life;
Thorns, also, and thistles, it shall bring thee forth,
Unbid, and thou shalt eat the herb of the field;
In the sweat of thy face shalt thou eat bread.
Till thou return unto the ground; for thou
Out of the earth wast taken, know thy birth,
For dust thou art, and shalt to dust return.[1]
    So judged he man, both Judge and Saviour sent.
And the instant stroke of death, denounced that day,
Removed far off. Then pitying how they stood
Before him, naked to the air, that now
Must suffer change, disdained not to begin
Thenceforth the form of servant to assume;
As when he washed his servants' feet; so now
As Father of his family, he clad
Their nakedness with skins of beasts, or slain.

1. *To dust return.*–Gen. iii. 15–19.

Or, as the snake, with youthful coat repaid.
And thought not much to clothe his enemies.
Nor he their outward only with the skins
Of beasts, but inward nakedness, much more
Opprobrious, with his robe of righteousness
Arraying, covered from his Father's sight.
To Him, with swift ascent, he up returned,
Into his blissful bosom reassumed.
In glory, as of old; to Him, appeased.
All, though all-knowing, what had passed with Man
Recounted, mixing intercession sweet
    Meanwhile, ere thus was sinned and judged on earth,
Within the gates of hell sat Sin and Death,
In counterview within the gates, that now
Stood open wide, belching outrageous flame
Far into Chaos, since the Fiend passed through,
Sin opening; who thus now to Death began :
    O son, why sit we here, each other viewing
Idly, while Satan, our great author, thrives
In other worlds, and happier seat provides
For us, his offspring dear ? It cannot be
But that success attends him; if mishap,
Ere this he had returned, with fury driven
By his avengers; since no place like this
Can fit his punishment, or their revenge.
Methinks I feel new strength within me rise,
Wings growing, and dominion given me large,
Beyond this deep; whatever draws me on,
Or sympathy, or some connatural force.
Powerful at greatest distance to unite.
With secret amity, things of like kind.
By secretest conveyance. Thou, my shade
Inseparable, must with me along.
For Death from Sin no power can separate.
But lest the difficulty of passing back
Stay his return, perhaps, over this gulf

Impassable, impervious, let us try
Adventurous work, yet to thy power and mine
Not unagreeable, to found a path
Over this main from Hell to that new World,
Where Satan now prevails; a monument
Of merit high to all the infernal host,
Easing their passage hence, for intercourse,
Or transmigration, as their lot shall lead,
Nor can I miss the way, so strongly drawn
By this new-felt attraction and instinct.
    Whom thus the meagre shadow answered soon :
Go, whither fate, and inclination strong.
Lead thee; I shall not lag behind, nor err
The way, thou leading; such a scent I draw
Of carnage, prey innumerable, and taste
The savour of death from all things there that live;
Nor shall I to the work thou enterprisest
Be wanting, but afford thee equal aid.
    So saying, with delight he snuffed the smell
Of mortal change on earth. As when a flock
Of ravenous fowl, though many a league remote,
Against the day of battle, to a field,
Where armies lie encamped, come flying, lured
With scent of living carcases designed
For death the following day, in bloody fight;
So scented the grim feature, and upturned
His nostril wide into the murky air,
Sagacious of his quarry from so far.
Then both, from out Hell gates, into the waste
Wide anarchy of Chaos, damp and dark,
Flew diverse; and with power – their power was great–
Hovering upon the waters, what they met,
Solid or slimy, as in raging sea
Tossed up and down, together crowded drove,
From each side shoaling towards the mouth of Hell:–
As when two polar winds, blowing adverse

Upon the Cronian sea,[1] together drive
Mountains of ice, that stop the imagined way
Beyond Petsora[2] eastward, to the rich
Cathaian coast.[3] The aggregated soil.
Death, with his mace petrific, cold and dry,
As with a trident smote, and fixed as firm
As Delos, floating once;[4] the rest his look
Bound with Gorgonian rigour[5] not to move;
And with asphaltic slime, broad as the gate,
Deep to the roots of Hell the gathered beach
They fastened, and the mole immense wrought on,
Over the foaming Deep, high-arched, a bridge
Of length prodigious, joining to the wall
Immovable of this now fenceless world.
Forfeit to Death; from hence a passage broad,
Smooth, easy, inoffensive, down to hell.
So, if great things to small may be compared,
Xerxes, the liberty of Greece to yoke.
From Susa, his Memnonian palace high.
Came to the sea, and, over Hellespont
Bridging his way, Europe with Asia joined,
And scourged with many a stroke the indignant waves.
Now had they brought the work by wondrous art
Pontifical, a ridge of pendent rock.
Over the vexed abyss, following the track
Of Satan to the self-same place where he
First lighted from his wing, and landed safe
From out of Chaos, to the outside bare
Of this round world. With pins of adamant

1. *Cronian sea.*–Name given to the Polar Seas.
2. *Petsora.*–A river descending to the Arctic Sea from the Ural mountains.
3. *Cathaian coast.*–China.
4. *As Delos, floating once*–One of the Cyclades group of islands, in the Ægean Sea, which was said to have been a floating island, until Jupiter chained it to the bottom of the sea.
5. *Gorgonian rigour.*–See Book II., line 611, and Note 3.

And chains they made all fast, too fast they made
And durable ! And now in little space
The confines met of empyrean heaven
And of this world; and, on the left hand hell
With long reach interposed; three several ways
In sight, to each of these three places led.
And now their way to earth they had descried,
To Paradise first tending; when, behold !
Satan, in likeness of an angel bright.
Betwixt the Centaur and the Scorpion[1] steering
His zenith, while the sun in Aries rose,
Disguised he came; but those his children dear
Their parent soon discerned, though in disguise.
He, after Eve seduced, unminded slunk
Into the wood fast by; and changing shape
To observe the sequel, saw his guileful act,
By Eve, though all unweeting, seconded
Upon her husband; saw their shame that sought
Vain covertures. But when he saw descend
The Son of God to judge them, terrified
He fled; not hoping to escape, but shun
The present; fearing, guilty, what His wrath
Might suddenly inflict; that past, returned
By night, and listening where the hapless pair
Sat in their sad discourse, and various plaint,
Thence gathered his own doom; which understood
Not instant, but of future time, with joy
And tidings fraught, to hell he now returned,
And at the brink of Chaos, near the foot
Of this new wondrous pontifice, unhoped
Met, who to meet him came, his offspring dear.
Great joy was at their meeting, and at sight
Of that stupendous bridge his joy increased.
Long he admiring stood, till Sin, his fair
Enchanting daughter, thus the silence broke :

---

1. *Centaur, Scorpion, Aries.*–Signs in the Zodiac.

O Parent, these are thy magnific deeds,
Thy trophies ! which thou view'st as not thine own;
Thou art their author, and prime architect;
For I no sooner in my heart divined –
My heart, which by a secret harmony
Still moves with thine, joined in connection sweet –
That thou on earth hadst prospered, which thy looks
Now also evidence, but straight I felt.
Though distant from thee worlds between, yet felt
That I must after thee, with this thy son;
Such fatal consequence unites us three.
Hell could no longer hold us in her bounds,
Nor this unvoyageable gulf obscure
Detain from following thy illustrious track.
Thou hast achieved our liberty, confined
Within Hell-gates till now; thou us empowered
To fortify thus far, and overlay.
With this portentous bridge, the dark abyss.
Thine now is all this world; thy virtue hath won
What thy hands builded not; thy wisdom gained,
With odds, what war hath lost, and fully avenged
Our foil in heaven. Here thou shalt monarch reign,
There didst not. There let Him still victor sway.
As battle hath adjudged; from this new world
Retiring, by his own doom alienated,
And henceforth monarchy with thee divide
Of all things, parted by the empyreal bounds,
His quadrature, from thy orbicular world;
Or try thee now more dangerous to his throne.
Whom thus the Prince of Darkness answered glad
Fair daughter, and thou son and grandchild both;
High proof ye now have given to be the race
Of Satan – for I glory in the name,
Antagonist of heaven's Almighty King –
Amply have merited of me, of all
The infernal empire, that so near heaven's door

Triumphal with triumphal act have met.
Mine, with this glorious work, and made one realm.
Hell and this world, one realm, one continent
Of easy thoroughfare. Therefore – while I
Descend through darkness, on your road, with ease,
To my associate Powers, them to acquaint
With these successes, and with them rejoice –
You two this way, among these numerous orbs,
All yours, right down to Paradise descend;
There dwell, and reign in bliss : thence on the earth
Dominion exercise, and in the air.
Chiefly on Man, sole lord of all declared.
Him first make sure your thrall, and lastly kill.
My substitutes I send ye, and create
Plenipotent on earth, of matchless might
Issuing from me. On your joint vigour now,
My hold of this new kingdom all depends,
Through Sin to Death exposed by my exploit.
If your joint power prevail, the affairs of hell
No detriment need fear; go, and be strong.
So saying, he dismissed them. They with speed
Their course through thickest constellations held,
Spreading their bane; the blasted stars looked wan;
And planets, planet-struck, real eclipse
Then suffered. The other way Satan went down
The causey to hell-gate. On either side
Disparted Chaos overbuilt exclaimed,[1]
And with rebounding surge the bars assailed,
That scorned his indignation. Through the gate,
Wide open and unguarded, Satan passed,
And all about found desolate; for those,
Appointed to sit there, had left their charge,
Flown to the upper world; the rest were all
Far to the inland retired, about the walls

1. *Exclaimed.*–"Deep calling unto deep." (Ps. xlii. 7.)

Of Pandemonium, city and proud seat
Of Lucifer, so by allusion called
Of that bright star to Satan paragoned:[1]
There kept their watch the legions, while the grand
In council sat, solicitous what chance
Might intercept their emperor sent; so he.
Departing, gave command, and they observed.
As when the Tartar, from his Russian foe,
By Astracan, over the snowy plains
Retires; or Bactrian Sophi, from the horns
Of Turkish crescent, leaves all waste beyond
The realm of Aladule, in his retreat
To Tauris or Casbeen : so these, the late
Heaven-banished host, left desert utmost hell
Many a dark league, reduced in careful watch[2]
Round their metropolis, and now expecting
Each hour their great adventurer, from the search
Of foreign worlds. He through the midst, unmarked,
In show plebeian angel militant
Of lowest order, passed; and from the door
Of that Plutonian hall, invisible
Ascended his high throne, which, under state
Of richest texture spread, at the upper end
Was placed in regal lustre. Down a while
He sat, and round about him saw, unseen.
At last, as from a cloud, his fulgent head
And shape star-bright appeared, or brighter, clad
With what permissive glory since his fall
Was left him, or false glitter. All amazed
At that so sudden blaze, the Stygian throng
Bent their aspect, and whom they wished beheld,
Their mighty chief returned. Loud was the acclaim;
Forth rushed in haste the great consulting peers,
Raised from their dark divan, and with like joy

1. *Paragoned.*–Compared, equalled.
2. *Reduced in careful watch.*–Contracted, drawn in.

Congratulant approached him, who with hand
Silence, and with these words, attention won :
Thrones, Dominations, Princedoms, Virtues, Powers !
For in possession such, not only of right,
I call ye, and declare ye now, returned
Successful beyond hope, to lead ye forth
Triumphant out of this infernal pit.
Abominable, accursed, the house of woe,
And dungeon of our tyrant – now possess,
As lords, a spacious world, to our native heaven
Little inferior, by my adventure hard.
With peril great, achieved. Long were to tell
What I have done, what suffered; with what pain
Voyaged the unreal, vast, unbounded Deep
Of horrible confusion; over which.
By Sin and Death, a broad way now is paved,
To expedite your glorious march; but I
Toiled out my uncouth passage, forced to ride
The untractable Abyss, plunged in the womb
Of unoriginal Night and Chaos wild.
That, jealous of their secrets, fiercely opposed
My journey strange, with clamorous uproar
Protesting fate supreme; thence, how I found
The new-created world, which fame in heaven
Long had foretold; a fabric wonderful,
Of absolute perfection; therein man,
Placed in a Paradise, by our exile
Made happy. Him by fraud I have seduced
From his Creator; and, the more to increase
Your wonder, with an apple. He, thereat
Offended – worth your laughter – hath given up
Both his beloved Man and all this world,
To Sin and Death a prey, and so to us.
Without our hazard, labour, or alarm.
To range in, and to dwell, and over man
To rule as over all He should have ruled.

True is, me also he hath judged, or rather
Me not, but the brute serpent, in whose shape
Man I deceived. That which to me belongs
Is enmity, which he will put between
Me and mankind. I am to bruise his heel;
His seed, when is not set, shall bruise my head.
A world who would not purchase with a bruise.
Or much more grievous pain ? Ye have the account
Of my performance. What remains, ye gods.
But up, and enter now into full bliss ?
So having said, awhile he stood, expecting
Their universal shout, and high applause,
To fill his ear; when, contrary, he hears,
On all sides, from innumerable tongues,
A dismal universal hiss, the sound
Of public scorn. He wondered, but not long
Had leisure, wondering at himself now more.
His visage drawn he felt to sharp and spare,
His arms clung to his ribs, his legs entwining
Each other, till, supplanted, down he fell
A monstrous serpent, on his belly prone.
Reluctant, but in vain;[1] a greater Power
Now ruled him, punished in the shape he sinned,
According to his doom. He would have spoke,
But hiss for hiss returned with forked tongue
To forked tongue. For now were all transformed
Alike, to serpents all, as accessories
To his bold riot. Dreadful was the din
Of hissing; through the hall, thick-swarming: now
With complicated monsters,[2] head and tail.
Scorpion, and Asp, and Amphisbæna dire.

---

1. *Reluctant, but in vain.*–Unwilling to move on the belly prone, but forced to do so.
2. *Complicated monsters.*–The "scorpion" mentioned among these "monsters" was not a serpent; the remainder are all mentioned by Lucan, Pliny, and other ancient writers.

Cerastes horned, Hydrus, and Ellops drear.
And Dipsas – not so thick swarmed once the soil
Bedropt with blood of Gorgon, or the isle
Ophiusa– but still greatest he the midst,
Now Dragon grown, larger than whom the sun
Ingendered in the Pythian vale on slime,
Huge Python,[1] and his power no less he seemed
Above the rest still to retain. They all
Him followed, issuing forth to the open field,
Where all yet left of that revolted rout.
Heaven-fallen, in station stood, or just array,
Sublime with expectation when to see
In triumph issuing forth their glorious chief
They saw, but other sight instead – a crowd
Of ugly serpents ! Horror on them fell.
And horrid sympathy – for, what they saw,
They felt themselves now changing. Down their arms,
Down fell both spear and shield; down they as fast,
And the dire hiss renewed, and the dire form
Catched, by contagion, like in punishment.
As in their crime. Thus the applause they meant,
Turned to exploding hiss, triumph to shame,
Cast on themselves from their own mouths. There stood
A grove hard by, sprung up with this their change,
His will who reigns above, to aggravate
Their penance, laden with fair fruit, like that
Which grew in Paradise, the bait of Eve
Used by the tempter. On that prospect strange
Their earnest eyes they fixed, imagining
For one forbidden tree a multitude
Now risen, to work them further woe or shame.
Yet, parched with scalding thirst and hunger fierce,
Though to delude them sent, could not abstain;
But on they rolled in heaps, and up the trees

1. *Huge Python.*–The great serpent said to have come from the slime left by the deluge in the time of Deucalion.

Climbing, sat thicker than the snaky locks
That curled Megæra.[1] Greedily they plucked
The fruitage fair to sight, like that which grew
Near, that bituminous lake where Sodom flamed;
This more delusive, not the touch, but taste
Deceived. They, fondly thinking to allay
Their appetite with gust, instead of fruit
Chewed bitter ashes, which the offended taste
With spattering noise rejected. Oft they assayed,
Hunger and thirst constraining; drugged as oft,
With hatefulest disrelish writhed their jaws.
With soot and cinders filled; so oft they fell
Into the same illusion, not as Man
Whom they triumphed once lapsed. Thus were they plagued,
And worn with famine, long and ceaseless hiss,
Till their lost shape, permitted, they resumed,
Yearly enjoined, some say, to undergo
This annual humbling, certain numbered days,
To dash their pride, and joy for man seduced.
However, some tradition they dispersed
Among the heathen, of their purchase got,
And fabled how the serpent, whom they called
Ophion,[2] with Eurynome, the wide-
Encroaching Eve, perhaps, had first the rule
Of high Olympus, thence by Saturn driven
And Ops, ere yet Dictæan Jove was born.
    Meanwhile in Paradise the hellish pair
Too soon arrived; Sin, there in power before,
Once actual; now in body, and to dwell
Habitual habitant; behind her, Death,
Close following pace for pace, not mounted yet

1. *Snaky locks that curled Megæra.*–A name given to the avenging deities–the Furies.

2. *Ophion* in Greek signifies a serpent, and Milton supposes the old Serpent may have been worshipped under that name. The reference to Eurynome and Eve is obscure, but it points, beyond doubt, to the element of ambition in Eve's fall.

On his pale horse : to whom Sin thus began :
Second of Satan sprung, all-conquering Death !
What thinkest thou of our empire now, though earned
With travail difficult ? Not better far
Than still at Hell's dark threshold to have sat watch,
Unnamed, undreaded, and thyself half-starved ?
Whom thus the sin-born monster answered soon :
To me, who with eternal famine pine.
Alike is Hell, or Paradise, or Heaven;
There best, where most with ravine I may meet.
Which here, though plenteous, all too little seems
To stuff this maw, this vast un-hide-bound[1] corpse.
To whom the incestuous mother thus replied :
Thou, therefore, on these herbs, and fruits, and flowers.
Feed first; on each beast next, and fish, and fowl.
No homely morsels; and whatever thing
The scythe of Time mows down, devour unspared.
Till I, in man residing, through the race.
His thoughts, his looks, words, actions, all infect.
And season him thy last and sweetest prey.
This said, they both betook them several ways,
Both to destroy, or unimmortal make
All kinds, and for destruction to mature
Sooner or later; which the Almighty seeing,
From his transcendent seat the saints among.
To those bright Orders uttered thus his voice :
See with what heat these dogs of hell advance
To waste and havoc yonder world, which I
So fair and good created, and had still
Kept in that state, had not the folly of man
Let in these wasteful furies, who impute
Folly to me; so doth the Prince of hell
And his adherents, that with so much ease
I suffer them to enter and possess

1. *Un-hide-bound.*–A body hanging loose, wanting filling up.

A place so heavenly; and, conniving, seem
To gratify my scornful enemies.
That laugh, as if, transported with some fit
Of passion, I to them had quitted all,
At random yielded up to their misrule;
And know not that I called, and drew them thither,
My hell-hounds, to lick up the draff and filth
Which man's polluting sin with taint hath shed
On what was pure; till, crammed and gorged, nigh burst
With sucked and glutted offal, at one sling
Of thy victorious arm, well-pleasing Son,
Both Sin and Death, and yawning grave, at last.
Through Chaos hurled, obstruct the mouth of hell
For ever, and seal up his ravenous jaws.
Then Heaven and Earth, renewed, shall be made pure
To sanctity, that shall receive no stain :
Till then, the curse pronounced on both precedes.
He ended, and the heavenly audience loud
Sung hallelujah, as the sound of seas,
Through multitude that sung: Just are thy ways.
Righteous are thy decrees on all thy works;
Who can extenuate Thee ? Next, to the Son,
Destined Restorer of mankind, by whom
New heaven and earth shall to the ages rise.
Or down from heaven descend. Such was their song,
While the Creator, calling forth by name
His mighty Angels, gave them several charge,
As sorted best with present things. The sun
Had first his precept so to move, so shine,
As might affect the earth with cold and heat
Scarce tolerable, and from the north to call
Decrepit winter; from the south to bring
Solstitial summer's heat. To the blank moon
Her office they prescribed; to the other five
Their planetary motions, and aspects.
In sextile, square, and trine, and opposite,

Of noxious efficacy, and when to join
In synod unbenign;[1] and taught the fixed
Their influence malignant when to shower.
Which of them rising with the sun, or falling,
Should prove tempestuous; to the winds they set
Their corners, when with bluster to confound
Sea, air, and shore; the thunder when to roll
With terror through the dark aerial hall.
Some say. He bid his Angels turn askance
The poles of earth, twice ten degrees and more,
From the sun's axle; they with labour pushed
Oblique the centric globe. Some say, the sun
Was bid turn reins from the equinoctial road
Like distant breadth to Taurus[2] with the seven
Atlantic Sisters, and the Spartan Twins,
Up to the tropic Crab; thence down amain
By Leo, and the Virgin, and the Scales,
As deep as Capricorn, to bring in change
Of seasons to each clime, Else had the spring
Perpetual smiled on earth with vernant flowers,
Equal in days and nights, except to those
Beyond the polar circles; to them day
Had unbenighted shone, while the low sun,
To recompense his distance, in their sight
Had rounded still the horizon, and not known
Or east or west, which had forbid the snow
From cold Estotiland,[3] and south as far
Beneath Magellan.[4] At that tasted fruit,

1. *In synod unbenign.*–One of Milton's faults, even in the judgment of friendly critics, is a somewhat ostentatious display of learning. In the text the reader is favoured with something from the lore of astrology, in which the poet would seem to have been in some sense a believer.

2. *To Taurus, &c*–This passage describes the supposed relation of the Earth to the signs of the Zodiac through the changes of seasons.

3. *Estotiland.*–Greenland.

4. *Magellan.*–The Straits of Magellan.

The sun, as from Thyestean[1] banquet, turned
His course intended; else, how had the world
Inhabited, though sinless, more than now,
Avoided pinching cold and scorching heat ?
These changes in the heavens, though slow, produced
Like change on sea and land; sidereal blast.
Vapour, and mist, and exhalation hot,
Corrupt and pestilent : now, from the north
Of Norumbega, and the Samoed[2] shore.
Bursting their brazen dungeon, armed with ice,
And snow, and hail, and stormy gust and flaw,
Boreas, and Cæcias,[3] and Argestes loud,
And Thrascias, rend the woods, and seas upturn
With adverse blasts upturns them from the south
Notus, and Afer, black with thunderous clouds
From Sierra Liona; thwart of these, as fierce.
Forth rushed the Levant and the Ponent winds,
Eurus and Zephyr, with their lateral noise,
Sirocco and Libecchio. Thus began
Outrage from lifeless things; but Discord first,
Daughter of Sin, among the irrational
Death introduced, through fierce antipathy.
Beast now with beast gan war, and fowl with fowl,
And fish with fish : to graze the herb all leaving,
Devoured each other; nor stood much in awe
Of man, but fled him, or, with countenance grim,
Glared on him passing. These were, from without,
The growing miseries which Adam saw

1. *Thyestean.*–A reference to the story which describes Atreus as giving to his brother Thyestes the flesh of his sons as food. From the sight of a father feeding upon his own children the sun is said to have turned away.
2. *Norumbega.*–In northern America. *Samoed.*–In the north-east of Muscovy.
3. *Boreas, and Cæcias, &c.* 6-v.–The names which follow are names of winds, or of places where winds of an unusual soil prevail.

Already in part, though hid in gloomiest shade.
To sorrow abandoned, but worse felt within;
And in a troubled sea of passion tost.
Thus to disburden sought with sad complaint :
Oh miserable of happy ! Is this the end
Of this new glorious world, and me so late
The glory of that glory ? who now, become
Accursed of blessed, hide me from the face
Of God, whom to behold was then my height
Of happiness ! Yet well, if here would end
The misery; I deserved it, and would bear
My own deservings. But this will not serve;
All that I eat or drink, or shall beget,
Is propagated curse. Oh voice, once heard
Delightfully – Increase and multiply;
Now death to hear ! for what can I increase,
Or multiply, but curses on my head ?
Who of all ages to succeed, but, feeling
The evil on him brought by me, will curse
My head ? Ill fare our ancestor impure !
For this we may thank Adam ! but his thanks
Shall be the execration. So, besides
Mine own that bide upon me, all from me
Shall with a fierce reflux on me redound;
On me, as on their natural centre, light
Heavy, though in their place. Oh fleeting joys
Of Paradise, dear bought with lasting woes !
Did I request thee, Maker, from my clay
To mould me man ? Did I solicit thee
From darkness to promote me, or here place
In this delicious garden ? As my will
Concurred not to my being, it were but right
And equal to reduce me to my dust;
Desirous to resign, and render back,
All I received; unable to perform
Thy terms too hard, by which I was to hold

The good I sought not. To the loss of that,
Sufficient penalty, why hast thou added
The sense of endless woes ? Inexplicable
Thy justice seems. Yet, to say truth, too late
I thus contest; then should have been refused
Those terms, whatever, when they were proposed.
Thou didst accept them : wilt thou enjoy the good,
Then cavil the conditions ? and, though God
Made thee without thy leave, what if thy son
Prove disobedient; and, reproved, retort,
Wherefore didst thou beget me ? I sought it not.
Wouldst thou admit for his contempt of thee
That proud excuse ? Yet him, not thy election,
But natural necessity, begot.
God made thee of choice his own, and of his own
To serve him; thy reward was of his grace;
Thy punishment, then, justly is at his will.
Be it so, for I submit; his doom is fair,
That dust I am, and shall to dust return.
Oh, welcome hour whenever ! Why delays
His hand to execute what his decree
Fixed on this day ? Why do I overlive ?
Why am I mocked with death, and lengthened out
To deathless pain ? How gladly would I meet
Mortality, my sentence, and be earth
Insensible ! How glad would lay me down,
As in my mother's lap ! There I should rest,
And sleep secure; his dreadful voice no more
Would thunder in my ears; no fear of worse
To me, and to my offspring, would torment me
With cruel expectation. Yet one doubt
Pursues me still, lest all I cannot die;
Lest that pure breath of life – the spirit of Man
Which God inspired, cannot together perish
With this corporeal clod; then, in the grave,
Or in some other dismal place, who knows

But I shall die a living death ? Oh thought
Horrid, if true ! Yet why ? It was but breath
Of life that sinned. What dies but what had life
And sin ? The body properly hath neither.
All of me, then, shall die : let this appease
The doubt, since human reach no farther knows :
For though the Lord of all be infinite,
Is his wrath also ? Be it, man is not so,
But mortal doomed. How can he exercise
Wrath without end on man, whom death must end ?
Can he make deathless death ? That were to make
Strange contradiction, which to God himself
Impossible is held, as argument
Of weakness, not of power. Will he draw out,
For anger's sake, finite to infinite
In punished man, to satisfy his rigour,
Satisfied never ? That were to extend
His sentence beyond dust and nature's law,
By which all causes else, according still
To the reception of their matter, act,
Not to the extent of their own sphere. But say
That death be not one stroke, as I supposed,
Bereaving sense, but endless misery
From this day onward – which I feel begun
Both in me, and without me – and so last
To perpetuity : ah, me ! that fear
Comes thundering back with dreadful revolution
On my defenceless head. Both death and I
Are found eternal, and incorporate both;
Nor I on my part single; in me all
Posterity stands cursed – fair patrimony
That I must leave ye, sons ! Oh, were I able
To waste it all myself, and leave ye none !
So disinherited, how would ye bless
Me, now your curse ! Ah, why should all mankind,
For one man's fault, thus guiltless be condemned.

If guiltless ? But from me what can proceed
But all corrupt; both mind and will depraved,
Not to do only, but to will the same
With me ? How can they, then, acquitted stand
In sight of God? Him, after all disputes,
Forced I absolve : all my evasions vain.
And reasonings, though through mazes, lead me still
But to my own conviction : first and last
On me – me only, as the source and spring
Of all corruption, all the blame lights due;
So might the wrath ! Fond wish ! couldst thou support
That burden, heavier than the earth to bear –
Than all the world much heavier, though divided
With that bad woman ? Thus, what thou desirest,
And what thou fearest, alike destroys all hope
Of refuge, and concludes thee miserable
Beyond all past example and future;
To Satan only like, both crime and doom.
O conscience ! Into what abyss of fears
And horrors hast thou driven me; out of which
I find no way, from deep to deeper plunged !
Thus Adam to himself lamented loud.
Through the still night; not now, as ere man fell,
Wholesome, and cool, and mild, but with black air
Accompanied; with damps and dreadful gloom,
Which to his evil conscience represented
All things with double terror, on the ground
Outstretched he lay, on the cold ground, and oft
Cursed his creation; Death as oft accused
Of tardy execution, since denounced
The day of his offence. Why comes not Death,
Said he, with one thrice-acceptable stroke
To end me ? Shall truth fail to keep her word,
Justice divine not hasten to be just ?
But Death comes not at call; justice divine
Mends not her slowest pace for prayers or cries.

O woods, O fountains, hillocks, dales, and bowers !
With other echo late I taught your shades
To answer, and resound far other song.
Whom thus afflicted, when sad Eve beheld,
Desolate where she sat, approaching nigh,
Soft words to his fierce passion she assayed;
But her, with stern regard, he thus repelled :
    Out of my sight, thou serpent ! That name best
Befits thee, with him leagued, thyself as false
And hateful. Nothing wants, but that thy shape,
Like his, and colour serpentine, may show
Thy inward fraud, to warn all creatures from thee
Henceforth, lest that too heavenly form, pretended
To hellish falsehood, snare them ! But for thee
I had persisted happy, had not thy pride
And wandering vanity, when least was safe.
Rejected my forewarning, and disdained
Not to be trusted; longing to be seen.
Though by the Devil himself, him overweening
To over-reach; but, with the serpent meeting,
Fooled and beguiled; by him thou, I by thee,
To trust thee from my side, imagined wise.
Constant, mature, proof against all assaults;
And understood not all was but a show,
Rather than solid virtue; all but a rib
Crooked by nature, bent, as now appears,
More to the part sinister, from me drawn;
Well if thrown out, as supernumerary
To my just number found. Oh ! why did God,
Creator wise, that peopled highest heaven
With spirits masculine, create at last
This novelty on Earth, this fair defect
Of nature, and not fill the world at once
With men, as angels, without feminine;
Or find some other way to generate
Mankind ? This mischief had not then befallen,

And more that shall befall; innumerable
Disturbances on earth through female snares.
And straight conjunction with this sex : for either
He never shall find out fit mate, but such
As some misfortune brings him, or mistake;
Or whom he wishes most shall seldom gain,
Through her perverseness, but shall see her gained
By a far worse; or, if she love, withheld
By parents; or his happiest choice too late
Shall meet, already linked and wedlock-bound
To a fell adversary, his hate or shame;
Which infinite calamity shall cause
To human life, and household peace confound.
He added not, and from her turned. But Eve,
Not so repulsed, with tears that ceased not flowing,
And tresses all disordered, at his feet
Fell humble; and, embracing them, besought
His peace, and thus proceeded in her plaint:
Forsake me not thus, Adam! witness. Heaven,
What love sincere, and reverence in my heart,
I bear thee, and unweeting have offended,
Unhappily deceived! Thy suppliant,
I beg, and clasp thy knees; bereave me not,
Whereon I live, thy gentle looks, thy aid,
Thy counsel, in this uttermost distress
My only strength and stay; forlorn of thee.
Whither shall I betake me, where subsist ?
While yet we live, scarce one short hour perhaps,
Between us two let there be peace; both joining,
As joined in injuries, one enmity
Against a foe by doom express assigned us,
That cruel serpent. On me exercise not
Thy hatred for this misery befallen;
On me, already lost, me than thyself
More miserable. Both have sinned; but thou
Against God only, I against God and thee;

And to the place of judgment will return.
There with my cries importune Heaven, that all
The sentence, from thy head removed, may light
On me, sole cause to thee of all this woe;
Me – me only, just object of His ire!
    She ended, weeping; and her lowly plight.
Immovable till peace obtained from fault
Acknowledged and deplored, in Adam wrought
Commiseration. Soon his heart relented,
Towards her, his life so late, and sole delight,
Now at his feet submissive in distress;
Creature so fair his reconcilement seeking,
His counsel, whom she had displeased, his aid.
As one disarmed, his anger all he lost,
And thus with peaceful words upraised her soon :
    Unwary, and too desirous, as before,
So now, of what thou knowest not, who desirest
The punishment all on thyself; alas !
Bear thine own first, ill able to sustain
His full wrath, whose thou feelcst as yet least part,
And my displeasure bearest so ill. If prayers
Could alter high decrees, I to that place
Would speed before thee, and be louder heard,
That on my head all might be visited;
Thy frailty and infirmer sex forgiven;
To me committed, and by me exposed.
But rise; let us no more contend, nor blame
Each other, blamed enough elsewhere; but strive.
In offices of love, how we may lighten
Each other's burden, in our share of woe,
Since this day's death denounced, if aught I see.
Will prove no sudden, but a slow-paced evil –
A long day's dying to augment our pain,
And to our seed (O hapless seed !) derived.
    To whom thus Eve, recovering heart, replied : –
Adam, by sad experiment I know

How little weight my words with thee can find,
Found so erroneous, thence by just event
Found so unfortunate : nevertheless.
Restored by thee, vile as I am, to place
Of new acceptance, hopeful to regain
Thy love, the sole contentment of my heart,
Living or dying, from, thee I will not hide
What thoughts in my unquiet breast are risen,
Tending to some relief of our extremes,
Or end; though sharp and sad, yet tolerable,
As in our evils, and of easier choice.
If care of our descent perplex us most,
Which must be born to certain woe, devoured
By death at last – and miserable it is
To be to others cause of misery,
Our own begotten, and of our loins to bring
Into this cursed world a woeful race.
That, after wretched life, must be at last
Food for so foul a monster – in thy power
It lies yet, ere conception, to prevent
The race unblest, to being yet unbegot.
Childless thou art, childless remain; so Death
Shall be deceived his glut, and with us two
Be forced to satisfy his ravenous maw.
But if thou judge it hard and difficult.
Conversing, looking, loving, to abstain
From love's due rights, nuptial embraces sweet,
And, with desire, to languish without hope,
Before the present object languishing
With like desire, which would be misery
And torment less than none of what we dread,
Then, both ourselves and seed at once to free
From what we fear for both, let us make short.
Let us seek Death; or, he not found, supply
With our own hands his office on ourselves.
Why stand we longer shivering under fears

That show no end but Death; and have the power,
Of many ways to die, the shortest choosing,
Destruction with destruction to destroy ?
    She ended here, or vehement despair
Broke off the rest; so much of Death her thoughts
Had entertained, as dyed her cheeks with pale.
But Adam, with such counsel nothing swayed,
To better hopes his more attentive mind
Labouring had raised; and thus to Eve replied :
    Eve, thy contempt of life and pleasure seems
To argue in thee something more sublime
And excellent than what thy mind contemns;
But self-destruction therefore sought, refutes
That excellence thought in thee; and implies,
Not thy contempt, but anguish and regret
For loss of life and pleasure overloved.
Or if thou covet death, as utmost end
Of misery, so thinking to evade
The penalty pronounced, doubt not but God
Hath wiselier armed his vengeful ire, than so
To be forestalled; much more I fear lest death,
So snatched, will not exempt us from the pain
We are by doom to pay; rather, such acts
Of contumacy will provoke the Highest
To make death in us live. Then let us seek
Some safer resolution, which methinks
I have in view, calling to mind with heed
Part of our sentence, that thy seed shall bruise
The serpent's head – piteous amends ! unless
Be meant, whom I conjecture, our grand foe,
Satan, who, in the serpent, hath contrived
Against us this deceit – to crush his head
Would be revenge indeed ! which will be lost.
By death brought on ourselves, or childless days
Resolved, as thou proposest; so our foe
Shall 'scape his punishment ordained, and we,

Instead, shall double ours upon our heads.
No more be mentioned then, of violence
Against ourselves, and wilful barrenness
That cuts us off from hope, and savours only
Rancour and pride, impatience and despite,
Reluctance against God, and his just yoke
Laid on our necks. Remember with what mild
And gracious temper he both heard and judged,
Without wrath or reviling. We expected
Immediate dissolution, which we thought
Was meant by death that day; when, lo ! to thee
Pains only in child-bearing were foretold,
And bringing forth, soon recompensed with joy,
Fruit of thy womb. On me the curse aslope
Glanced on the ground; with labour I must earn
My bread – what harm ? Idleness had been worse;
My labour will sustain me; and, lest cold
Or heat should injure us, his timely care
Hath, unbesought, provided, and his hands
Clothed us, unworthy, pitying while he judged;
How much more, if we pray him, will his ear
Be open, and his heart to pity incline.
And teach us further by what means to shun
The inclement seasons, rain, ice, hail, and snow !
Which now the sky, with various face, begins
To show us in this mountain; while the winds
Blow moist and keen, shattering the graceful locks
Of these fair-spreading trees; which bids us seek
Some better shroud, some better warmth, to cherish
Our limbs benumbed, ere this diurnal star
Leave cold the night, how we his gathered beams
Reflected may with matter sere foment;
Or, by collision of two bodies, grind
The air attrite to fire : as late the clouds
Justling, or pushed with winds, rude in their shock.

Tine[1] the slant lightning, whose thwart flame, driven down,
Kindles the gummy bark of fir or pine,
And sends a comfortable heat from far,
Which might supply the sun : such fire to use.
And what may else be remedy or cure
To evils which our own misdeeds have wrought,
He will instruct us praying, and of grace
Beseeching him. So as we need not fear
To pass commodiously this life, sustained
By him with many comforts, till we end
In dust, our final rest and native home.
What better can we do, than, to the place
Repairing where he judged us, prostrate fall
Before him, reverent; and there confess
Humbly our faults, and pardon beg, with tears
Watering the ground, and with our sighs the air
Frequenting,[2] sent from hearts contrite, in sign
Of sorrow unfeigned, and humiliation meek ?
Undoubtedly he will relent, and turn
From his displeasure; in whose look serene,
When angry most he seemed, and most severe,
What else but favour, grace, and mercy, shone ?
    So spake our father, penitent; nor Eve
Felt less remorse : they, forthwith to the place
Repairing where he judged them, prostrate fell
Before him, reverent, and both confessed
Humbly their faults, and pardon begged, with tears
Watering the ground; and with their sighs the air
Frequenting, sent from hearts contrite, in sign
Of sorrow unfeigned, and humiliation meek.

1. *Tine.*– Kindle. Anglo-Saxon.

2. *Frequenting.*–Filling.

BOOK - XI

THE Son of God presents to His Father the prayers of our first parents now repenting, and intercedes for them : God accepts them, but declares that they must no longer abide in Paradise; sends Michael with a band of cherubim to dispossess them; but first to reveal to Adam future things: Michael's coming down. Adam shows to Eve-certain ominous signs : he discerns Michael's approach; goes out to meet him : the angel denounces their departure. Eve's lamentation. Adam pleads, but submits : the angel leads him up to a high hill; sets before him in vision what shall happen till the flood.

Thus they, in lowliest plight, repentant stood,
Praying; for from the mercy-seat above
Prevenient[1] grace descending had removed
The stony from their hearts, and made new flesh
Regenerate grow instead, that sighs now breathed
Unutterable, which the Spirit of prayer
Inspired, and winged for Heaven with speedier flight
Than loudest oratory. Yet their port
Not of mean suitors; nor important less
Seemed their petition, than when the ancient pair,
In fables old, less ancient yet than these,
Deucalion and chaste Pyrrha, to restore
The race of mankind drowned, before the shrine
Of Themis stood devout. To Heaven their prayers
F lew up, nor missed the way, by envious winds
Blown vagabond or frustrate :[2] in they passed
Dimensionless through Heavenly doors; then clad
With incense, where the golden altar fumed.
By their great Intercessor, came in sight

1. *Prevenient.*–Going before, before sought.

2. *Vagabond or frustrate.*–Not diverted or made vain.

Before the Father's throne : them the glad Son
Presenting, thus to intercede began :
    See, Father, what first-fruits on Earth are sprung
From thy implanted grace in man; these sighs
And prayers, which, in this golden censer, mixed
With incense, I, thy priest, before thee bring;
Fruits of more pleasing savour, from thy seed
Sown with contrition in his heart, than those
Which, his own hand manuring, all the trees
Of Paradise could have produced, ere fallen
From innocence. Now, therefore, bend thine ear
To supplication; hear his sighs, though mute,
Unskilful with what words to pray; let me
Interpret for him, me, his Advocate
And propitiation; all his works on me.
Good, or not good, ingraft; my merit those
Shall perfect, and for these my death shall pay.
Accept me; and, in me, from these receive
The smell of peace toward mankind; let him live
Before thee reconciled, at least his days
Numbered, though sad, till death, his doom – which I
To mitigate thus plead, not to reverse –
To better life shall yield him, where with me
All my redeemed may dwell in joy and bliss,
Made one with me, as I with thee am one.
    To whom the Father, without cloud, serene :
All thy request for Man, accepted Son,
Obtain; all thy request was my decree.
But, longer in that Paradise to dwell.
The law I gave to nature him forbids;
Those pure immortal elements that know
No gross, no unharmonious mixture foul.
Eject him, tainted now, and purge him off,
As a distemper gross, to air as gross.
And mortal food, as may dispose him best
For dissolution wrought by sin, that first
Distempered all things, and of incorrupt

Corrupted. I, at first, with two fair gifts
Created him endowed, with happiness,
And immortality; that fondly lost.
This other served but to eternise woe,
Till I provided death : so death becomes
His final remedy, and, after life,
Tried in sharp tribulation, and refined
By faith and faithful works, to second life,
Waked in the renovation of the just,
Resigns him up with heaven and earth renewed.
But let us call to synod all the blest
Through heaven's wide bounds; from them I will not hide
My judgments, how with mankind I proceed.
As how with peccant Angels late they saw.
And in their state, though firm, stood more confirmed.
He ended, and the Son gave signal high
To the bright minister that watched. He blew
His trumpet, heard in Oreb since, perhaps.
When God descended, and, perhaps, once more
To sound a general doom. The angelic blast
Filled all the regions. From their blissful bowers
Of amaranthine shade, fountain, or spring,
By the waters of life, where'er they sat
In fellowships of joy, the Sons of Light
Hasted, resorting to the summons high,
And took their seats, till, from his throne supreme,
The Almighty thus pronounced his sovereign will :
O Sons, like one of us Man is become.
To know both good and evil, since his taste
Of that defended[1] fruit; but let him boast
His knowledge of good lost, and evil got;
Happier, had it sufficed him to have known
Good by itself, and evil not at all.
He sorrows now, repents, and prays contrite,
My motions in him; longer than they move,

1. *Defended.*–Forbidden.

His heart I know how variable and vain,
Self-left. Lest, therefore, his now bolder hand
Reach also of the tree of life, and eat.
And live for ever, – dream at least to live
For ever – to remove him I decree,
And send him from the garden forth to till
The ground whence he was taken, fitter soil.
Michael, this my behest have thou in charge;
Take to thee from among the cherubim
Thy choice of flaming warriors, lest the Fiend,
Or in behalf of man, or to invade
Vacant possession, some new trouble raise.
Haste thee, and from the Paradise of God,
Without remorse, drive out the sinful pair;
From hallowed ground the unholy; and denounce
To them, and to their progeny, from thence
Perpetual banishment. Yet, lest they faint
At the sad sentence rigorously urged –
For I behold them softened, and with tears
Bewailing their excess– all terror hide.
If patiently thy bidding they obey,
Dismiss them not disconsolate; reveal
To Adam what shall come in future days,
As I shall thee enlighten; intermix
My covenant in the woman's seed renewed.
So send them forth, though sorrowing, yet in peace.
And, on the east side of the garden, place.
Where entrance up from Eden easiest climbs,
Cherubic watch; and of a sword the flame
Wide-waving, all approach far off to fright,
And guard all passage to the tree of life,
Lest Paradise a receptacle prove
To spirits foul, and all my trees their prey,
With whose stolen fruit Man once more to delude.
He ceased; and the archangelic Power prepared
For swift descent; with him the cohort bright

Of watchful Cherubim. Four faces each
Had, like a double Janus;[1] all their shape
Spangled with eyes more numerous than those
Of Argus[2] and more wakeful than to drowse,
Charmed with Arcadian pipe, the pastoral reed
Of Hermes, or his opiate rod. Meanwhile,
To re-salute the world with sacred light,
Leucothea[3] waked, and with fresh dews embalmed
The earth; when Adam and first matron Eve
Had ended now their orisons, and found
Strength added from above, new hope to spring
Out of despair, joy, but with fear yet linked;
Which thus to Eve his welcome words renewed :
　　Eve, easily may faith admit that all
The good which we enjoy from heaven descends;
But that from us aught should ascend to Heaven
So prevalent, as to concern the mind
Of God, high-blest, or to incline His will,
Hard to belief may seem; yet this will prayer,
Or one short sigh of human breath, upborne
Even to the seat of God. For since I sought
By prayer the offended Deity to appease,
Kneeled, and before him humbled all my heart,
Methought I saw him placable and mild,
Bending his ear; persuasion in me grew
That I was heard with favour; peace returned
Home to my breast, and to my memory
His promise, that thy seed shall bruise our Foe;
Which, then not minded in dismay, yet now
Assures me that the bitterness of death

1. *Double Janus.*–A favourite Roman deity, described as having two faces.

2. *Argus.*–Son of Jupiter, who had a hundred eyes; but being hushed to sleep by the pipe of Hermes (Mercury), that deity cut off his head.

3. *Leucothea.*–A Grecian divinity–a goddess of the morning and of the sea.

Is past, and we shall live. Whence, hail to thee,
Eve, rightly called Mother of all Mankind,
Mother of all things living, since by thee
Man is to live, and all things live for Man.
To whom thus Eve, with sad demeanour, meek :
Ill-worthy I such title should belong
To me, transgressor, who, for thee ordained
A help, became thy snare : to me reproach
Rather belongs, distrust, and all dispraise.
But infinite in pardon was my Judge,
That I, who first brought death on all, am graced
The source of life; next favourable thou,
Who highly thus to entitle me vouchsafest,
Far other name deserving. But the field
To labour calls us, now with sweat imposed.
Though after sleepless night; for see ! the Morn,
All unconcerned with our unrest, begins
Her rosy progress, smiling. Let us forth,
I never from thy side henceforth to stray,
Where'er our day's work lies, though now enjoined
Laborious till day droop. While here we dwell,
What can be toilsome in these pleasant walks ?
Here let us live, though in fallen state, content.
So spake, so wished, much-humbled Eve; but fate
Subscribed not. Nature first gave signs, impressed
On bird, beast, air – air suddenly eclipsed,
After short blush of morn. Nigh, in her sight.
The bird of Jove, stooped from his aery tour,
Two birds of gayest plume before him drove;
Down from a hill, the beast that reigns in woods.
First hunter then, pursued a gentle brace.
Goodliest of all the forest, hart and hind;
Direct to the eastern gate was bent their flight.
Adam observed, and, with his eye the chase
Pursuing, not unmoved, to Eve thus spake :
O Eve, some further change awaits us nigh,

Which Heaven, by these mute signs in Nature, shows
Forerunners of His purpose; or to warn
Us, haply too secure of our discharge
From penalty, because from death released
Some days; how long, and what till then our life,
Who knows ? or more than this, that we are dust,
And thither must return, and be no more ?
Why else this double object in our sight,
Of flight pursued in the air, and o'er the ground.
One way the self-same hour ? Why, in the east,
Darkness ere day's mid-course, and morning-light
More orient in yon western cloud, that draws
O'er the blue firmament a radiant white.
And slow descends with something heavenly fraught ?
He erred not; for, by this, the heavenly bands
Down from a sky of jasper lighted now
In Paradise, and on a hill made halt;
A glorious apparition, had not doubt
And carnal fear that day dimmed Adam's eye.
Not that more glorious, when the Angels met
Jacob in Mahanaim,[1] where he saw
The field pavilioned with his guardians bright;
Nor that which on the flaming mount appeared
In Dothan,[2] covered with a camp of fire.
Against the Syrian king, who, to surprise
One man, assassin-like, had levied war.
War unproclaimed. The princely hierarch
In their bright stand there left his Powers, to seize
Possession of the garden. He alone,
To find where Adam sheltered, took his way,
Not unperceived of Adam; who to Eve,
While the great visitant approached, thus spake :
Eve, now expect great tidings, which, perhaps,
Of us will soon determine, or impose

1. *Jacob in Mahanaim.*–Gen. xxxii.

2. *Dothan.*– 2 Kings vi. 13–17.

New laws to be observed; for I descry.
From yonder blazing cloud that veils the hill,
One of the heavenly host, and, by his gait.
None of the meanest; some great Potentate,
Or of the Thrones above, such majesty
Invests his coming; yet not terrible,
That I should fear, nor sociably mild.
As Raphael, that I should much confide.
But solemn and sublime; whom, not to offend.
With reverence I must meet, .and thou retire.
He ended; and the Archangel soon drew nigh,
Not in his shape celestial, but as man
Clad to meet man. Over his lucid arms
A military vest of purple flowed.
Livelier than Meliboean, or the grain
Of Sarra, worn by kings and heroes old
In time of truce: Iris had dipt the woof.
His starry helm unbuckled showed him prime
In manhood where youth ended; by his side,
As in a glistering zodiac, hung the sword,
Satan's dire dread, and in his hand the spear.
Adam bowed low. He, kingly, from his state
Inclined not, but his coming thus declared :
Adam, Heaven's high behest no preface needs
Sufficient that thy prayers are heard; and Death,
Then due by sentence when thou didst transgress,
Defeated of his seizure many days,
Given thee of grace, wherein thou mayst repent,
And one bad act with many deeds well done
Mayst cover : well may, then, thy Lord, appeased,
Redeem thee quite from Death's rapacious claim.
But longer in this Paradise to dwell
Permits not. To remove thee I am come,
And send thee from the garden forth, to till
The ground whence thou wast taken, fitter soil.
He added not; for Adam, at the news

Heart-struck, with chilling gripe of sorrow stood,
That all his senses bound : Eve, who unseen,
Yet all had heard, with audible lament
Discovered soon the place of her retire:[1]
O unexpected stroke, worse than of Death !
Must I thus leave thee, Paradise ? thus leave
Thee, native soil ! these happy walks and shades,
Fit haunt of gods ? where I had hope to spend.
Quiet, though sad, the respite of that day
That must be mortal to us both ? O flowers,
That never will in other climate grow,
My early visitation, and my last
At even, which I bred up with tender hand
From the first opening bud, and gave ye names !
Who now shall rear ye to the sun, or rank
Your tribes, and water from the ambrosial fount ?
Thee, lastly, nuptial bower, by me adorned
With what to sight or smell was sweet, from thee
How shall I part, and whither wander down
Into a lower world, to this obscure
And wild ? How shall we breathe in other air
Less pure, accustomed to immortal fruits ?
Whom thus the Angel interrupted mild:
Lament not, Eve, but patiently resign
What justly thou hast lost, nor set thy heart.
Thus over fond, on that which is not thine.
Thy going is not lonely; with thee goes
Thy husband; him to follow thou art bound;
Where he abides, think there thy native soil.
Adam, by this from the cold sudden damp
Recovering, and his scattered spirits returned,
To Michael thus his humble words addressed :
Celestial, whether among the Thrones, or named
Of them the Highest, for such of shape may seem
Prince above princes ! gently hast thou told

1. *Her retire*–Her retirement, retreat.

Thy message, which might else in telling wound,
And, in performing, end us. What besides
Of sorrow, and dejection, and despair,
Our frailty can sustain, thy tidings bring,
Departure from this happy place – our sweet
Recess, and only consolation left
Familiar to our eyes – all places else
Inhospitable appear, and desolate.
Nor knowing us, nor known : and if, by prayer
Incessant, I could hope to change the will
Of Him who all things can, I would not cease
To weary him with my assiduous cries.
But prayer against his absolute decree
No more avails than breath against the wind,
Blown stifling back on him that breathes it forth.
Therefore to His great bidding I submit.
This most afflicts me; that, departing hence,
As from His face I shall be hid, deprived
His blessed countenance. Here I could frequent.
With worship, place by place where he vouchsafed
Presence Divine, and to my sons relate,
On this mount He appeared; under this tree
Stood visible; among these pines his voice
I heard; here with Him at this fountain talked.
So many grateful altars I would rear
Of grassy turf, and pile up every stone
Of lustre from the brook, in memory
Or monument to ages, and thereon
Offer sweet-smelling gums, and fruits, and flowers.
In yonder nether world where shall I seek
His bright appearances, or footstep trace ?
For though I fled him angry, yet, recalled
To life prolonged and promised race, I now
Gladly behold though but his utmost skirts
Of glory, and far off his steps adore.
To whom thus Michael, with regard benign :

Adam, thou knowest heaven His, and all the earth;
Not this rock only. His omnipresence fills
Land, sea, and air, and every kind that lives,
Fomented by his virtual power, and warmed.
All the earth he gave thee to possess and rule,
No despicable gift. Surmise not, then.
His presence to these narrow bounds confined
Of Paradise, or Eden; this had been
Perhaps, thy capital seat, from whence had spread,
All generations, and had hither come.
From all the ends of the Earth, to celebrate
And reverence thee, their great progenitor,
But this pre-eminence thou hast lost, brought down
To dwell on even ground now with thy sons.
Yet doubt not but in valley and in plain,
God is, as here, and will be found alike
Present; and of his presence many a sign
Still following thee, still compassing thee round
With goodness and Paternal love, his face
Express, and of his steps the track divine.
Which that thou mayst believe, and be confirmed
Ere thou from hence depart, know, I am sent
To shew thee what shall come in future days
To thee, and to thy offspring; good with bad
Expect to hear, supernal grace contending
With sinfulness of men; thereby to learn
True patience, and to temper joy with fear
And pious sorrow, equally inured
By moderation either state to bear,
Prosperous or adverse. So shalt thou lead
Safest thy life, and best prepared endure
Thy mortal passage when it comes. Ascend
This hill; let Eve – for I have drenched her eyes –
Here sleep below, while thou to foresight wakest;
As once thou sleptest, while she to life was formed.
    To whom thus Adam gratefully replied :

Ascend, I follow thee, safe guide, the path
Thou leadest me; and to the hand of Heaven submit,
However chastening; to the evil turn
My obvious breast, arming to overcome
By suffering, and earn rest from labour won,
If so I may attain. So both ascend
In the visions of God. It was a hill,
Of Paradise the highest, from whose top,
The hemisphere of earth, in clearest ken,
Stretched out to the amplest reach of prospect, lay.
Not higher that hill, nor wider looking round.
Whereon, for different cause, the Tempter set
Our second Adam, in the wilderness.
To show him all Earth's kingdoms,[1] and their glory.
His eye might there command wherever stood
City of old or modern fame, the seat
Of mightiest empire, from the destined walls
Of Cambalu, seat of Cathaian[2] Cham,
And Samarcand by Oxus, Temir's[3] throne,
To Paquin, of Sinaean kings; and thence
To Agra, and Labor, of Great Mogul,
Down to the golden Chersonese;[4] or where
The Persian in Ecbatan sat, or since
In Hispahan; or where the Russian Czar
In Moscow; or the Sultan in Bizance,[5]
Turchestan-born;[6] nor could his eye not ken
The empire of Negus to his utmost port

1. *All Earth's kingdoms.*–This description is in part literal; or seems to be so; but Milton must have known that, from many causes, his readers could only regard it as a vision.
2. *Cathaian.*– Cathai was accounted the residence of the great Zinghis Khan.
3. *Temir.*–Timur Lung–Tamerlane.
4. *Golden Chersonese.*–Peninsula of Molucea.
5. *Bizance.*–Byzantium, Constantinople.
6. *Turchestan-born.*–Descended from a race whieh had migrated from Turchcstan.

Ercoco, and the less maritime kings,
Mombaza, and Quiloa, and Melind,
And Sofala – thought Ophir – to the realm
Of Congo, and Angola farthest south :
Or thence from Niger flood to Atlas mount,
The kingdoms of Almanzor, Fez and Sus,
Morocco, and Algiers, and Tremisen;
On Europe thence, and where Rome was to sway
The world. In spirit, perhaps, he also saw
Rich Mexico, the seat of Montezume,
And Cusco in Peru, the richer seat
Of Atabalipa, and yet unspoiled
Guiana, whose great city Geryon's sons
Call El Dorado.[1] But to nobler sights
Michael from Adam's eyes the film removed,
Which that false fruit, that promised clearer sight,
Had. bred; then purged with euphrasy and rue[2]
The visual nerve, for he had much to see.
And from the well of life three drops instilled.
So deep the power of these ingredients pierced,
Even to the inmost seat of mental sight,
That Adam, now enforced to close his eyes,
Sunk down, and all his spirits became entranced;
But him the gentle angel by the hand
Soon raised, and his attention thus recalled :
    Adam, now ope thine eyes, and first behold
The effects which thy original crime hath wrought
In some to spring from thee, who never touched
The excepted tree, nor with the snake conspired,
Nor sinned thy sin; yet from that sin derive
Corruption, to bring forth more violent deeds.
    His eyes he opened, and beheld a field,

1. *El Dorado.*–The country in whieh the unfortunate Raleigh had hoped to realise large wealth.

2. *Euphrasy and rue.*–Fomentations from the plants so named were supposed to be good for the sight.

Part arable and tilth, whereon were sheaves
New reaped; the other part, sheep-walks and folds;
In the midst an altar, as the landmark stood,
Rustic, of grassy sward. Thither, anon,
A sweaty reaper from his tillage brought
First-fruits, the green ear, and the yellow sheaf,
Unculled, as came to hand; a shepherd next,
More meek, came with the firstlings of his flock,
Choicest and best; then, sacrificing, laid
The inwards and their fat, with incense strewed,
On the cleft wood, and all due rites performed.
His offering soon propitious fire from heaven
Consumed with nimble glance, and grateful steam;
The other's not, for his was not sincere.
Whereat he inly raged, and, as they talked,
Smote him into the midriff with a stone
That beat out life.[1] He fell, and, deadly pale.
Groaned out his soul, with gushing blood effused.
Much at that sight was Adam in his heart
Dismayed, and thus in haste to the Angel cried :
O Teacher, some great mischief hath befallen
To that meek man, who well had sacrificed;
Is piety thus, and pure devotion, paid?
To whom Michael thus, he also moved, replied:
These two are brethren, Adam, and to come
Out of thy loins. The unjust the just hath slain,
For envy that his brother's offering found
From Heaven acceptance; but the bloody fact

1. "And Abel was a keeper of sheep, but Cain was a tiller of the ground. And in process of time it came to pass, thnt Cain brought of the fruit of the ground an offering unto the Lord. And Abel, he also brought of the firstlings of his flock, and of the fat thereof. And the Lord had respect unto Abel and to his offering : but unto Cain and to his offering he had not respect. And Cain was very wroth, and his countenance fell.…And Cain talked with Abel his brother : and it came to pass, when they were in the field, that Cain rose up against Abel his brother, and slew him." (Gen. iv. 2–8.)

Will be avenged, and the other's faith, approved,
Lose no reward, though here thou see him die,
Rolling: in dust and gore. To which our sire :
Alas ! both for the deed, and for the cause !
But have I now seen death ? Is this the way
I must return to native dust ? O sight
Of terror, foul and ugly to behold !
Horrid to think, how horrible to feel !
To whom thus Michael : Death thou hast seen
In his first shape on Man; but many shapes
Of Death, and many are the ways that lead
To his grim cave; all dismal, yet to sense
More terrible at the entrance than within.
Some, as thou sawest, by violent stroke shall die;
By fire, flood, famine; by intemperance more
In meats and drinks, which on earth shall bring
Diseases dire, of which a monstrous crew
Before thee shall appear, that thou mayst know
What misery the inabstinence of Eve
Shall bring on men. Immediately a place
Before his eyes appeared, sad, noisome, dark,
A lazar-house[1] it seemed, wherein were laid
Numbers of all diseased; all maladies
Of ghastly spasm, or racking torture, qualms
Of heart-sick agony, all feverous kinds,
Convulsions, epilepsies, fierce catarrhs,
Intestine stone and ulcer, cholic pangs,
Demoniac frenzy, moping melancholy.
And moon-struck madness, pining atrophy,[2]
Marasmus,[3] and wide-wasting pestilence,
Dropsies, and asthmas, and joint-racking rheums,
Dire was the tossing, deep the groans. Despair

1. *A lazar-house.*–A hospital.
2. *Atrophy.*–When a body wastes away from disease in the digestive organs.
3. *Marasmus.*–Consumption.

Tended the sick, busiest from couch to couch;
And over them triumphant Death his dart
Shook, but delayed to strike, though oft invoked
With vows, as their chief good, and final hope.
Sight so deform what heart of rock could long
Dry-eyed behold ? Adam could not, but wept.
Though not of woman born; compassion quelled
His best of man, and gave him up to tears
A space, till firmer thoughts restrained excess;
And, scarce recovering words, his plaint renewed :
    O miserable mankind, to what fall
Degraded, to what wretched state reserved !
Better end here unborn. Why is life given
To be thus wrested from us ? Rather, why
Obtruded on us thus ? who, if we knew
What we receive, would either not accept
Life offered, or soon beg to lay it down,
Glad to be so dismissed in peace. Can thus
The image ot God in man, created once
So goodly and erect, though faulty since.
To such unsightly sufferings be debased
Under inhuman pains ? Why should not man.
Retaining still Divine similitude
In part, from such deformities be free,
And, for his Maker's image sake, exempt
    Their Maker's image, answered Michael, then
Forsook them, when themselves they vilified
To serve ungoverned appetite, and took
His image whom they served, a brutish vice,
Inductive mainly to the sin of Eve.
Therefore so abject is their punishment.
Disfiguring not God's likeness, but their own;
Or, if His likeness, by themselves defaced;
While they pervert pure nature's healthful rules
To loathsome sickness; worthily, since they
God's image did not reverence in themselves.

I yield it just, said Adam, and submit :
But is there yet no other way, besides
These painful passages, how we may come
To death, and mix with our connatural dust ?
There is, said Michael, if thou well observe
The rule of : Not too much – by temperance taught,
In what thou eat'st and drink'st; seeking from thence
Due nourishment, not gluttonous delight.
Till many years over thy head return,
So mayst thou live, till, like ripe fruit, thou drop
Into thy mother's lap, or be with ease
Gathered, not harshly plucked, for death mature.
This is old age; but, then, thou must outlive
Thy youth, thy strength, thy beauty; which will change
To withered, weak, and gray; thy senses then,
Obtuse, all taste of pleasure must forego.
To what thou hast; and for the air of youth,
Hopeful and cheerful, in thy blood will reign
A melancholy damp of cold and dry,
To weigh thy spirits down, and last consume
The balm of life. To whom our ancestor :
Henceforth I fly not Death, nor would prolong
Life much; bent, rather, how I may be quit,
Fairest and easiest, of this cumbrous charge,
Which I must keep till my appointed day
Of rendering up, and patiently attend
My dissolution. Michael replied :
Nor love thy life, nor hate, but what thou livest
Live well; how long, or short, permit to Heaven.
And now prepare thee for another sight.
He looked, and saw a spacious plain, whereon
Were tents of various hues.[1] By some were herds

1. *Were tents of various hues.*–"And Adah bare Jabal : he was the father of such as dwell in tents, and of such as have cattle. And his brother's name was Jubal : he was the father of all such as handle the harp and organ. And Zillah, she also bare Tubal-Cain, an instructor of every artificer in brass and iron." (Gen. iv.-20–22.)

Of cattle grazing; others, whence the sound
Of instruments, that made melodious chime,
Was heard, of harp and organ, and who moved
Their stops and chords was seen, his volant touch,
Instinct through all proportions, low and high.
Fled and pursued transverse the resonant fugue.
In other part stood one who, at the forge
Labouring, two massy clods of iron and brass
Had melted – whether found where casual fire
Had wasted woods on mountain or in vale,
Down to the veins of earth, thence gliding hot
To some cave's mouth, or whether washed by stream
From under ground. The liquid ore he drained
Lito fit moulds prepared, from which he formed
First, his own tools, then, what might else be wrought
Fusil or graven[1] in metal. After these.
But on the hither side, a different sort,
From the high neighbouring hills, which was their seat,
Down to the plain descended; by their guise
Just men they seemed, and all their study bent
To worship God aright, and know his works
Not hid, nor those things last, which might preserve
Freedom and peace to men. They on the plain
Long had not walked, when from the tents, behold
A bevy of fair women, richly gay
In gems and wanton dress; to the harp they sung
Soft amorous ditties, and in dance came on.
The men, though grave, eyed them, and let their eyes
Rove without rein; till, in the amorous net
Fast caught, they liked, and each his liking chose.
And now of love they treat, till the evening star,
Love's harbinger, appeared; then, all in heat,
They light the nuptial torch, and bid invoke
Hymen, then first to marriage rites invoked;
With feast and music all the tents resound.

1. *Fusil or graven.*–Fused or graven.

Such happy interview, and fair event
Of love and youth not lost, songs, garlands, flowers.
And charming symphonies, attached the heart[1]
Of Adam, soon inclined to admit delight,
The bent of nature; which he thus expressed :
True opener of mine eyes, prime Angel blest,
Much better seems this vision, and more hope
Of peaceful days portends, than those two past;
Those were of hate and death, or pain much worse :
Here nature seems fulfilled in all her ends.
To whom thus Michael : Judge not what is best
By pleasure, though to nature seeming meet;
Created, as thou art, to nobler end
Holy and pure, conformity divine
Those tents thou sawest so pleasant were the tents
Of wickedness, wherein shall dwell his race
Who slew his brother; studious they appear
Of arts that polish life, inventors rare,
Unmindful of their Maker, though his Spirit
Taught them,[2] but they his gifts acknowledged none.
Yet they a beauteous offspring shall beget;
For that fair female troop thou sawest, that seemed
Of goddesses, so blithe, so smooth, so gay,
Yet empty of all good, wherein consists
Woman's domestic honour and chief praise;
Bred only and completed to the taste
Of lustful appetance, to sing, to dance,
To dress, and troll the tongue, and roll the eye:
To these that sober race of men, whose lives
Religious titled them the sons of God,

1. *Attached the heart.*–"And it came to pass when men began to multiply on the face of the earth, and daughters were born unto them, that the sons of God saw the daughters of men that they were fair; and they took them wives of all which they chose." (Gen. vi. I, 2.)

2. *Though his Spirit taught them.*–"And he hath filled him with the spirit of God, in wisdom, in understanding, and iu knowledge, and in all manner of workmanship." (Exod. xxxv. 31.)

Shall yield up all their virtue, all their fame,
Ignobly, to the trains and to the smiles
Of these fair atheists; and now swim in joy.
Ere long to swim at large; and laugh, for which
The world ere long a world of tears must weep.
To whom thus Adam, of short joy bereft :
O pity and shame, that they, who to live well
Entered so fair, should turn aside to tread
Paths indirect, or in the midway faint !
But still I see the tenor of man's woe
Holds on the same, from woman to begin.
From man's effeminate slackness it begins,
Said the angel, who should better hold his place
By wisdom, and superior gifts received.
But now prepare thee for another scene.
He looked, and saw wide territory spread
Before him, towns, and rural works between,
Cities of men with lofty gates and towers,
Concourse in arms, fierce faces threatening war,
Giants of mighty bone and bold emprise.[1]
Part wield their arms, part curb the foaming steed,
Single, or in array of battle ranged.
Both horse and foot, nor idly mustering stood.
One way a band select from forage drives
A herd of beeves, fair oxen and fair kine.
From a fat meadow-ground; or fleecy flock,
Ewes and their bleating lambs over the plain.
Their booty; scarce with life the shepherds fly,
But call in aid, which makes a bloody fray.
With cruel tournament the squadrons join;
Where cattle pastured late, now scattered lies
With carcases and arms, the ensanguined field
Deserted. Others to a city strong
Lay siege, encamped; by battery, scale, and mine.
Assaulting; others from the wall defend

1. *Bold emprise.*–Courageous deeds.

With dart and javelin, stones, and sulphurous fire;
On each hand slaughter, and gigantic deeds.
In other part the sceptred heralds call
To council, in the city gates. Anon
Gray-headed men and grave, with warriors mixed,
Assemble, and harangues are heard; but soon
In factious opposition, till, at last.
Of middle age one rising, eminent
In wise deport, spake much of right and wrong,
Of justice, of religion, truth, and peace,
And judgment from above; him old and young
Exploded,[1] and had seized with violent hands,
Had not a cloud descending snatched him thence,
Unseen amid the throng. So violence
Proceeded, and oppression, and sword law,
Through all the plain, and refuge none was found.
Adam was all in tears, and to his guide
Lamenting, turned full sad : O what are these ?
Death's ministers, not men ! who thus deal death
Inhumanly to men, and multiply
Ten thousand fold the sin of him who slew
His brother; for of whom such massacre
Make they, but of their brethren, men of men ?
But who was that just man, whom had not Heaven
Rescued, had in his righteousness been lost ?
To whom thus Michael: These are the product
Of those ill-mated marriages[2] thou sawest;

1. *Exploded.*–Denounced, hissed. The poet's account of Enoch is taken in part from the Apocryphal Book of Enoch cited in the Epistle of Jude–"Enoch also, the seventh from Adam, prophesied of these, saying, Behold, the Lord cometh with ten thousand of his saints." (Jude 14.) "And Enoch walked with God : and he was not; for God took him." (Gen. v. 24.)

2. *Ill-mated marriages.*–"There were giants in the earth in those days; and also after that, when the sons of God came in unto the daughters of men, and they bare children to them, the same became mighty men which were of old, men of renown." (Gen. vi. 4.)

Where good with bad were matched, who of themselves
Abhor to join, and, by imprudence mixed,
Produce prodigious births of body or mind.
Such were those giants, men of high renown;
For in those days might only shall be admired,
And valour and heroic virtue called.
To overcome in battle, and subdue
Nations, and bring home spoils, with infinite
Manslaughter, shall be held the highest pitch
Of human glory; and for glory done
Of triumph, to be styled great conquerors,
Patrons of mankind, gods, and sons of gods;
Destroyers rightlier called, and plagues of men.
Thus fame shall be achieved, renown on earth;
And what most merits fame, in silence hid.
But he, the seventh from thee, whom thou beheldest
The only righteous in a world perverse,
And therefore hated, therefore so beset
With foes, for daring single to be just,
And utter odious truth, that God would come
To judge them with His saints, him the Most High,
Rapt in a balmy cloud with winged steeds,
Did, as thou sawest, receive, to walk with God
High in salvation and the climes of bliss.
Exempt from death; to shew thee what reward
Awaits the good; the rest what punishment,
Which now direct thine eyes and soon behold.
He looked, and saw the face of things quite changed.
The brazen throat of war had ceased to roar.
All now was turned to jollity and game,
To luxury and riot, feast and dance;
Marrying or prostituting, as befell,
Rape or adultery, where passing fair
Allured them – thence from cups to civil broils.
At length a reverend sire among them came,
And of their doings great dislike declared,

And testified against their ways. He oft
Frequented their assemblies, whereso met.
Triumphs or festivals, and to them preached
Conversion and repentance, as to souls
In prison, under judgment imminent.
But all in vain. Which, when he saw, he ceased
Contending, and removed his tents far off
Then, from the mountain hewing timber tall,
Began to build a vessel of huge bulk;
Measured by cubit, length, and breadth, and height,
Smeared round with pitch, and in the side a door
Contrived, and of provisions laid in large
For man and beast. When, lo ! a wonder strange !
Of every beast, and bird, and insect small.
Came sevens and pairs, and entered in, as taught
Their order. Last, the sire and his three sons,
With their four wives, and God made fast the door.
Meanwhile the south wind rose, and, with black wings
Wide-hovering, all the clouds together drove
From under heaven; the hills to their supply
Vapour, and exhalation, dusk and moist,
Sent up amain. And now the thickened sky
Like a dark ceiling stood; down rushed the rain
Impetuous, and continued till the earth
No more was seen; the floating vessel swum
Uplifted, and secure, with beaked prow,
Rode tilting o'er the waves; all dwellings else
Flood overwhelmed, and them, with all their pomp,
Deep under water rolled; sea covered sea,
Sea without shore, and in their palaces.
Where luxury late reigned, sea monsters whelped
And stabled : of mankind, so numerous late.
All left in one small bottom swum embarked.
How didst thou grieve then, Adam, to behold
The end of all thy offspring, end so sad,
Depopulation ! Thee, another flood,

Of tears and sorrow a flood, thee also drowned,
And sunk thee as thy sons; till, gently reared
By the Angel, on thy feet thou stood'st at last,
Though comfortless – as when a father mourns
His children, all in view destroyed at once;
And scarce to the angel uttered'st thus thy plaint :
O visions ill foreseen ! better had I
Lived lgnorant of future : so had borne
My part of evil only, each day's lot
Enough to bear. Those now, that were dispensed
The burden of many ages, on me light
At once, by my foreknowing gaining birth
Abortive, to torment me, ere their being.
With thought that they must be. Let no man seek
Henceforth to be foretold what shall befall
Him or his children; evil, he may be sure,
Which neither his foreknowing can prevent.
And he the future evil shall no less
In apprehension than in substance feel,
Grievous to bear. But that care now is past;
Man is not whom to warn; those few escaped.
Famine and anguish will at last consume.
Wandering that watery desert. I had hope.
When violence was ceased, and war on earth.
All would have then gone well; peace would have crowned,
With length of happy days, the race of man;
But I was far deceived; for now I see
Peace to corrupt, no less than war to waste.
How comes it thus ? Unfold, celestial guide,
And whether here the race of man will end.
To whom thus Michael : Those, whom last thou sawest
In triumph and luxurious wealth, are they
First seen in acts of prowess eminent,
And great exploits, but of true virtue void,
Who, having spilt much blood, and done much waste,
Subduing nations, and achieved thereby

Fame in the world, high titles, and rich prey,
Shall change their course to pleasure, ease, and sloth,
Surfeit, and lust; till wantonness and pride
Raise out of friendship hostile deeds in peace.
The conquered, also, and enslaved by war.
Shall, with their freedom lost, all virtue lose.
And fear of God, from whom their piety feigned.
In sharp contest of battle, found no aid
Against invaders; therefore, cooled in zeal.
Thenceforth shall practise how to live secure.
Worldly or dissolute, on what their lords
Shall leave them to enjoy; for the earth shall bear
More than enough, that temperance may be tried.
So all shall turn degenerate, all depraved,
Justice and temperance, truth and faith, forgot;
One man except, the only son of light
In a dark age, against example good.
Against allurement, custom, and a world
Offended. Fearless of reproach or scorn,
Or violence, he of their wicked ways
Shall them admonish; and before them set
The paths of righteousness, how much more safe,
And full of peace; denouncing wrath to come
On their impenitence, and shall return
Of them derided. But of God observed.
The one just man alive, by his command
Shall build a wondrous ark, as thou beheld'st,
To save himself and household from amidst
A world devote to universal wrack.
No sooner he, with them of man and beast
Select for life, shall in the ark be lodged,
And sheltered round, but all the cataracts
Of heaven set open on the earth shall pour
Rain day and night; all fountains of the deep,
Broke up, shall heave the ocean to usurp
Beyond all bounds, till inundation rise

Above the highest hills; then shall this mount
Of Paradise by might of waves be moved
Out of his place, pushed by the horned flood.
With all his verdure spoiled, and trees adrift,
Down the great river to the opening gulf,
And there take root, an island salt and bare,
The haunt of seals, and ores, and sea-mews' clang
To teach thee that God attributes to place
No sanctity, if none be thither brought
By men who there frequent, or therein dwell;
And now, what further shall ensue, behold.

He looked, and saw the ark hull on the flood,
Which now abated. For the clouds were fled.
Driven by a keen north wind, that, blowing dry,
Wrinkled the face of deluge, as decayed;
And the clear sun on his wide watery glass
Gazed hot, and of the fresh wave largely drew.
As after thirst; which made their flowing shrink
From standing lake to tripping ebb, that stole.
With soft foot, towards the deep, who now had stopt
His sluices, as the heaven his windows shut.
The ark no more now floats, but seems on ground,
Fast on the top of some high mountain fixed.
And now the tops of hills, as rocks, appear;
With clamour thence the rapid currents drive,
Towards the retreating sea, their furious tide.
Forthwith from out the ark a raven flies;
And after him, the surer messenger,
A dove, sent forth once and again to spy
Green tree or ground, whereon his foot may light.
The second time returning, in his bill
An olive leaf he brings, pacific sign.
Anon dry ground appears, and from his ark
The ancient sire descends, with all his train :
Then, with uplifted hands, and eyes devout,
Grateful to Heaven, over his head beholds

A dewy cloud, and in the cloud a bow
Conspicuous, with three listed colours gay,
Betokening peace from God, and covenant new
Whereat the heart of Adam, erst so sad,
Greatly rejoiced, and thus his joy broke forth :
O Thou, who future things canst represent
As present, heavenly instructor, I revive
At this last sight; assured that man shall live,
With all the creatures, and their seed preserve.
Far less I now lament for one whole world
Of wicked sons destroyed, than I rejoice
For one man found so perfect, and so just.
That God vouchsafes to raise another world
From him, and all his anger to forget.
But say, what mean those coloured streaks in heaven
Distended, as the brow of God appeased ?
Or serve they, as a flowery verge, to bind
The fluid skirts of that same watery cloud.
Lest it again dissolve and shower the earth ?
To whom the Archangel : Dexterously thou aimest;
So willingly doth God remit his ire,
Though late repenting him of man depraved;
Grieved at his heart, when, looking down, he saw
The whole earth filled with violence, and all flesh
Corrupting each their way. Yet, those removed,
Such grace shall one just man find in his sight,
That he relents, not to blot out mankind;
And makes a covenant, never to destroy
The earth again by flood, nor let the sea
Surpass his bounds, nor rain to drown the world,
With man therein or beast; but when he brings
Over the earth a cloud, will therein set
His triple-coloured bow, whereon to look
And call to mind His covenant. Day and night,
Seed-time and harvest, heat and hoary frost.
Shall hold their course, till fire purge all things new,
Both heaven and earth, wherein the just shall dwell.

BOOK - XII

The Angel Michael continues, from the flood, to relate what shall succeed; then, in the mention of Abraham, comes by degrees to explain who that seed of the woman shall be which was promised Adam and Eve in the fall: His in-carnation, death, resurrection, and ascension; the state of the Chinch till His second coming. Adam, greatly satisfied and re-comforted by these relations and promises, descends the hill with Michael; wakens Eve, who all this while had slept, but with gentle dreams composed to quietness of mind and submission. Michael, in either hand leads them out of Paradise, the fiery sword waving behind them, and the cherubim taking their stations to guard the place.

As one who, in his journey, bates at noon.
Though bent on speed, so here the Archangel paused
Betwixt the world destroyed and world restored,
If Adam aught, perhaps, might interpose;
Then, with transition sweet, new speech resumes :
    Thus thou hast seen one world begin, and end,
And man, as from a second stock, proceed.
Much thou hast yet to see; but I perceive
Thy mortal sight to fail; objects divine
Must needs impair and weary human sense.
Henceforth what is to come I will relate;
Thou, therefore, give due audience, and attend :
    This second source of men, while yet but few,
And while the dread of judgment past remains
Fresh in their minds, fearing the Deity,
With some regard to what is just and right
Shall lead their lives, and multiply apace,
Labouring the soil, and reaping plenteous crops,
Corn, wine, and oil; and, from the herd or flock,

Oft sacrificing bullock, lamb, or kid,
With large wine-offerings poured, and sacred feast,
Shall spend their days in joy unblamed, and dwell
Long time in peace, by families and tribes,
Under paternal rule; till one shall rise,[1]
Of proud, ambitious heart, who, not content
With fair equality, fraternal state,
Will arrogate dominion undeserved
Over his brethren, and quite dispossess
Concord and law of nature from the earth :
Hunting, – and men, not beasts, shall be his game, –
With war, and hostile snare, such as refuse
Subjection to his empire tyrannous !
A mighty hunter thence he shall be styled
Before the Lord, as, in despite of Heaven,
Or from Heaven, claiming second sovereignty;
And from rebellion shall derive his name,
Though of rebellion others he accuse.
He, with a crew, whom like ambition joins
With him, or under him, to tyrannise,
Marching from Eden towards the west, shall find
The plain wherein a black, bituminous gurge
Boils out from under ground, the mouth of Hell.
Of brick, and of that stuff, they cast to build
A city and tower, whose top may reach to heaven,
And get themselves a name, lest, far dispersed
In foreign lands, their memory be lost:
Regardless whether good or evil fame.
But God, who oft descends to visit men
Unseen, and through their habitations walks
To mark their doings, them beholding soon,
Comes down to see their city, ere the tower

1. *Till one shall rise.*–"And Cush begat Nimrod : he began to be a mighty one in the earth. He was a mighty hunter before the Lord: and the beginning of his kingdom was Babel, in the land of Shinar." (Gen. x. 8–10.)

Obstruct Heaven-towers, and in derision sets
Upon their tongues a various spirit, to rase
Quite out their native language, and, instead,
To sow a jangling noise of words unknown.
Forthwith a hideous gabble rises loud
Among the builders; each to other calls,
Not understood, till hoarse, and all in rage,
As mocked they storm. Great laughter was in Heaven,
And looking down to see the hubbub strange,
And hear the din. Thus was the building left
Ridiculous, and the work Confusion named.[1]
Whereto thus Adam, fatherly displeased :
O execrable son ! so to aspire
Above his brethren; to himself assuming
Authority usurped, from God not given.
He gave us only over beast, fish, fowl,
Dominion absolute; that right we hold
By his donation, but man over men
He made not lord; such title to Himself
Reserving, human left for human free.
But this usurper his encroachment proud
Stays not on man; to God his tower intends
Siege and defiance ! Wretched man ! what food
Will he convey up thither, to sustain
Himself and his rash army, where thin air
Above the clouds, will pine his entrails gross,
And famish him of breath, if not of bread ?
To whom thus Michael : Justly thou abhor'st

1. *The work Confusion named.*–"And it came to pass as they journeyed from the east, that they found a plain in the valley of Shinar; and they dwelt there. And they said, Go to, let us make brick, and burn them throughly: And they had brick for stone, and slime had they for mortar. And they said, Go to, let us build us a city and a tower, whose top may reach unto heaven; and let us make us a name, lest we be scattered abroad upon the face of the whole earth.…And the Lord came down to see the city and tower," &c. &c. (Gen. xi. 2 *et seq*)

That son, who on the quiet state of men
Such trouble brought, affecting to subdue
Rational liberty; yet know withal,
Since thy original lapse, true liberty
Is lost, which always with right reason dwells,
Twinned, and from her hath no dividual being.
Reason in man obscured, or not obeyed,
Immediately inordinate desires
And upstart passions catch the government
From reason, and to servitude reduce
Man, till then free. Therefore, since he permits.
Within himself, unworthy powers to reign
Over free reason, God, in judgment just,
Subjects him from without to violent lords.
Who oft as undeservedly enthral
His outward freedom. Tyranny must be,
Though to the tyrant thereby no excuse.
Yet sometimes nations will decline so low
From virtue, which is reason, that no wrong,
But justice, and some fatal curse annexed
Deprives them of their outward liberty.
Their inward lost. Witness the irreverent son
Of him who built the ark, who, for the shame,
Done to his father, heard this heavy curse,
Servant of servants, on his vicious race.
Thus will this latter, as the former, world.
Still tend from bad to worse, till God, at last,
Wearied with their iniquities, withdraw
His presence from among them, and avert
His holy eyes, resolving from thenceforth
To leave them to their own polluted ways,
And one peculiar nation to select
From all the rest, of whom to be invoked,
A nation from one faithful man to spring :
Him on this side Euphrates yet residing,
Bred up in idol worship. O that men –

Canst thou believe ? – should be so stupid grown.
While yet the patriarch lived who 'scaped the flood,
As to forsake the living God, and fall
To worship their own work in wood and stone
For gods! Yet him, God the Most High vouchsafes
To call, by vision, from his father's house,
His kindred, and false gods, into a land
Which He will show him; and from him will raise
A mighty nation, and upon him shower
His benediction so, that in his seed
All nations shall be blest.[1] He straight obeys,
Not knowing to what land, yet firm believes.
I see him, but thou canst not, with what faith
He leaves his gods, his friends, and native soil,
Ur of Chaldea, passing now the ford
To Haran; after him a cumbrous train
Of herds and flocks, and numerous servitude;
Not wandering poor, but trusting all his wealth
With God, who called him, in a land unknown.
Canaan he now attains. I see his tents
Pitched about Sechem, and the neighbouring plain
Of Moreh. There, by promise, he receives
Gift to his progeny of all that land,
From Hamath, northward to the desert south –
Things by their names I call, though yet unnamed –
From Herrnon east, to the great western sea;
Mount Hermon, yonder sea; each place behold
In prospect, as I point them. On the shore,
Mount Carmel; here, the double-founted stream,[2]

1. *In his seed all nations shall be blest.*–"Now the Lord had said unto Abram, Get thee out of thy country, and from thy kindred, and from thy father's house, unto a land that I will show thee. And I will make of thee a great nation, and in thee shall all the families of the earth be blessed." (Gen. xii. I, 2.)

2. *The double-founted stream.*–The Jordan has its origin in two fountains or springs –the one about twenty miles north of Cæsarea Philippi, the other about eighteen miles south of that spot.

Jordan, true limit eastward; but his sons
Shall dwell to Senir,[1] that long ridge of hills.
This ponder, that all nations of the earth
Shall in his seed be blessed. By that seed
Is meant thy great Deliverer, who shall bruise
The Serpent's head; whereof to thee anon
Plainlier shall be revealed. This patriarch blest,
Whom faithful Abraham due time shall call,
A son, and of his son a grandchild, leaves.
Like him in faith, in wisdom, and renown.
The grandchild, with twelve sons increased, departs
From Canaan to a land hereafter called
Egypt, divided by the river Nile.
See where it flows, disgorging at seven mouths
Into the sea : to sojourn in that land
He comes, invited by a younger son
In time of dearth – a son, whose worthy deeds
Raise him to be the second in that realm
Of Pharaoh. There he dies, and leaves his race
Growing into a nation. And, now grown
Suspected to a sequent king, who seeks
To stop their overgrowth, as inmate guests
Too numerous; whence of guests he makes them slaves,
Inhospitably; and kills their infant males:
Till by two brethren – those two brethren call
Moses and Aaron – sent from God to claim
His people from enthralment, they return,
With glory and spoil, back to their promised land.
But first, the lawless tyrant, who denies
To know their God, or message to regard,
Must be compelled by signs and judgments dire.
To blood unshed the rivers must be turned;
Frogs, lice, and flies, must all his palace fill
With loathed intrusion, and fill all the land;
His cattle must of rot and murrain die;

1. *Senir.*–The Amorites gave this name to Mount Hermon.

Botches and blains must all his flesh emboss.
And all his people; thunder mixed with hail.
Hail mixed with fire, must rend the Egyptian sky.
And wheel on the earth, devouring where it rolls;
What it devours not, herb, or fruit, or grain,
A darksome cloud of locusts swarming down
Must eat, and on the ground leave nothing green;
Darkness must overshadow all his bounds.
Palpable darkness, and blot out three days;
Last, with one midnight stroke, all the first-born
Of Egypt must lie dead. Thus, with ten wounds.
The river-dragon, tamed, at length submits
To let his sojourners depart, and oft
Humbles his stubborn heart, but still as ice
More hardened after thaw ! till, in his rage
Pursuing whom he late dismissed, the sea
Swallows him with his host, but them lets pass,
As on dry land, between two crystal walls;
Awed by the rod of Moses so to stand
Divided, till his rescued gain their shore :
Such wondrous power God to his saint will lend,
Though present in his Angel, who shall go
Before them in a cloud, and pillar of fire;
By day a cloud, by night a pillar of fire;
To guide them in their journey, and remove
Behind them, while the obdurate king pursues.
All night he will pursue, but his approach
Darkness defends between till morning watch;[1]
Then through the fiery pillar and the cloud,
God, looking forth, will trouble all his host,
And craze their chariot-wheels; when, by command,

1. *Till morning watch.*– "And it came to pass, that in the morning watch the Lord looked unto the host of the Egyptians through the pillar of fire and of the cloud, and troubled the host of the Egyptians, and took off their chariot wheels, so that they drave heavily," &c. &c. (Exod. xiv. 24–28.)

Moses once more his potent rod extends
Over the sea; the sea his rod obeys;
On their embattled ranks the waves return,
And overwhelm their war. The race elect
Safe towards Canaan, from the shore, advance
Through the wild desert; not the readiest way,
Lest, enterinor on the Canaanite alarmed,
War terrify them, inexpert, and fear
Return them back to Egypt, choosing rather
Inglorious life with servitude. For life,
To noble and ignoble, is more sweet
Untrained in arms, where rashness leads not on.
This also shall they gain by their delay
In the wide wilderness; there they shall found
Their government, and their great senate choose
Through the twelve tribes, to rule by laws ordained;
God, from the mount of Sinai, whose grey top
Shall tremble, He descendmg, will Himself,
In thunder, lightning, and loud trumpets' sound,
Ordain them laws; part, such as appertain
To civil justice; part, religious rites
Of sacrifice; informing them, by types
And shadows, of that destined Seed to bruise
The Serpent, by what means He shall achieve
Mankind's deliverance. But the voice of God
To mortal ear is dreadful : they beseech
That Moses might report to them his will.
And terror cease. He grants what they besought,
Instructed that to God is no access
Without mediator, whose high office now
Moses in figure bears, to introduce
One greater, of whose day he shall foretell,
And all the prophets in their age, the times
Of great Messiah shall sing. Thus, laws and rites
Established, such delight hath God in men
Obedient to his will, that he vouchsafes

Among them to set up his tabernacle –
The Holy One with mortal men to dwell :
By his prescript a sanctuary is framed
Of cedar, overlaid with gold; therein
An ark, and in the ark his testimony,
The records of his covenant; over these
A mercy-seat of gold, between the wings
Of two bright cherubim; before him burn
Seven lamps, as in a zodiac, representing
The heavenly fires; over the tent a cloud
Shall rest by day, a fiery gleam by night,
Save when they journey, and at length they come,
Conducted by his Angel,[1] to the land
Promised to Abraham and his seed. The rest
Were long to tell; how many battles fought;
How many kings destroyed, and kingdoms won;
Or how the sun shall in mid heaven stand still
A day entire, and night's clue course adjourn,
Man's voice commanding, Sun, in Gibeon stand,
And thou, moon, in the vale of Ajalon,
Till Israel overcome ! – so call the third
From Abraham, son of Isaac; and from him
His whole descent, who thus shall Canaan win.
    Here Adam interposed: O sent from Heaven
Enlightener of my darkness, gracious things
Thou hast revealed, those chiefly which concern
Just Abraham and his seed. Now first I find
Mine eyes true opening, and my heart much eased,
Erewhile perplexed with thoughts, what would becom
Of me and all mankind; but now I see
His day, in whom all nations shall be blest;
Favour unmerited by me, who sought
Forbidden knowledge by forbidden means.
This yet I apprehend not; why to those

1. *Conducted by his Angel.*–"For my Angel shall go before thee, and bring thee," &c.

Among whom God will deign to dwell on earth,
So many and so various laws are given ?
So many laws argue so many sins
Among them; how can God with such reside ?
To whom thus Michael : Doubt not but that sin
Will reign among them, as of thee begot;
And, therefore, was law given them, to evince
Their natural pravity, by stirring up
Sin against law[1] to fight; that when they see
Law can discover sin, but not remove,
Save by those shadowy expiations weak.
The blood of bulls and goats, they may conclude
Some blood more precious must be paid for man;
Just for unjust; that in such righteousness,
To them by faith imputed, they may find
Justification towards God, and peace
Of conscience, which the law by ceremonies
Cannot appease, nor man the moral part
Perform, and, not performing, cannot live.
So law appears imperfect, and but given
With purpose to resign them, in full time,
Up to a better covenant, disciplined
From shadowy types to truth, from flesh to spirit,
From imposition of strict laws to free
Acceptance of large grace, from servile fear
To filial – works of law to works of faith.
And, therefore, shall not Moses, though of God
Highly beloved, being but the minister
Of law, his people into Canaan lead;
But Joshua, whom the Gentiles Jesus call,[2]
His name and office bearing, who shall quell.

---

1. *Stirring vp sin against law.*–"The law entered that the offence might abound." (Rom v. 20.) "By the law is the knowledge of sin." (Rom. iii. 20.)

2. *The Gentiles Jesus call.–The* Septuagint always gives this name to Joshua.

The adversary Serpent, and bring back,
Through the world's wilderness, long-wandered Man
Safe to eternal Paradise of rest.
Meanwhile they, in their earthly Canaan placed,
Long time shall dwell and prosper, but when sins
National interrupt their public peace,
Provoking God to raise them enemies;
From whom as oft he saves them penitent,
By Judges first, then under Kings; of whom
The second, both for piety renowned
And puissant deeds, a promise shall receive
Irrevocable, that his regal throne
For ever shall endure. The like shall sing
All prophecy, that of the royal stock
Of David – so I name this king – shall rise
A son, the Woman's Seed to thee foretold,
Foretold to Abraham, as in whom shall trust
All nations; and to kmgs foretold, of kings
The last – for of His reion shall be no end.
But first, a long succession must ensue;
And his next son, for wealth and wisdom famed,
The clouded ark of God, till then in tents
Wandering, shall in a glorious temple enshrine.
Such follow him as shall be registered
Part good, part bad; of bad the longer scroll;
Whose foul idolatries, and other faults,
Heaped to the popular sum, will so incense
God, as to leave them, and expose their land,
Their city, his temple, and his holy ark,
With all his sacred things, a scorn and prey
To that proud city, whose high walls thou sawest
Left in confusion – Babylon thence called.
There in captivity he lets them dwell
The space of seventy years; then brings them back,
Remembering mercy, and his covenant sworn
To David, 'stablished as the days of heaven.

Returned from Babylon by leave of kings.
Their lords, whom God disposed, the house of God
They first re-edify, and for a while
In mean estate live moderate, till, grown
In wealth and multitude, factious they grow.
But first among the priests dissension springs[1]
Men who attend the altar, and should most
Endeavour peace. Their strife pollution brings;
Upon the temple itself At last they seize
The sceptre, and regard not David's sons;
Then lose it to a stranger, that the true
Anointed king, Messiah, might be born
Barred of his right. Yet at his birth a star,
Unseen before in heaven, proclaims him come,
And guides the eastern sages, who inquire
His place, to offer incense, myrrh, and gold :
His place of birth a solemn angel tells
To simple shepherds, keepmg watch by night;
They gladly thither haste, and by a quire
Of squadroned angels hear his carol sung.
A Virgin is his mother, but his sire
The power of the Most High. He shall ascend
The throne hereditary, and bound his reign
With earth's wide bounds, his glory with the heavens.
He ceased; discerning Adam, with such joy
Surcharged, as had, like grief, been dewed in tears.
Without the vent of words; which these he breathed :
O prophet of glad tidings, finisher
Of utmost hope ! now clear I understand
What oft my steadiest thoughts have searched in vain;
Why our great Expectation should be called

---

1. *Among the priests dissension springs.*–This is a reference to the struggle for the high, priesthood between Jason and Menelaus, in the time of Antiochus Epiphanes; and later between Aristobulus and Hyrcanus. Aristobulus united the kingly and priestly office in his person.

The Seed of Woman : Virgin Mother, hail !
High in the love of Heaven; yet from my loins
Thou shalt proceed, and from thy womb the Son
Of God Most High; so God with man unites.
Needs must the Serpent now his capital bruise
Expect with mortal pain; say where and when
Their fight; what stroke shall bruise the Victor's heel ?
To whom thus Michael : Dream not of their fight.
As of a duel, or the local wounds
Of head or heel; not, therefore, joins the Son
Manhood to Godhead, with more strength to foil
Thy enemy; nor so is overcome
Satan, whose fall from heaven, a deadlier bruise,
Disabled not to give thee thy death's wound;
Which He, who comes thy Saviour, shall re-cure,
Not by destroying Satan, but his works
In thee, and in thy seed : nor can this be,
But by fulfilling that which thou didst want,
Obedience to the law of God, imposed
On penalty of death; and suffering death.
The penalty to thy transgression due,
And due to theirs, which out of thine will grow;
So only can high justice rest appaid.[1]
The law of God exact he shall fulfil.
Both by obedience and by love, though love
Alone fulfil the law; thy punishment
He shall endure, by coming in the flesh
To a reproachful life and cursed death;
Proclaiming life to all who shall believe
In his redemption, and that his obedience.
Imputed, becomes theirs by faith; His merits
To save them, not their own, though legal, works.
For this he shall live hated, be blasphemed.
Seized on by force, judged, and to death condemned.
A shameful and accursed, nailed to the cross

1. *Appaid.* – Paid; *appagato,* Italian.

By his own nation; slain for bringing life.
But to the cross He nails thy enemies,
The law that is against thee, and the sins
Of all mankind with him there crucified.
Never to hurt them more who rightly trust
In this his satisfaction. So he dies.
But soon revives; death over Him no power
Shall long usurp. Ere the third dawning light
Return, the stars of morn shall see him rise
Out of his grave, fresh as the dawning light.
Thy ransom paid, which man from death redeems,
His death for man, as many as offered life
Neglect not, and the benefit embrace
By faith not void of works. This Godlike act
Annuls thy doom, the death thou shouldst have died,
In sin for ever lost from life; this act
Shall bruise the head of Satan, crush his strength,
Defeating Sin and Death, his two main arms,
And fix far deeper in his head their stings
Than temporal death shall bruise the Victor's heel,
Or theirs whom he redeems – a death like sleep,
A gentle wafting to immortal life.
Nor after resurrection shall he stay
Longer on earth than certain times to appear
To his disciples, men who in his life
Still followed him; to them shall leave in charge
To teach all nations what of him they learned,
And his salvation; them who shall believe
Baptising in the profluent stream,[1] the sign
Of washing them from guilt of sin to life
Pure, and in mind prepared, if so befall.
For death, like that which the Redeemer died.
All nations they shall teach; for, from that day,
Not only to the sons of Abraham's loins

1. *Profluent stream.*–Milton seems to have thought that baptism should be administered in running, not in stagnant water.

Salvation shall be preached, but to the sons
Of Abraham's faith wherever through the world;
So in his seed all nations shall be blest.
Then to the Heaven of heavens he shall ascend
With victory, triumphing through the air,
Over his foes and thine; there shall surprise
The Serpent, prince of air, and drag in chains
Through all his realm, and there confounded leave;
Then enter into glory, and resume
His seat at God's right hand, exalted high
Above all names in Heaven; and thence shall come,
When this world's dissolution shall be ripe,
With glory and power, to judge both quick and dead;
To judge the unfaithful dead, but to reward
His faithful, and receive them into bliss,
Whether in heaven or earth; for then the earth
Shall all be Paradise, far happier place
Than this of Eden, and far happier days.
    So spake the Archangel Michael; then paused.
As at the world's great period; and our sire.
Replete with joy and wonder, thus replied :
    O Goodness infinite. Goodness immense !
That all this good of evil shall produce.
And evil turn to good; more wonderful
Than that which by creation first brought forth
Light out of darkness ! Full of doubt I stand,
Whether I should repent me now of sin
By me done, and occasioned, or rejoice
Much more, that much more good thereof shall spring;
To God more glory, more good-will to men
From God, and over wrath grace shall abound.
But say, if our Deliverer up to Heaven
Must reascend, what will betide the few,
His faithful, left among the unfaithful herd.
The enemies of truth ? Who, then, shall guide
His people – who defend ? Will they not deal

Worse with His followers than with Him they dealt?
Be sure they will, said the Angel; but from Heaven
He to his own a Comforter will send,
The promise of the Father, who shall dwell
His Spirit within them; and the law of faith,
Working through love, upon their hearts shall write,
To guide them in all truth, and also arm
With spiritual armour able to resist
Satan's assaults, and quench his fiery darts;
What man can do against them, not afraid,
Though to the death; against such cruelties
With inward consolations recompensed,
And oft supported so as shall amaze
Their proudest persecutors; for the Spirit,
Poured first on his apostles, whom he sends
To evangelise the nations, then on all
Baptised, shall them with wondrous gifts endue
To speak all tongues, and do all miracles.
As did their Lord before them. Thus they win
Great numbers of each nation to receive
With joy the tidings brought from Heaven: at length,
Their ministry performed, and race well run,
Their doctrine and their story written left,
They die; but in their room, as they forewarn.
Wolves shall succeed for teachers, grievous wolves,
Who all the sacred mysteries of Heaven
To their own vile advantages shall turn,
Of lucre and ambition, and the truth
With superstitions and traditions taint,
Left only in those written records pure.
Though not but by the Spirit understood.[1]
Then shall they seek to avail themselves of names,

1. *Though not but by the Spirit understood.*–One of many passages which showed that Milton believed in Divine influence as a teaching power in man. Not an influence to render one man infallible against another, but tending to general enlightenment when rationally understood.

Places, and titles, and with these to join
Secular power, though feigning still to act
By spiritual, to themselves appropriating
The Spirit of God, promised alike, and given
To all believers; and from that pretence,
Spiritual laws by carnal power shall force
On every conscience; laws which none shall find
Left them enrolled,[1] or what the spirit within
Shall on the heart engrave. What will they, then,
But force the Spirit of Grace itself, and bind
His consort Liberty ? What but unbuild
His living temples, built by faith to stand.
Their own faith, not another's ? For, on earth,
Who against faith and conscience can be heard
Infallible. Yet many will presume:
Whence heavy persecution shall arise
On all who in the worship persevere
Of spirit and truth; the rest, far greater part,
Will deem in outward rites and specious forms
Religion satisfied; truth shall retire
Bestuck with slanderous darts, and works of faith
Rarely be found. So shall the world go on,
To good malignant, to bad men benign.
Under her own weight groaning, till the day
Appear of respiration to the just,
And vengeance to the wicked, at return
Of Him so lately promised to thy aid,
The woman's Seed; obscurely then foretold,
Now ampler known thy Saviour and thy Lord;
Last, in the clouds, from Heaven, to be revealed,
In glory of the Father, to dissolve
Satan with his perverted world; then raise
From the conflagrant mass, purged and refined,
New Heavens, new Earth, ages of endless date,
Founded in righteousness, and peace, and love,

1. *Left them enrolled.*–Left written, written in the Scriptures.

To bring forth fruits, joy and eternal bliss.
He ended; and thus Adam last replied:
How soon hath thy prediction. Seer blest,
Measured this transient world, the race of time,
Till time stand fixed ! Beyond is all abyss,
Eternity, whose end no eye can reach.
Greatly instructed I shall hence depart;
Greatly in peace of thought; and have my fill
Of knowledge, what this vessel can contain;
Beyond which was my folly to aspire.
Henceforth I learn, that to obey is best.
And love, with fear, the only God; to walk
As in His presence, ever to observe
His providence, and on him sole depend,
Merciful over all his works, with good
Still overcoming evil, and by small
Accomplishing great things; by things deemed weak
Subverting worldly strong, and worldly wise
By simply meek; that suffering for truth's sake
Is fortitude to highest victory;
And, to the faithful, death the gate of life;
Taught this by His example, whom I now
Acknowledge my Redeemer ever blest.
To whom thus also the Angel last replied :
This having learned, thou hast attained the sum
Of wisdom; hope no higher, though all the stars
Thou knewest by name, and all the ethereal power
All secrets of the Deep, all Nature's works,
Or works of God in heaven, air, earth, or sea,
And all the riches of this world enjoyedst.
And all the rule, one empire. Only add
Deeds to thy knowledge answerable; add faith,
Add virtue, patience, temperance; add love,
By name to come called charity, the soul
Of all the rest : then wilt thou not be loath
To leave this Paradise, but shalt possess

A paradise within thee, happier far.
Let us descend now, therefore, from this top
Of speculation; for the hour precise
Exacts our parting hence. And, see ! the guards.
By me encamped on yonder hill, expect
Their motion, at whose front a flaming sword,
In signal of remove, waves fiercely round.
We may no longer stay : go, waken Eve;
Her also I with gentle dreams have calmed,
Portending good, and all her spirits composed
To meek submission; thou, at season fit,
Let her with thee partake what thou hast heard,
Chiefly, what may concern her faith to know.
The great deliverance by her seed to come –
For by the Woman's seed – on all mankind;
That ye may live, which will be many days.
Both in one faith unanimous, though sad,
With cause, for evils past, yet much more cheered
With meditation on the happy end.
He ended, and they both descend the hill
Descended, Adam to the bower, where Eve
Lay sleeping, ran before, but found her waked;
And thus with words not sad she him received :
Whence thou return'st, and whither went'st, I know;
For God is also in sleep; and dreams advise,
Which He hath sent propitious, some great good
Presaeine, since, with sorrow and heart's distress
Wearied, I fell asleep. But now lead on,
In me is no delay; with thee to go.
Is to stay here; without thee here to stay,
Is to go hence unwilling; thou to me
Art all things under heaven, all places thou.
Who for my wilful crime art banished hence.
This further consolation yet secure
I carry hence; though all by me is lost,
Such favour I, unworthy, am vouchsafed.

By me the Promised Seed shall all restore.
        So spake our mother Eve; and Adam heard,
Well pleased, but answered not; for now, too nigh
The Archangel stood; and from the other hill
To their fixed station, all in bright array,
The Cherubim descended, on the ground
Gliding meteorus, as evening mist.
Risen from a river, o'er the marish glides,
And gathers ground fast at the labourer's heel.
Homeward returning. High in front advanced.
The brandished sword of God before them blazed,
Fierce as a comet; which, with torrid heat.
And vapour as the Lybian air adust.
Began to parch that temperate clime; whereat
In either hand the hastening Angel caught
Our lingering parents, and to the eastern gate
Led them direct, and down the cliff as fast
To the subjected plain; then disappeared.
They, lookuig back, all the eastern side beheld
Of Paradise, so late their happy seat.
Waved over by that flaming brand; the gate
With dreadful faces thronged, and fiery arms.
Some natural tears they dropt, but wiped them soon;
The world was all before them, where to choose
Their place of rest, and Providence their guide :
They, hand in hand, with wandering steps and slow,
Through Eden took their solitary way.